INSIDE CORK

This is the first and only independent guide to Cork City and County. As well as comprehensive touring information, historical background and detailed descriptions of all the major attractions in the county, and many lesser known ones, it includes the definitive guide to the best hospitality available in the area. Hotels, guest houses, B & Bs, restaurants and bars have been selected by the author after extensive research, and are described in detail to enable you to make an informed choice about where to stay, where to eat, and where to socialise. There are also detailed listings of recreational facilities including golfing, angling, horse riding, tennis, boat and bicycle hire. This guide carries no advertising, and has received no sponsorship. Nobody can buy their way into INSIDE CORK: they have to be among the best of their kind to get a mention. Whether you live in the county, or are just passing through, this is the book that you need to make the most of it.

While every care has been taken to ensure the accuracy of the information in this guide, changes can occur at short notice, and consequently, neither the publisher nor the author can accept responsibility for any errors that may occur.

INSIDE CORK will be updated regularly, and we would like to hear about your experiences. Any establishment that fails to live up to its recommendation will be investigated, and our entries revised where warranted. We would also be pleased to receive any additional information or suggestions. Please write to us, or fill in the form at the back of the book. Writers of the best suggestions will receive a free copy of the new edition of the guide.

Alannah Hopkin is a freelance writer based in Kinsale. She has published two novels and a highly acclaimed work of non-fiction, *The Living Legend of St. Patrick*. She writes regularly for *The Financial Times* and *The Irish Times*, and since 1982 she has been Area Editor of *Fodor's Travel Guide to Ireland*. She is an active member of the Committee of *An Taisce Corcaigh* (The Cork Association of The National Trust for Ireland). She has travelled extensively around the county by foot, by boat, on horseback, by bicycle and by car, and is known for her extraordinary knowledge of the county's pubs which, she claims, are as good as museums as a source of local history.

INSIDE CORK

Alannah Hopkin

The Collins Press

Published by The Collins Press, Carey's Lane, Cork.

Printed in Ireland by Colour Books Ltd., Dublin.

Typesetting by Upper Case Ltd., Cork.

Cover Design by Upper Case Ltd., Cork.

ISBN-0-9516036-5-5

CONTENTS

AUTHOR'S FOREWORD

INSIDE CORK is a unique publication. It has been produced independently, and is based on local knowledge supplemented by active research. It has been compiled by one person. It is not trying to sell you anything, and neither is it an anonymous team effort. It is not an official publication of the Irish Tourist Board, neither is it in any way connected with their regional office, Cork-Kerry Tourism. It is not, in fact, written specifically for tourists, although tourists will certainly benefit from it. It is aimed at anyone who is interested in finding out more about the area, and enjoying the best that Cork city and county have to offer.

I have tried to be non-critical in my descriptions, whether I am writing about a fashionable restaurant or a historic castle, because I have only included places that can be positively recommended. But, inevitably, I have certain preferences of my own that have influenced my choices, and there is no point in trying to hide them. I do not like noisy, crowded places, whether they are pubs or beaches. I like unusual bed and breakfast places well off the main road, and prefer a farmhouse or a period house to a modern bungalow. I have nothing against modern B & B's, some of which set very high standards in comfort, but I have given preference to places off the main road for the logical reason that you do not need a guide book to find a modern B & B on the main road. If I am eating out, in whatever price bracket, I look for somewhere offering fresh local produce, which will be treated with respect and competently served in pleasant surroundings. I do not eat "fast food". I try not to have strong views on decor, but I do get annoyed if the decor and the building are wildly at odds with each other, and I tend to prefer light, sunny rooms to dark gloomy ones.

Some of the places mentioned here I have known all my life, as I come from a family that loves "a day out". Others I first discovered about twenty years ago when I began sailing around the west coast. My interest in horses opened up the north and east of the county to me, in the annual round of point-to-points. My work for an American guide book filled in the gaps. In fact, I thought I knew Cork pretty well, until I started writing this book, and discovered that there is far more to it than I had expected.

The county is changing, certainly, and has adopted the god of tourism in an alarmingly enthusiastic way, something which must continue to be closely monitored. Mistakes have been made, but they are few, and we are learning. An undeniable spin-off from tourist development is the great improvement in the quality of places to stay and places to eat out, which is a bonus for those of us who live here.

Which brings me to the "thanks yous". I am not going to name names, because there are too many of them. Friends, colleagues, and even total strangers have been generous with details of their favourite pubs, restaurants, hotels, bed and breakfasts, walks, and the loan of books. Then there are the people, mostly voluntary, involved in local tourism organisations who do such a great job compiling and distributing information on their immediate locality. I must also thank the people working so hard on the heritage side, from the often-voluntary curators of local museums to employees of the Office of Public Works and other state bodies, through to individuals who open their homes or gardens to the public, or allow access to historic sites on their land. Then there is Bord Failte, and the team at Cork-Kerry Tourism, who do so much to improve and promote the county's facilities. And, finally, there are all those people "at the coal face" - owners and staff of pubs, restaurants and accommodation, who have done so much to put Cork on the map. Without the persistent hard work, and the patient response to my very detailed enquiries, of all these people, I could not have written this book; in a way it is as much their book as mine.

INTRODUCTION

Cork is the largest county in Ireland, with an area of 2890 square miles. It stretches from Youghal in the east to the Dursey Head in the west, from Charleville in the north to Cape Clear in the south. It is bordered on the south by a long and varied coastline, and from west to east by Kerry, Limerick, Tipperary and Waterford. Nowhere in the county are you more than an hour's drive from the sea, and distances within it are modest, yet there is great variety of scenery. The county is shaped by ridges of sandstone running from east to west, divided by the three main rivers, the Blackwater, the Lee and the Bandon, which run along limestone valleys to the sea. The north and east of the county and the river valleys consist of rich farming country, mainly dairying. Top class race horses are reared on the limestone pastures.

The coast beyond Kinsale has a different character altogether, increasing in ruggedness as you travel west, but with a strangely mild climate because of the nearby Gulf Stream which allows palm trees and other sub-tropical plants to flourish. The combination of a long unspoilt coastline and a relatively mild climate have turned rocky west Cork, once an impoverished area of small farmers, into a popular holiday resort. Although the popular image of traffic-free roads is no longer a reality in July and August, for the rest of the year driving is a pleasure around here, a throw-back to the days before traffic jams and parking restrictions when vehicles were so scarce on the roads that drivers saluted each other, and any pedestrians, as they passed. In some parts people still do, and everyone is expected to join in.

Visitors should be warned that back roads in some parts of the county are still used for the sport of "road bowling", which is unique to counties Cork and Armagh. A heavy metal "bowl", or ball, is used in this game. Large groups congregate on the road to follow the players as they compete to see who can complete the course in the fewest throws. There is much shouting and cheering, and large sums of money sometimes change hands. If you encounter an animated group of people on the road, this is probably what they are doing. Pull up and wait, and you will be waved on when it is safe to pass - usually after only a minute or two.

Both coastal and inland areas are rich in natural produce, from the trout and salmon of the Blackwater to the mussels, and shrimps on the shoreline, and ling, cod, monkfish, John Dory and other fish from the deep sea. Mackerel and herring still have their seasons, although they are less numerous than in the past. Lovers of wild flowers will be surprised by the abundance of primroses, violets, bluebells, wild garlic, camomile, sea pinks, scabious, cornflowers, poppies, montbretia, and other species which have become rare in more industrialised areas. Glorious banks of red fuchsia bloom in the roadside hedgerows from mid-July into October. Blackberry, elderflower, whitethorn and honeysuckle also grow wild in hedges. Add to this a rich bird life, with larks often heard above the cliffs, heron, plover, curlews and oyster catchers frequenting the mud flats, rare migratory birds passing off the south coast, a good supply of woodcock, wild duck and pheasant, plus numerous colonies of nesting sea birds, and it becomes clear why the area is so popular with people who love the outdoors. Walking, camping, sailing, swimming, diving, fishing, golfing, cycling and hill climbing are all enhanced by the beauty of the unpolluted countryside and coast.

The mountains of Cork would be called hills in other parts of the world, but they provide excellent walks, and unspoilt rugged scenery. The Ballyhoura Mountains in the north, the Nagles Mountains to the south of the Blackwater, the Boggeragh, Derrynasaggart and Shehy Mountains near the Kerry border, and the Slieve Miskish Mountains on the Beara peninsula are all dotted with forest parks offering walking trails. They are also criss-crossed by small roads, ideal for walking or cycling. The

Pass of Keimaneigh, on the road between Macroom and Kealkil, is an unusual drive, while the county offers two routes through the mountains to Kerry - the Tim Healy Pass, and the Glengarriff-Kenmare "tunnel road" - which can compete with anywhere in Europe for scenic beauty.

The coast to the east of Cork harbour offers a selection of long sandy beaches between Garryvoe and Youghal, while the coast to the west of the city tends more to high cliffs and rocky coves - notable exceptions being the long sandy beaches of Courtmacsherry, Clonakilty and Rosscarbery Bays. In the far west, the Mizen Head peninsula, the Sheep's Head peninsula and the Beara peninsula provide a variety of spectacular unspoilt coastal scenery, and a wealth of bird life.

The county has a long and eventful history, and past generations have left their mark on it. Cork has been inhabited since about 6000 B.C., and small worked flints from that period are sometimes discovered in ploughed fields. Stone circles, standing stones, cooking pits and wedge tombs from the Megalithic age (pre 2000 B.C.) can still be seen, although we can only guess at the rituals behind them. Ringforts - circular earthworks built by farmers from around 500 A.D. to 1000 A.D. - have been excavated, and the remains of promontory forts, built on spectacular coastal sites in that time, can still be seen. There are early Christian remains, possibly pre-dating the arrival of Saint Patrick in the 6th century A.D., on Cape Clear Island, and there are several other shrines and monastic remains connected with early Christian saints. Two round towers, and several ruined abbeys survive from the later monastic period.

The invasion of the Anglo-Normans in 1157 led to the first walled towns, and a rash of castle building. There are the remains of some 400 castles to be found around the county, from the moated sites of the Normans to the 15th century tower houses and the large fortified mansions favoured after the Elizabethan "plantation" of Munster in the 16th century. The 17th century saw the building of the great star-shaped fortifications, Charles Fort and James Fort, in Kinsale. Further coastal defence works, including a number of Martello towers, were built at the end of the 18th century for fear of French invasion. Many fine 18th and 19th-century "big houses" with ornamental grounds and plantations, are still standing, and some of them are open to the public.

The towns of the county are also rich in historical interest, particularly Cork, Youghal and Kinsale, which were walled towns in medieval times. Cobh, with its wonderful location on Cork harbour, its fine cathedral and its long connections with emigration, has many well-preserved Victorian buildings, and is well worth getting to know. Other towns - Fermoy, Mallow, Mitchelstown, Kanturk, Bandon, Macroom, Skibbereen, and Bantry have interesting histories, but are not immediately so attractive. Clonakilty, with its hand-painted shop-signs and renovated mills, shows what can be done to revive the fading looks of a simple market town.

HOW TO USE THIS BOOK

Basic touring information for the whole county and useful addresses and phone numbers are contained in the section entitled INSIDE INFORMATION. This section also contains specialised information not listed in Chapters One to Twelve,including camping and caravanning sites, hostel accommodation, self-catering contacts, residential activity holidays, and yacht marinas.

The county has been divided into twelve touring areas. These are organised in itineraries following the main roads of the county, and exploring interesting places off them. It is not necessary to follow the routes exactly as set out. The intention is that, as you travel from one place to another, you will be aware of the options along that route. The touring information is followed by a list of special events, and contacts for sporting activities in that area, which covers, where available, golf, tennis, horse-riding, bicycle hire, boat hire and angling.

WALKS are included in the touring sections as they are encountered, and are indicated by capitals. Most of the walks are within the 20 minute to two hour category, but I must warn you that I am a fast walker, so allow more time if you are not.

I have used Imperial measures throughout. To convert to metric, multiply as follows:
Inches to millimetres: x 25.4
Feet to metres: x 0.3048
Yards to metres: x 0.9144
Miles to kilometres: x 1.609
Acres to hectares: x 0.4047

Every effort has been made to ensure that the touring directions are clear, but you are well advised to travel with a good map. Anyone who claims that they never get lost in Cork is lying, or else never leaves the main road, and so misses some of the best places. The Ordnance Survey covers the county in four half-inch to the mile maps, but for most purposes their Ireland South Holiday Map (1:250,000 - 4 miles to the inch) or an equivalent, is adequate. The 12 miles-to-an-inch touring map of Ireland is not. Maps are sold in good bookshops, newsagents and Tourist Information Offices. Off the main road, the signposting is terrible; you just have to learn to live with it.

The listings at the end of each chapter contain recommended bars, restaurants and places to stay, and interesting shops and galleries along the route. These represent the best of their kind in all styles and price ranges. The entries are designed to give you enough information to decide for yourself whether the place is one that suits your taste and your budget. They are listed alphabetically under the name of the nearest town or village.

Bar food is normally well under £5 for a main course.

Restaurants are divided into 3 categories, based on the price of a three-course meal excluding drinks and service:
Expensive: over £20
Moderate: £13-£20
Inexpensive: under £13.

Places to stay are divided into four categories based on the price of bed and breakfast per person, sharing a double room:
Very Expensive: over £50
Expensive: £36-£50
Moderate: £18-£36
Inexpensive: under £18.
Credit Cards: Mastercard is accepted by places that take its Irish equivalent, Access.

INSIDER'S CHOICE

Pre-Historic Sites
Drombeg Stone Circle - Chapter Eleven
Kealkil Stone Circle - Chapter Five
Labbacallee Wedge Tomb - Chapter Eight

Early Christian Sites
Lisnagun Ring Fort - Chapter Ten
Knockdrum Ring Fort - Chapter Eleven
St. Gobnait's Shrine - Chapter Seven

Monastic Remains
Timoleague Abbey - Chapter Ten
Ballybeg Abbey, Buttevant - Chapter Six
Kilcrea Abbey, Aherla - Chapter Seven

Churches
St. Colman's Cathedral, Cobh - Chapter Two
St. Mary's Collegiate Church, Youghal - Chapter Four
Timoleague Church of Ireland, - Chapter Ten

Castles
Charles Fort - Chapter Nine
Blarney Castle - Chapter Seven
Liscarroll Castle - Chapter Six

Romantic Ruins
Coppinger's Court - Chapter Eleven
Downeen Castle - Chapter Ten
Dunboy Castle - Chapter Twelve

Houses to Visit
Bantry House - Chapter Eight
Doneraile Court - Chapter Six
Dunkathel House, Glanmire - Chapter Two

Gardens to Visit
Annes Grove Gardens, Castletownroche - Chapter Five
Creagh Gardens, Skibbereen - Chapter Eleven
Illnacullen Gardens, Glengarriff - Chapter Twelve

Outings For Children
Trabolgan Holiday Centre - Chapter Two
Sherkin Island Marine Centre - Chapter Eleven
Fota Wildlife Park - Chapter Two

Sandy Beaches
Garryvoe - Chapter Four
Inchydoney - Chapter Ten
Barley Cove - Chapter Twelve

Scenic Drives
The Ring of Beara - Chapter Twelve
Rosscarbery to Castletownshend via Glandore- Chapter Eleven
The Healy Pass - Chapter Twelve

Walks
Lough Hyne - Chapter Eleven

Allihies Copper Mines - Chapter Twelve
Old Head of Kinsale - Chapter Nine

Forest Trails
Gougane Barra National Park - Chapter Seven
Farran Regional Park - Chapter Six
Currabinny Woods - Chapter Three

Festivals
Cork Jazz Festival - October Bank Holiday
Clonakilty Busking Festival - mid-August
Kinsale Gourmet Festival - late September

Luxury Hotels
Morrison's Island Hotel, Cork - Chapter One
Ballymaloe House - Chapter Four
Longueville House - Chapter Five

Hotels (Moderate)
Marine Hotel, Glandore - Chapter Nine
Ashbourne House, Glounthaune - Chapter One
The West Cork Hotel, Skibbereen - Chapter Four

Country House Accommodation
Ballyvolane House, Castlelyons - Chapter Five
Assolas House, Kanturk - Chapter Six
Bantry House - Chapter Eight

Guest Houses
The Castle, Castletownshend - Chapter Eleven
The Bank House, Kinsale - Chapter Nine
Corthna Lodge Country House, Schull - Chapter Eleven

Farmhouse B & B's
Ballymakeigh House, Killeagh - Chapter Four
Hillcrest, Ahakista - Chapter Twelve
Kilfinnan House, Glandore - Chapter Eleven

Country B & B's
Lissardagh House, Macroom - Chapter Seven
Rathmore House, Baltimore - Chapter Eleven
Glebe House, Ballinadee - Chapter Eight

Restaurants (Expensive)
Arbutus Lodge, Cork - Chapter One
Clifford's, Cork - Chapter One
Shiro Japanese Dinner House, Ahakista - Chapter Twelve

Restaurants (Moderate)
Dunworley Cottage, Butlerstown - Chapter Ten
Lettercollum House, Timoleague - Chapter Ten
Chez Youen, Baltimore - Chapter Eleven

Restaurants (Inexpensive)
Bully's, Cork - Chapter One
Piazetta, Kinsale - Chapter Nine
O'Connor's Seafood, Bantry - Chapter Eight

Bars worth a detour
Reidy's Wine Vaults, Cork - Chapter One
Bunnyconnellan, Myrtleville - Chapter Two
The Pink Elephant, Harbour View - Chapter Ten
Mary Ann's, Castletownshend - Chapter Eleven

INSIDE INFORMATION

Useful Addresses and Phone Numbers

Travel
Cork Airport, Ballygarvan. Tel. 021/313131.
Kent Railway Station, Lower Glanmire Rd. Tel. 021/504422.
Cork Bus Station, Parnell Place. Tel. 021/508188.
B & I Line, 42 Grand Parade, Cork. Tel. 021/273024.
Brittany Ferries, Tourist House, 42 Grand Parade, Cork. Tel. 021/277801.
Swansea Cork Ferries, Grand Parade, Cork. Tel. 021/271166.
Aer Lingus, 38 Patrick St. Cork. Tel. 021/274331.
Ryanair, Passenger Reservations nationwide: Tel. 1-850-567890.

Tourist Information Offices (TIOs)
   The Tourist Advisers in these offices will book your accommodation anywhere in Ireland, (in return for a nominal fee), and provide useful information for visitors. They also sell maps and Bord Failte approved publications. In most towns the local travel agent is usually a source of tourist information off-season. Many towns in the county produce their own tourist information, and, for technical reasons, not all of it is approved and distributed by Bord Failte (neither is this book), but some of it is very useful. This "unofficial" tourist information will usually be given away free in bars, hotels, and banks.
   The following is a list of Bord Failte's TIOs in the county. With the exception of the offices in Cork and Skibbereen they are only open from mid-June to mid-Sept. Normal hours are 9-6 Mon.-Fri, 9-1 Sat., but these may vary locally. It is not possible to give addresses for the smaller TIOs, because many of them do not have a permanent base, but the towns are all so small that you will have no problem in finding them.
   Cork - Tourist House, Grand Parade, Cork - Tel. 021/273251.
   Skibbereen - Town Hall - 028/21766.
   Bantry - Tel. 027/50229.
   Clonakilty - Tel. 023/33226.
   Cork Airport - Tel. 021/964347.
   Cork Ferryport (Ringaskiddy) - services passenger arrivals.
   Glengarriff - Tel. 027/63084.
   Kinsale - Tel. 021/772234.
   Youghal - 024/92390

Car Hire
   Johnson & Perrott Ltd., Emmet Place, Cork. Tel. 021/273295.
   Avis Rent A Car, Cork Airport. Tel. 021/965045.
   Budget Rent A Car, Cork Airport. Tel. 021/314000
   Carental Ireland, Monahan Rd. Cork. Tel. 021/963456.
   Clancy Car Rentals, 47 MacCurtain St. Cork. Tel. 021/503536.
   Deasy Rent A Car, Comons Rd. Cork. Tel. 021/395024.
   Hertz Rent A Car, Cork Airport. Tel. 021/965849.
   Murray's Europcar, Cork Airport. Tel. 021/966736.

Taxis
   Cork Taxi Co-Op, Tel. 021/272222.
   Joyce Russell Cabs Ltd. Tel. 021/509011
   ABC Taxis, Tel. 021/961961.
   Shandon Cabs, Tel. 021/502255.

Emergency Services - Motorists
Automobile Association, Emmet Place, Cork. Tel. 021/276922.
AA Emergency Breakdown, Tel. 021/276922.
Fastfit Exhaust, 37 Patrick's Quay, Cork. Tel. 021/504411.
Auto Exhausts and Windscreens Ltd., Clarkes Bridge, Cork. Tel. 021/273567.
Kirwan & Murphy Kars Ltd. Windscreen Hospital, 38 Patrick's Quay, Cork.
Tel. 021/505668.

24-hour Towing and Breakdown Services:
Casey's Garage, Pine St. Cork. Tel. 021/505050.
A-A-A Autoservices Ltd., Glanmire, Cork. Tel. 021/821276.
Frank Cronin, Greenmount Ave. Cork. Tel. 021/275775.
D. Dennehy, Ltd., Carrigtwohill, Cork. Tel. 021/883300; after hours: 021/822413.
Great Island Motors, Rushbrooke, Cobh. Tel. 021/811609.
Ballinrea Motor Spares, Carrigaline. Tel. 021/372410.
Dempsey's Garage, Kinsale. Tel. 021/772124; after hours: 021/772683.

Police
In emergency dial 999. There are Superintendents' Offices in the following towns:
Bandon - 023/41145; *Bantry* - 02750045; *Clonakilty* - 023/33202; *Cobh* -
021/334002; *Cork*, Barrack St. - 021/271220; *Macroom* - 026/41724; *Mallow* -
022/21105; *Midleton* - 021/631324. Motorists are warned to lock their boots and not
to leave anything visible inside the car, whether valuable or not. Unfortunately visitors' cars are especially vulnerable to attack.

Emergency Services - Health
Ambulance - dial 999.
Southern Health Board, Tel. 021/545011 for the name of your
nearest doctor or dentist.
Cork Regional Hospital, Wilton, Cork. (24-hour casualty dept.). Tel. 021/546400.
Sexually Transmitted Diseases Clinic, Victoria Hospital, Inifrmary Rd. Cork.
Tel. 021/966844.
Cork Family Planning Clinic, Tuckey St. Cork. Tel. 021/277906.
The Samaritans, Coach St. Cork. Tel. 021/271323.
Alcohol and Drug Prevention Centre - Tel. 021/969833.
CURA (Pregnancy counselling service) - 021/277544.
Rape Crisis Centre - 26 MacCurtain St. Tel. 021/968465; after hours: 021/968086.

Gay and Lesbian Contacts
The main gay pub in Cork is *Loafers,* Dougals Street. Women gather there fairly
late on Thursday nights, and the crowd sometimes moves on the the "Sweat Dance"
at *Sir Henry's*, South Main Street. For further information contact *Gay Switchboard*
(mixed) - Weds. 7-9PM - 021/317926, or *Lesbian Line* on the same number Thurs. 8-
10PM. News of gay and lesbian events is usually posted on the noticeboard at the
Quay Co-Op, Sullivan's Quay, tel. 021/967660, which is also the headquarters of the
Lesbian Collective. There is a women-only bed and breakfast at *Amazonia*, Coast
Road, Fountainstown, Tel. 021/831115, Penny Norris or Toni Burgess.

Disabled People
These places have en-suite bedrooms especially adapted for disabled people:
Jury's Hotel, Cork (Chapter One); *Morrison's Island Hotel*, Cork (Chapter One);
Midleton Park Hotel, Midleton (Chapter Four); *Ballymaloe House*, Shanagarry
(Chapter Four); *Ballyvolane House*, Castlelyons (Chapter Five); *Seaview Hotel*,
Ballylickey (Chapter Eight); *Corthna Lodge Country House*, Schull (Chapter Eleven);
West Cork Hotel, Skibbereen (Chapter Eleven). Self-catering facilities suitable for
disabled people are provided at the *Trabolgan Holiday Centre* (see below - *Self-
Catering*).

Self Catering

Cork Kerry Tourism, Tourist House, Grand Parade, Cork (Tel. 021/273251) manages a number of independently owned self-catering properties in the county. They also sell the Irish Tourist Board's *Self Catering Guide* (£4) which covers the whole country. *Mrs. Rosemary Salter-Townshend* manages a wide selection of self-catering premises in the Castletownshend area. Contact her at The Castle, Castletownshend, near Skibbereen. Tel. 028/36100. This is a list of the major self-catering centres in County Cork. Most of them are purpose built cottages or apartments, or modern conversions of existing premises:

Brookfield Self-Catering Accommodation, College Rd. Cork. Tel. 021/344032. *Castlewhite Apartments,* University College, Western Rd. Cork. Tel. 021/341473. *Trabolgan Holiday Centre,* near Midleton. Tel. 021/661511. *The Old Stableyard*, Coolmore, Carrigaline. Tel. 021/372141. *Lovett's,* Churchyard Lane, off Well Rd. Douglas. Tel. 021/294909. *Douglas Village Holiday Homes*, 22 Adare Mews, Douglas. Tel. 021/891885. *Kinsale Holiday Homes*, c/o Joe Cotter, Auctioneer, Newman's Mall, Kinsale. Tel. 021/772510. *The Grove Apartments*, Compass Hill, Kinsale. Tel. 021/772190. *Celtic Cottages*, Rosscarbery, *Ballinglanna Holiday Homes*, Clonakilty, both c/o Nora Wycherley, 13 Ashfield Park, Dublin 4. Tel 01/691000. *Lavalley Cottages*, Desert, Clonakilty. Tel. 023/33472. *Blair's Cove House*, Durrus, near Bantry. Tel. 027/61041. *Colla Pier Cottages, Schull Holiday Cottages*, both c/o Main St. Schull. Tel. 028/28122. *Fastnet Residential Hotel*, Main St. Schull. Tel. 028/28393. *Coastguard Cottages*, Courtmacsherry. Tel. 023/46222. *Courtmacsherry Hotel*, Courtmascsherry. Tel. 023/46198. *Lislee House*, Courtmacsherry. Tel. 023/40126. *Baltimore Harbour Cottages*, Baltimore. Tel. 028/20319. *Beacon Park Hotel*, Baltimore. Tel. 028/20361. *Barley Cove Hotel*, near Goleen. Tel. 028/35234.

Camping and Caravan Sites

Places marked * offer mobile homes for hire by the week.

*Cork City Camping and Caravan Park, Togher Rd. Tel. 021/961866. Open Easter-30 Sept. and October Bank Holiday. *Bienvenue Caravan and Camping Park*, Ballygarvan, near Cork Airport. Tel. 021/312711. Open Easter-31 Oct. *Eagle Point Caravan and Camping Park*, Ballylickey. Tel. 027/50630. Open 1 May-30 Sept. *Sonas Caravan and Camping Park*, Ballymacoda, Near Youghal. Tel. 024/98132. Open Easter-15 Sept. *Murray's Caravan and Camping Park*, Bandon. Tel. 023/41232. Open 1 April-30 Sept. **Barleycove Caravan and Camping Park*, Barleycove. Tel. 028/35302 or 021/54244. Open 2 May-20 Sept. *Cuas An Uisce*, South Harbour, Cape Clear Island. Tel. 028/31149. Open 1 June-30 Sept. *Jasmine Villa Camping and Caravan Park*, Carrigtwohill. Tel. 021/88234. Open all year. *Desert House Caravan and Camping Park*, Clonakilty. Tel. 023/33331. Open Easter week and 3 May-30 Sept. *The Meadow Camping Park*, near Glandore. Tel. 028/33280. Open all year. *Dowling's Caravan and Camping Park*, Glengarriff. Tel. 027/63154. Open 15 March-31 Oct. *O'Shea's Caravan andCamping Park*, Glengarriff. Tel. 027/63140. Open 17 March-18 Oct. **Garrettstown House Holiday Park*, Ballinspittle, Near Kinsale. Tel. 021/778156. Open 16 May-30 Sept. *Trabolgan Holiday Centre*, Near Midleton. Tel. 021/661551. Open 17 March-October Bank Holiday. **Burke's Caravan and Camping Park*, Shanagarry. Tel. 021/646796. Open 1 April-1 Oct. *Sexton's Caravan and Camping Park*, Timoleague. Tel. 023/46347. Open all year. *Summerfield Camping and Caravan Park,* Youghal. Tel. 024/93537. Open 29 May- 6 Sept.

Youth Hostels

An Oige (Irish Youth Hostel Association) has four hostels in county Cork, which are open only to members of *An Oige* or other affiliated youth hostel organisations. They open every evening at 5.30 and close at 11pm, and provide simple dormitory accommodation and cooking facilities. Overnight accommodation costs under £6, less for juniors. Membership costs £7.50 senior, £4.00 under 18. Membership enquiries to *An Oige*, 39 Mountjoy Square, Dublin 1. Tel. 01/363111.

Cork International Hostel, 1 Redclyffe, Western Rd. Cork. Tel. 021/543289. Open all year. *Kinsale Hostel,* Summercove, Kinsale. Tel. 021/772309. Open 1 March-31 Dec. *Cape Clear Island Hostel*, Skibbereen. Tel. 028/39144. Open 1 March-31 Oct. *Allihies Hostel*, Allihies, Bantry. Tel. 027/73014. Open 1 March-30 Sept.

There are two "holiday hostels" in Cork city which provide dormitory accommodation and have no membership requirement and no curfew. Overnight accommodation costs from £5.50.

Isaac's Hostel, 48 MacCurtain St. Tel.021/500011. Open all year. *Kinlay House* (USIT Accommodation Centre), Bob and Joan Walk, Shandon. Tel. 021/508966. Open all year.

The county also has 11 "independent hostels", all of which are members of the Independent Hostel Owners Association of Ireland. Hostels displaying the IHO logo conform to strict fire and hygiene requirements. They offer a combination of dormitory accommodation and private rooms, and charge £4.50 a night for a dormitory bed and up to £7 for a private room. Showers and simple cooking facilities are provided, there is no membership requirement, they are open all day and have no curfew. Young and old are welcome, and they aim to provide a friendly, informal atmosphere. Some have small, inexpensive restaurants and sell organic food and produce. Most people bring their own sleeping bags, although sleeping sheets can be rented, and extra blankets and duvets will be provided free.

Those marked * also offer camping facilities. *Sheila's Tourist Hostel*, Wellington Rd. Cork. Tel. 021/505562. Open all year. *Campus House*, 3 Woodland View, Western Rd. Cork. Tel.021/343531. *Dempsey's Hostel*, Eastern Rd. Kinsale. Tel.021/772124. Open all year. *Lettercollum House*, Timoleague. Tel. 023/46251. Open 1 March-31 Dec. *Shiplake Hostel*, near Dunmanway. Tel.023/45750. Open 15 March-15 Nov. *Tigbarra*, Ballingeary. Tel. 026/47016. Open 14 March- 30 Oct. *Rolf's Hostel*, Baltimore. Tel. 028/20289. Open all year. *Bantry Independent Hostel*, Bishop Lucey Place, Bantry. Tel. 027/51050. Open 15 March-1 Nov. *Tooreen Hostel*, Kenmare Rd. Glengarriff. Tel. 027/63075. Open 1 March-30 Oct. *Beara Hostel*, Castletownbere. Tel. 027/70184. Open all year. *Garranes Farmhouse Hostel*, Allihies, Beara. Tel. 027/73032.

OPEN ALL YEAR.

Residential Activity Holidays

General: *Trabolgan Holiday Centre*, Midleton, Tel.021/661551 offers 18-hole golf, indoor sports centre, indoor swimming pool, badminton, ten pin bowling and snooker, as well as a wide variety of amusements for children. *Oysterhaven Boardsailing Centre*, Oysterhaven, near Kinsale (see Chapter Nine) offers residential courses in self-catering accommodation for a weekend or 7 days. You can either opt for a "multi-activity" holiday, or specialise in improving your tennis, boardsailing, dinghy sailing, or canoeing. Bicycles are available for guests, and there are special rates for group programmes. *Whispering Pines*, Crosshaven (see Chapter Three) offers deep-sea fishing or bicycling holidays. *Streamline Fishing Holidays*, Snave, Ballylickey, near Bantry. Tel. 027/51297 organises tailor-made sporting holidays with the emphasis on trout and salmon fishing, and can also include golf, walking and deep sea fishing. Accommodation is in the Seaview Hotel (see Chapter Eight), or self-catering cottages, and a chauffeur-driven Range Rover is included in the package. **Cookery**: *The Ballymaloe Cookery School*, Shanagarry, Tel. 021/646785, run by the famous TV cook, Darina Allen, offers residential courses at all levels, including specialised weekend courses. *Assolas Country House* (see Chapter Six) offers short courses off season for home cooks wishing to improve their skills. *Lettercollum House*, Timoleague (see Chapter Ten) organises residential weekends in the autumn with tuition in cookery or art. **Yoga and Meditation:** *The Dzogchen Buddhist Centre*, Garranes, Allihies, Tel. 027/73032, offers residential courses with simple cottage accommodation and communal vegetarian meals. **Horse Riding**: *Ardnavaha House Hotel*, Ballinascarthy (See Chapter Ten) offers horse riding holidays with tuition. Hunting can be arranged by request. *Clonmeen Lodge*, Banteer (See Chapter Six) offers tuition, trekking, and hunting with the Duhallow. *Skevanish Riding Centre*, Innishannon, tel. 021/775746 will organise riding holidays with accommodation in local farmhouses or at the Innishannon House Hotel (See Chapter Eight). *Arbutus Lodge*, Cork(See Chapter One) will arrange hunting holidays. *Matt O'Connor*, The Square, Bantry, tel. 027/50221, organises trekking holidays in the West Cork mountains from his Bantry base, with guest house or country house accommodation. **Bicycling**: *Freewheelin' Holidays Ireland Ltd.*, Cotter's Yard, Main St. Schull. tel. 028/28165 organises 7 or 14 day cycling tours based in bed and breakfast accommodation and provide touring or mountain bikes, mechanical back-up, luggage transfer and cycling routes. *Irish Cycling Safaris*, 7 Dartry Park, Dublin 6, tel. 01/978440 offers week long tours of west Cork in groups of up to 20, with guide, tour van, bike rental and bed and breakfast accommodation. **Sailing**: The following offer residential courses at all levels: *Eddie English's International Sailing Centre*, East Beach. Cobh. Tel. 021/811237. *Baltimore Sailing School*, The Pier, Baltimore. Tel. 028/20141. *Glenans Irish Sailing Club Ltd.* have bases at Baltimore and Bere Island, Castletownbere. Contact 28 Merrion Square, Dublin 3. Tel. 01/611481 for details. **Yacht Charter**: *Yachting International Ireland*, Trident Hotel, Kinsale, Tel. 021/772301. **Deep Sea Fishing**: Most hotels and guesthouses in coastal towns offer a deep sea fishing package. *The East Cork Angling Centre*, Loughcarrig House, Ballinacurra, Midleton, tel. 021/631952 specialise in wreck, reef and shark fishing, and their package includes bed and breakfast accommodation in an attractive Georgian house near East Ferry pier. **Angling**: The following hotels and guest houses have private fishing rights either in the grounds or nearby: *Ballyvolane House*, Castlelyons (Chapter Five), *Longueville House*, Mallow (Chapter Five), *Avonmore Country House*, Fermoy (Chapter Five), *Assolas Country House*, Kanturk (Chapter Six), *Clonmeen Lodge*, Banteer (Chapter Six), *Lissardagh House*, Macroom (Chapter Seven), *Coolcower House*, Macroom (Chapter Seven), *Blanchfield House*, Ballinhassig (Chapter Eight), *Innishannon House Hotel* (Chapter Eight), *Courtmacsherry Hotel* (Chapter Ten).

Yacht Clubs and Marinas

The following places offer marina facilities to visitors: *Royal Cork Yacht Club*, Crosshaven. Tel. 021/831023. *Kinsale Yacht Club*, Kinsale. Tel. 021/772196. *East Ferry Marina*, Cobh. Tel. 021/811342.

Hunts and Point to Points

Point to point meetings are held on Sundays from January to May. The entrance fee is about £5 per car, pedestrians free.

The venues are announced in Saturday's *Cork Examiner*. There are eight hunts in the county, all of whom will accommodate visitors by prior arrangement. The name of the hunt and master to contact are listed in *The Irish Field Directory*, or will be given to you by your nearest riding school.

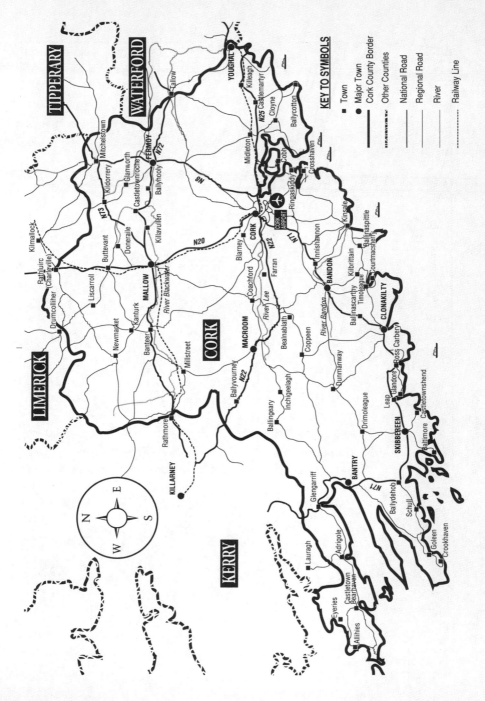

KEY TO SYMBOLS

■ Town
● Major Town
Cork County Border
Other Counties
National Road
Regional Road
River
Railway Line

TIPPERARY

WATERFORD

LIMERICK

CORK

KERRY

YOUGHAL
Killeagh
Castlemartyr
Cloyne
Ballycotton
N25
Midleton
Cobh
Crosshaven
Ringaskiddy
CORK AIRPORT
CORK
Kinsale
Nohaval
Innishannon
Ballinspittle
BANDON
Kilbrittain
Courtmacsherry
Timoleague
Ballinascarthy
CLONAKILTY
Ross Carbery
Glandore
Leap
Castletownshend
Ballymore
SKIBBEREEN
Drimoleague
Castletownshend
BANTRY
Ballydehob
Schull
Goleen
Crookhaven
Glengarriff
N71
Adrigole
Lauragh
Castletown Bearhaven
Eyeries
Allihies

Mitchelstown
Kildorrery
Glanworth
FERMOY
N72
Castletownroche
Ballyhooly
Tallow
Kilmallock
N73
Rathluirc (Charleville)
Drumcolliher
Liscarroll
Buttevant
Doneraile
Killavullen
N20
Blarney
N8
Kanturk
Banteer
MALLOW
River Blackwater
Newmarket
Millstreet
Coachford
Farran
N22
River Lee
Bealnablath
Coppen
MACROOM
N22
Ballyvourney
Inchigeelagh
Dunmanway
River Bandon
Ballingeary
Rathmore
KILLARNEY

N
E
W
S

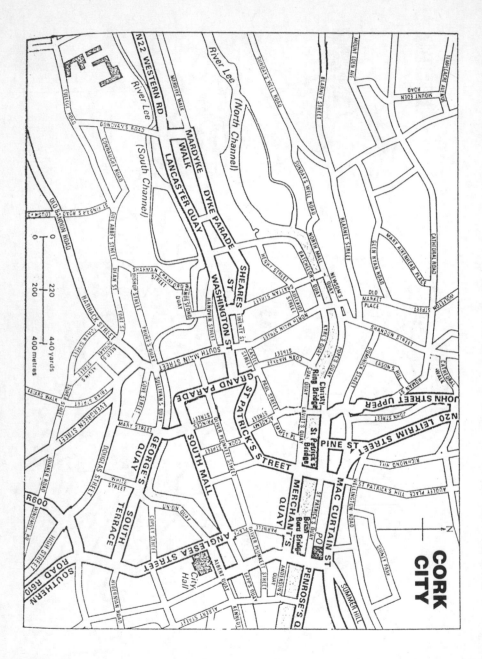

CORK CITY

1 CHAPTER ONE

Cork City

Cork is known as Ireland's "second city", and has an official population of 138,500. Compare this with the estimated one and a half million living in Dublin, and you will have some grasp of the gap between first and second city. Corkonians, however, are intensely chauvinistic. They do not care for comparisons with Dublin, but would rather praise the friendliness of their compact city, and stress the richness of its historic past and the prominence of its citizens' contribution to the sporting and cultural life of the country.

At its best, Cork has great provincial charm and undeniable character. But the twentieth century has not been kind to the fabric of the city, nor has its economic life prospered. Parts of the city are extremely run-down, long-term unemployment is a chronic problem, and emigration is taking a heavy toll on the younger generation. Nevertheless, the physical potential of Cork is great; all it needs is an economic boost.

First impressions of Cork are of water lined by numerous quays and bridges, and it can take newcomers a long time to get their bearings. The north side of the city is built on a steep hill punctuated with church spires which add greatly to the picturesqueness of the place.

Corcaigh means "marshy", and the first historically recorded settlement in the area was made by Saint Finbar in the seventh century A.D., traditionally on the site of the existing St. Finbarre's Cathedral. The Vikings settled nearby in the 900's, and lived in relative harmony with the original Celtic community until the Normans arrived in Cork in 1177. Henry II granted the city its first charter in 1185. The walled medieval city grew up in the area west of the Grand Parade and north of Washington Street, with sea channels coming right up to its gates. As the city grew, other parts of the marsh were drained, and the channels of the River Lee diverted, so that today the main commercial area of the city is on an island connected to the north and south banks by a sequence of bridges.

Cork city reached the height of its prosperity in the 18th century, when its wealth derived from the export of butter and beef and other trading activities that centred on the port. Most of its best buildings date from this period, and from the still self-confident Victorian years. The War of Independence (1916-21) was fought in the streets of Cork, destroying most notably one side of Patrick Street, and the City Hall. Industry came to Cork in the 20th century with the establishment of factories by Dunlop Tyres, Ford Motors and Sunbeam Wolsey. By the early 1980s they had all gone. The docks are still in use, but not to anything like the extent that they once were. Consequently, Cork remains, as it always was, a city of merchants, a port and a commercial centre, not a manufacturing one. The last ten years have seen much urban renewal in the inner city, but much still remains to be done.

One reason why the population of Cork is so low is that many people who work there choose to live outside the city, either in the suburbs or on its rural edges. As a consequence, it can appear something of a ghost town after 6 o'clock. Once you have explored the surrounding countryside, you will understand why. Many people share my ambivalence about Cork City: on a good day, its compactness, its friendliness and the strong character of its buildings and geography combine to make it a delightful spot; if we must have cities, then they should all be as small and as easy to negotiate as this one. On a bad day it looks grim, uncared-for, grey and near-derelict, and I cannot get out of it quickly enough. If you only have one day, or even half a day to explore, then follow Walk One, concentrating on the Crawford Gallery and the pedestrianized area around Paul Street.

Walk One: *the City Centre*

This walk around the commercial centre of Cork can be done in under an hour, but to do justice to its points of interest, allow at least two hours, with a break for coffee and cakes in the Crawford Gallery. It starts at the **Tourist Information Office** in Grand Parade. This short, wide street connects the main shopping area, Patrick Street, to the banking and legal area of the South Mall. A couple of houses across the road from the TIO have retained the bow-windowed slated facades so typical of 18th-century domestic architecture in Cork. Standing with your back to the TIO, you will see the gates of the **Bishop Lucey Park** across the road, which was opened in 1985 as part of Cork's celebrations of the 800th anniversary of the granting of the city charter. The limestone archway originally belonged to the Cornmarket. Inside the small green space is a sculpture park dominated by a fountain with eight bronze swans. Part of the old city walls were found during excavations and they are exposed just inside the entrance. In a narrow lane to the right of the park is the **Triskel Arts Centre** *(Tel. 021/272022. Tobin St. Admission free. Open Mon.-Fri. 11-6, Sat. 11-5)* which holds exhibitions of contemporary art and has a small auditorium used for poetry readings and plays. To the left of the park is a view of the three spires of **St. Finbarre's Cathedral**.

From the TIO turn to your left into the **South Mall**, a wide tree-lined street which is the legal and financial centre of Cork. Both the South Mall and Grand Parade were waterways until the late 18th century; a few houses still have stone steps up to the front door with an arch underneath where boats could unload goods directly into the cellars. **The Imperial Hotel**, on the left-hand side of the street, dates from 1816; Maria Edgeworth, W.M. Thackeray, Dickens, Lizst, Eamon de Valera and Michael Collins are among those who have enjoyed its hospitality down the years. It is worth walking up to the traffic lights at the end of the South Mall to look across the river to the classical limestone facade of the **City Hall**, re-opened by de Valera in 1936. It is the city's main venue for large orchestral concerts. The ornate Corinthian facade of the **Provincial Bank** (now the Allied Irish Bank) at your back has some amusing carvings around its door and window frames.

Return to the Imperial Hotel and turn up Pembroke Street at its side. This leads into **Oliver Plunkett Street**, one of Cork's main shopping streets, and the **General Post Office**, a neo-classical building on the site of the 18th-century Theatre Royal. The pedestrianised way in front of the GPO leads to **Patrick Street**, the main shopping street of Cork city. It has probably seen its heyday, and it is fast being eclipsed by the Paul Street area. But up to the mid-60s, a walk down busy Patrick Street was considered the height of sophistication, both for natives of the city and their country cousins, and itinerant photographers used to do a great business snapping the elegantly dressed shoppers and selling them the result.

Up to 1800 Patrick Street was also a waterway, with boats moored under tall steps such as those in front of the Chateau bar. Pause for a minute, looking across at the other side of the broad, curving street. This is the side that survived the damage of the civil war, and above the level of the modern shop facades, some of the original 18th-century bow-fronted windows can still be seen.

Turn right and walk up to the bridge. On that corner is the £30 million **Merchant's Quay Shopping Centre**, opened in 1989. Its design, which recalls the old warehouses where the tall ships used to take on cargo, is best appreciated from the other side of **Patrick's Bridge**, which is in front of you. The steeple to the left on the opposite bank of the river with a clock face and a fish weather vane is the famous **Shandon Steeple**. In the centre of the street, facing the bridge, is the **Father Mathew Statue**, a memorial to the temperance pioneer (1790-1861) who, besides running a successful campaign against the ingestion of alcohol, was also a great champion of the city's poor. It is the work of the sculptor John Foley (1818-1874), who also worked on the Albert memorial in London. "De Statcha", as it is known colloquially in Cork, has never been the same since the popular local musician Jimmy Crowley revived the old Cork song, "The Boys of Fair Hill", with its immortal opening lines "The smell on Patrick's Bridge is wicked/How does Father Mathew stick it?" To which, in all fairness, must be added the fact that these days the only smell on Patrick's Bridge comes from the traffic.

Turn left at Patrick's Bridge and walk up **Lavitt's Quay** towards the **Cork Opera House**, an ungainly concrete building designed by Michael Scott which opened in 1965, the original having burnt down in 1955. **The Christy Ring Bridge** beside the Opera House, named after the famous Cork hurler, was opened in 1990. Follow the curve of Emmet Place to arrive at the **Crawford Art Gallery**, *(Tel. 021/273377. Admission free. Open Mon.-Fri. 9-5, Sat. 9-1.)* which is indisputably Ireland's leading provincial gallery. It mounts regular exhibitions by contemporary artists from Ireland and abroad, and has a fine permanent collection of paintings and sculpture.

Turn right out of the Crawford Gallery and cross the road in front of you, entering the pedestrianised lane which leads to the **Paul Street Plaza**. This is a popular venue for buskers and street theatre, and is the centre of a revitalized shopping district which was rescued over the past ten years from virtual dereliction. The House of James, for example, a large shop on the left hand side, was a disused warehouse not so long ago.

Continue up Paul Street until you come to a pub called The Roundy House. The area to your right, **The Cornmarket**, is better known as the **Coal Quay** and was once a thriving outdoor market. Today it is a sad affair with one or two stalls selling electrical goods and a number of tables displaying tatty heaps of second-hand clothing. In its prime the Coal Quay (pronounced "kay" in Cork City) was as famous for its prostitutes as for its market, and in the 1920s the city burghers decided to get rid of the former by discouraging the latter, and it never really recovered, despite recent efforts to persuade craft workers to sell there on Saturdays as a tourist attraction.

Return to the junction of Patrick Street and Grand Parade and turn left. If you are interested in churches, take a look at the Gothic facade of Saints Peter and Paul in the narrow street next to the pedestrian crossing; it was designed by E.W. Pugin. Cross Patrick Street and walk up Grand Parade until you come to the wrought iron arch which is one of several entries to the **English Market** *(Open Mon.-Sat. 9-5.30,)*. Anyone who likes food will enjoy a tour of this covered market. The first stall sells the ingredients for the famous Cork dish, tripe and drisheen - cow's intestines and blood sausage. The interior is divided into sections for fishmongers, butchers, poulterers and greengrocers. Be sure to get right to the back where a courtyard with a fountain allows you to appreciate the elegantly designed cast iron infrastructure of the building.

Come out into Grand Parade again. The shopping centre across the road on the right, the **Queen's Old Castle**, is on the site of a castle that guarded the watergates to the medieval city of Cork. Cross Grand Parade and walk up Washington Street. The site of medieval Cork is on your right. Today it is an unfashionable shopping area, and visitors curious about its medieval past will have to wait until the promised Interpretative Centre, which will explain medieval Cork in detail, opens in the area. **The Courthouse**, on Washington Street is an unmistakable building with an imposing classical portico dating from 1830, another of Cork's landmarks.

If you are interested in having a closer look at St. Finbarre's Cathedral, you can extend this walk by crossing the road outside the courthouse and walking down **South Main Street**, then crossing the river at the **South Gate Bridge**. A right turn on the opposite bank of the river will bring you to the cathedral. On the way you have the chance to look at a sadly neglected monument, **Elizabeth Fort**. It is reached by going up a narrow entrance on the left, as you walk along the river bank, called **Keyser's Lane**. This was a star-shaped fort built in 1603, in the reign of Elizabeth I. It was badly damaged in the Great Siege of 1690 by the Duke of

Marlborough, and was subsequently used as a prison, and an artillery barracks. Today there is a Garda Station in the internal courtyard. One curtain wall remains from the original fort, and from its summit there is an unusual view of Cork with the Beamish Brewery in the foreground.

Walk Two - *North Cork City*

You can walk from the city centre to Shandon steeple and back in about an hour. Not everyone will find this excursion satisfying, so the walk is extended as far as Montenotte, making a round trip of about one and a half hours.

Start at the Courthouse, taking the right-hand turn above it, then the wide road on your left, Sheares Street. Turn right into Prospect Row, and pass **The Mercy Hospital**. This Italianate building, designed by David Ducart, was originally erected in 1767 as the Mansion House for the Lord Mayor of the city. It has fine internal plasterwork, and is open to the public. It has been run as a hospital by the Sisters of Mercy since 1857. Grenville Place will take you down to the quays again, where you can cross the north channel of the River Lee by **St. Vincent's Footbridge**. Pause for a minute to admire the open stretch of river on the left, which, with any luck, should be graced by a flock of swans floating beneath the old industrial buildings of the Maltings and the Distillery.

Turn right along the tree-lined **North Mall**, a favourite promenade in the 18th century, much neglected today. Note the ornate fanlights above the front doors of the houses, a typical feature of Cork's domestic architecture. At the **North Gate Bridge**, turn left up the steep hill of Shandon Street. The steeple is clearly visible, and is also signposted on the right. Take a few minutes to explore the lanes around the church; they are too narrow for motor traffic, and are lined with beautifully-kept one and two-storey cottages. The lane on the left (facing St.Anne's) will lead you to **St. Mary's Pro-Cathedral**, a 19th-century Catholic church of no great architectural merit. It does, however, have records of baptism and marriages dating from 1748 which are a good source of family history.

The famous **Shandon Steeple** belongs to an early 18th-century parish church, **St. Anne's** (*Admission £1, £1.50 with bell tower. Open Mon.-Sat. 9.30- 5, May-Oct.; 10-3.30, Nov.-April*). The name *Sean Dun* means "old fort", and there was once a Barry castle near the site. The steeple is faced on two sides with white limestone, on the other two with red sandstone, and has four clock faces. It is topped with an 11 foot long weather vane in the shape of a salmon, thus giving the citizens of Cork both the time and the weather forecast. Its bells were made famous by a Cork wit, "Father Prout", alias Francis Mahony, (1804-1866) who is buried here, but I cannot bring myself to quote his awful doggerel. It is not widely known that Mahony abandoned the priesthood in 1834, and led a rather interesting life henceforth as a journalist in Paris and Rome. If you climb the bell tower your £1.50 entitles you to play tunes such as "Danny Boy" on the bells by pulling the ropes according to instructions on cards. The red-carpeted interior of the small church is of an austere Georgian design with a dark wood barrel ceiling.

Opposite the church is the newly restored **Butter Market**. Once the centre of Cork's economic life, it is now the **Shandon Craft Centre** (*Tel. 021/397711. Open 9-6, Mon.-Sat.*). The beautiful rotunda beside it, known as the **Firkin Crane**, is used for concerts, lectures and other events.

Make your way back downhill to the quays again, turning left when you reach them. At **Patrick's Bridge** turn left and look up **Patrick's Hill**, a street so steep that it has steps cut in the pavement. Walk up to the junction with **MacCurtain Street** and turn right, continuing on to the next traffic lights. On the right is the newly restored **Everyman Palace Theatre** (*Tel.021/501673*) which hosts theatrical touring companies from Ireland and abroad. If it is open, ask to have a look at the auditorium whose gilded boxes have been restored to their Victorian glory.

MacCurtain street divides into three at the first traffic lights, straight on leading to

Kent Station, Cork's rail terminus, and the left, **Summerhill**, up to **St. Luke's Cross** and the Victorian suburb, **Montenotte**, still considered " a good address" among upwardly-mobile Corkonians. If you want to extend your walk, continue up Summerhill; otherwise turn sharp right and return to the city centre across **Brian Boru Bridge**, which leads to the **Bus Station**.

St. **Luke's Church**, on the right at St. Luke's Cross, is a good example of the stye of decoration nicknamed "streaky bacon" which is so typical of Cork. It results from the combination of white limestone and red sandstone already observed on the Shandon Steeple. The booth in the middle of the road was once a toll booth. Note the fine Victorian facade of **Henchy's Pub**.

To explore Montenotte, take the right hand turn here, the **Middle Glanmire Road**, which passes the famous Arbutus Lodge Hotel, and offers fine views of Cork City and the lower harbour. Large Victorian villas behind high stone walls are typical of the area. Across the river is **Blackrock Castle**, a battlemented limestone building on the water's edge, which matches the castles on the city's coat of arms. It was built in 1830, to replace an earlier fortification, and is now a restaurant and function room.

Walk Three: *West of the City*

This walk visits the campus of University College and the Cork City Museum in Fitzgerald Park, and takes about an hour and a half. To avoid the dull stretch up Washington Street and the Western road, take any bus heading in that direction and get off at the gates of UCC. Otherwise start walking from the Courthouse, leaving the Grand Parade at your back.

The portico at the pedestrian entrance to **University College** *(Tel. 021/276871. Admission free. Open Mon.-Fri. 9-5, but phone to confirm during vacations.)* is part of the facade of the County Gaol, which stood on that site. On your left is a pleasant sunken shrubbery, reached by a single-span stone arch, leading to a short but pleasant river-side walk. The main path leads to the quadrangle built in the Tudor-Gothic style, reminiscent of many Oxbridge colleges, in the mid-19th century. The university was opened by Queen Victoria in 1849, and currently has a student population of about 8000. In the corridors of the quad there is a good collection of Ogham stones - prehistoric standing stones with inscriptions in an early alphabet. The **Aula Maxima**, a high ceilinged room with panelled walls, is used for chamber music recitals.

Opposite the quad is the **Boole Library**, a modern building named after a 19th century professor of mathematics whose Boolean logic became the basis of modern computer science. A signpost in front of the library will direct you to the **Honan Chapel**, built in 1916 and modelled on the 12th century Hiberno-Romanesque style. The interior is well worth looking at, with 8 stained glass windows by Sarah Purser and 11 by Harry Clarke. Note also the mosaic floor and the unusual semi-circular Stations of the Cross. Mass is said here at 12.15 daily.

Return to the Gaol gates, and cross to the other side of the Western road, where a signpost for Fitzgerald Park will direct you to the left. This is **The Mardyke**, a popular riverside walk with Cork citizens since it was laid out in 1719, nowadays, alas, lacking its tall elms which were victims of the Dutch elm disease. On the right is a cricket ground, cricket having remained an active sport in Cork even after the departure of the British Army who introduced it. *(Tel. 021/364735 for details of fixtures)*. The gates of **Fitzgerald Park** *(Open 8.30-5 1 Oct.-31 Mar.; 8.30-8 April & Sept.; 8.30 10 June and July; open 10AM Suns. and Bank Holidays.)* are on the right. It is an unexceptional city park on the banks of the Lee, with formal rose beds, some interesting sculptures and a duck pond. The suburb on the other side of the river is known as **Sunday's Well**. The large Georgian house near the entrance to the park is the **Cork Public Museum** *(Tel. 021/270679. Admission free. Open Mon.-Fri. 11-1 and 2.15-5; Sun. 3-5. Closed Sat. and Bank Holiday weekends.)* The displays will answer any questions you may have about Cork City. They are designed to appeal to all age groups, and include such homely items as the hat and rifle of Cork's Lord Mayor Terence MacSwiney (who died on hunger strike in Brixton Gaol in 1920), the top-coat of Daniel O'Connell, "the Liberator", (1745-1833), as well as examples of the work of 18th century silversmiths and glass-makers, and archaeological displays. Don't miss the push-button illuminated mural of the Crossbarry ambush which is totally ingenious, but also absolutely baffling.

Parking

A disc system is in operation, and parking areas throughout the city centre are indicated by a P sign. A plaque underneath tells you whether the disc is good for one, two or three hours. Discs can be bought singly for 40p or in books of 10 for £4 at the Tourist Information Office and shops displaying the Parking Disc logo in the window. There are two multi-storey car parks, the **City Centre Car Park** with an entrance on Lavitt's Quay one block west of the Opera House, and **Roches Stores Car Park** with an entrance in Parnell Place.

Important Addresses and Phone Numbers
(See also INSIDE INFORMATION)
Cork Tourist Information Office, Grand Parade. Tel. 021/273251.
Kent Railway Station, Lower Glanmire Rd. Tel. 021/504422.
Bus Station, Parnell Place. Tel. 021/508188
Cork Airport, Ballygarvan. Tel. 021/313131.
Gardai, Barrack St. Tel. 021/271220.

Sporting Facilities

Golf: *Mahon Golf Course,* off Skehard Rd. Blackrock, tel. 021/362480. 18-hole municipal course with golf equipment for hire. (See also Chapters Two and Six). **Tennis**: *Tennis Village Cork Ltd.*, Ballygoggin, Model Farm Rd. Tel. 021/342727: 24 hours facilities indoor and out. For details of tennis courts provided by *Cork Corporation* tel. 021/ 966222, ext. 333 or 323. **Horse Riding**: *Pine Grove Equestrian Centre*, White's Cross. Tel. 021/303857. *Castlewhite Riding Centre*, The Viaduct, Waterfall. Tel. 021/543646. *Greybrook Riding School*, Waterfall. Tel. 021/873194. **Bicycle Hire**: *A.A. Bike Shop*, 68 Shandon St. Tel. 021/304154. *Carroll Cycles*, Dillon's Cross. Tel. 021/508923. *Cycle Centre*, Kyle St. Tel. 021/276255. **Indoor Swimming**: *Jury's Hotel*, Western Road. Tel. 021/276622. The indoor-outdoor heated pool, sauna and jacuzzi are open to the public until 5PM daily, admission £6, £3 children. For details of public swimming pools, contact *Cork Corporation*, tel. 021/966222, ext.333 or 323. **Fishing**: Salmon and Trout: details from *The Tackle Shop*, Lavitt's Quay. Tel. 021/272842. Coarse fishing: The Lough, Lough Rd.

PUBS, RESTAURANTS, SHOPS AND ACCOMMODATION

(Price Categories are explained in HOW TO USE THIS BOOK)

Cork City Bars
THE HI-B
Oliver Plunkett St. Tel. 021/227581.
This is a small first-floor bar opposite the GPO, and could politely be described as eccentric. The music, which comes from a cassette player behind the horseshoe-shaped bar, will probably be grand opera. The place is, frankly, shabby, but it is famous for its conversation, not for its looks. If you sit up at the bar be prepared to discuss the latest developments in art and literature with your neighbours, or your host, Brian O'Donnell.

Cork City Bar Food

THE VINEYARD
Market Lane, Patrick St. Tel. 021/274793. Bar food 12.30-2.15 Mon.-Fri.
This atmospheric old bar is in an alley that runs between the Grand Parade end of Patrick Street and the English Market. It has been in the Mackesy family since 1911, and was recently refurbished and extended without losing any of the charm of its wood-panelled interior. The carvery lunch offers a roast of the day and a selection of 8 or 9 other main courses.

BEECHER'S INN
Faulkener's Lane, Patrick St. Tel. 021/273144. Bar food 12.30-3.
This is a chic little bar up a narrow street opposite Winthrop Street on the middle bend of Patrick's Street. The tables are a bit cramped, but the food is good, and includes light seafood options as well as substantial hot dishes.

THE LONG VALLEY
Winthrop St. Tel. 021/272144. Bar food available all day.
With your back to the GPO in Oliver Plunkett street, you will see the Long Valley on the right-hand side of the pedestrian precinct. The sandwiches at the Long Valley are legendary, and visitors with an interest in food should not leave the city without trying one. Thick slices of white or brown bread are filled with salad and/or meat, carved from freshly cooked joints of ham, pork or corned beef behind the bar by motherly ladies in white overalls. The clientele is from all walks of life, but student types predominate, especially in the evenings. The owner has a strange collection of military marching music and hits from old American musicals which provide a good talking point.

CLANCY'S
15 Prince's St. Tel. 021/271726. Bar food 12.30-2.30 Mon.-Sat. This large Victorianized bar runs right across the block from Marlboro Street to Prince's Street with entrances in both. It is dimly lit and a little smoky but enormously popular and has a major bar food operation from a small self-service counter. If at all possible, avoid the 1 o'clock to 1.40 rush. There are salads and sandwiches and a choice of hot dishes including the roast of the day, chicken of some sort, a casserole, lasagna, and deep-fried fish, all served with either salad or two veg. and two kinds of potatoes. There is a wide choice of seating areas, the nicest being the marble-topped tables under large Tiffany lamps near the Prince's Street entrance. Unusually among Cork bars, this one seems even more popular with women than with men, at least at lunchtime. I found the scruffy plants hanging in unruly fringes from the ceiling very worrying; either they were plastic and dirty, or they were dying.

LE CHATEAU
Patrick St. Tel. 021/270370. Bar food 10.30-9.30, 7 days.
The Chateau in the middle of Patrick street has been a Cork landmark since 1783. It is also known as the traditional watering hole for workers at the Cork Examiner who have their offices above it, and is therefore the closest Cork can offer to a journalist's pub. The front bar was totally refurbished in 1992, with stylish Victorian fittings, and has a reliable selection of casual bar food - lasagna, pates, soup, chicken dishes, smoked salmon - with plenty of space to eat it in the back.

IMPERIAL HOTEL
South Mall. Tel. 021/274040. Bar food 12.30-2.30.
The spacious front bar of the Imperial Hotel serves a good quality, self-service carvery lunch, where the roast joint of the day is carved in front of you by a chef. Soup, salads (including seafood salads) and a selection of puddings are also available. There is a quieter back bar adjoining a small restaurant, where women on their own can feel perfectly at ease, and the coffee is excellent.

REIDY'S WINE VAULT
Western Rd. Tel. 021/275751. Bar food 10.30-9.30, 7 days.
This quiet, family-run Victorian bar opposite Jury's Hotel was Black and White Pub

of the Year in 1987 and has received several other awards for its food. It deserves one for its decor as well. If you are not familiar with Irish pubs and want to have a look at a prime example, then this is the place to go. It is hard to believe that it has only been here four years; before that the long, high-ceilinged room was indeed a wine vault. The massive carved mahogany bar backed by mirrors came from a hotel in Leeds. Globe lamps sit on brass pillars along the counter. The two large lanterns in the ceiling have been fitted with art-deco stained glass. Black and white tiling around the bar area lightens the place up, and the tall ceiling stops it getting smoky. Brown velvet banquettes encircle antique tables, and the walls are covered in interesting framed prints. There are always Irish specials on the menu, such as Irish stew or smoked salmon; there is fresh sea food daily, home-made soup, sandwiches and the usual stand-bys like lasagna and chicken curry.

DAN LOWREY'S
MacCurtain St. Tel. 021/505071. Bar food 12-3, Mon.-Fri.
Situated north of the River Lee between the Metropole Hotel and the Everyman Palace, Lowrey's is a small, old fashioned bar serving primarily seafood. There are salads or sandwiches of prawn, smoked salmon, fresh salmon, crab, chicken or beef, plus home-made soup with brown bread.

HENCHY'S
St. Luke's Cross. Tel. 021/501115. Bar food 12.30-2.30 Mon.-Sat.
St. Luke's Cross is above the railway station at the junction of Wellington road and the Middle Glanmire road. Henchy's was a grocery and bar until 1983, and has retained many of the features of its original 1884 interior, including the snug at the front of the bar, much of the original Victorian stained and leaded glass, and the solid mahogany bar top which was once the grocer's counter. The bar menu has interesting hot dishes like savoury pancake, chicken pie, cod and garlic crumb, as well as soup, sandwiches and salads.

ARBUTUS LODGE - see below - Restaurants, Expensive.

Cork City Music Bars and Nightlife
The best guide to what's on tonight is the **Evening Echo** which is sold in the city every afternoon except Sunday. Friday to Sunday are the best nights, and some places also have music on Wednesdays.

Jury's Hotel, Western Road, tel. 021/276622 have Irish cabaret, mainly for the package tour trade from mid-May to mid-Sept. Check out *Fitzpatrick Silver Springs Hotel*, Tivoli, tel. 021/507533, for big-name cabaret and the best local (soul and R &B) bands. The best places for jazz are The Metropole Tavern at the *Metropole Hotel*, MacCurtain St., tel.021/508122, and the bar of *Morrison's Island Hotel*, Morrison's Island, tel. 021/275858. For nightclubs try *Mangan's*, (disco), 16 Carey's Lane, tel. 021/276531; *The Pav*, (disco and live bands), 13 Carey's Lane, tel. 021/276330; *Sir Henry's*, (disco and live bands), Grand Parade Hotel, tel. 021/274391; *Fast Eddy's*, (disco and live bands), Tuckey St. tel. 021/272252. The main musics bars are: *De Lacy House*, (separate venues for rock and new wave, traditional and folk), Oliver Plunkett St. tel. 021/270074; *Rearden's Mill*, (rock bands in bar, disco or bands upstairs), 26 Washington St. tel. 021/271969; *The Lobby*, (traditional music sessions in bar, Irish and international folk music upstairs), Union Quay, tel. 021/31113; *Nancy Spain's*, (rock bands), 48 Barrack St. tel. 021/313722; *Mojo's*, (Rock and Rhythm and Blues), 1 Buckingham Place, George's Quay, tel. 021/311786; *The Joshua Tree*, (rock and some traditional), 70 Blarney St. tel. 021/393848; *The Bodhran*, (very loud traditional), 42 Oliver Plunkett St. tel. 021/274544; *An Spalpin Fanach*, (traditional sessions in bar, traditional bands upstairs), 28 South Main St. tel.021/277949. Some of these bars charge about £2 admission if there is a band playing.

Cork City Restaurants

Expensive - over £20 for a three course meal excluding drinks and service.

ARBUTUS LODGE

Middle Glanmire Rd. Montenotte. Tel. 021/501237. Open: bar food 12.30-2.30, restaurant 1-2 and 7-9.30 Mon.-Sat. Reservations advised. Fully licensed. Credit Cards: Visa, Access, Amex, Diners.

The Arbutus is one of the most famous restaurants in Ireland, and its wine list is reckoned by two independent authorities to be among the best in the world. It is run by the Ryan family who are all catering professionals, and whose attention to detail is legendary. The dining room is in a Victorian villa overlooking the harbour from the heights of the up-market suburb of Montenotte. It has a tall ceiling and a large bay window, and is furnished with polished mahogany sideboards and original Irish paintings. Each table is beautifully laid with monogrammed napery and specially designed tableware, and has its own elaborate fresh flower arrangement. The menu is highly sophisticated with dishes such as baked sea bass in sea urchin sauce or haute cuisine interpretations of traditional Irish dishes, and uses only the best fresh local produce. The bar food menu gives travellers on a budget a chance to sample the Arbutus' style; it is served in a large room with a panoramic view over the river Lee and a tree shaded terrace, and features traditional dishes like tripe and drisheen or steak and kidney pie as well as salads.

CLIFFORD'S

18 Dyke Parade. Tel. 021/275333. Open 12.30-2.30 and 7-10.30 Mon.-Fri.;7-10.30 Sat. Booking advisable. Wine licence only. Credit Cards: Visa, Access, Amex, Diners.

This fashionable little restaurant is a short walk from Jury's hotel. The 50-seater room in a Georgian house has been strikingly modernized with art deco style tall-backed chairs and jazzy black and white curtains, while retaining original features like the plasterwork on the ceiling. The combination gives the room a very special, and usually very lively, ambience. Owner-chef Michael Clifford was once the head chef at the Arbutus, and keeps standards high by offering a set menu with limited choice, while his wife Deirdre copes admirably with the front of house. Since going independent about 5 years ago, he has established himself as a chef to be reckoned with. All food is freshly prepared to order and beautifully presented but without the over-fussiness of some nouvelle cuisine. Typical starters could be saute of pigeon and rabbit in a chestnut sauce, or warm scallop and avocado salad, with main courses like black sole and prawn in a pepper and lime sauce, or medallions of beef on a bed of spinach in a light port and Chetwynd cheese sauce.

THE FASTNET

Jury's Hotel, Western Rd. Tel. 021/276622. Open dinner only Tues.-Sat. Booking advisable. Credit Cards: Visa, Access, Amex, Diners.

This is Jury's luxury restaurant, installed in a well-designed corner of the open-plan hotel with screens of hanging plants and split level floors. The menu offers a wide-ranging selection of international cuisine with a strong emphasis on seafood. The a la carte menu changes every month, and the set dinner changes weekly. This is luxury food: Beluga caviar at £40 and foie gras at £19.75 are the most expensive starters. Main courses include the option of Chateaubriand for two, or dishes like roast magret of duck in an Armagnac sauce. For pudding you can have crepes flambéd at your table. There is a choice of 140 wines on their list.

FLEMING'S

Silvergrange House, Tivoli. Tel. 021/821621. Open 12.30-3 and 6-10.30, 7 days. Booking advisable PM. Wine licence only. Credit Cards: Visa, Access, Amex, Diners.

Fleming's overlooks the river from a hill just beyond the Silver Springs Hotel on the main N22. The entrance is through a Victorian glass porch at the back of the 3-storey Georgian house. The dining room occupies two inter-connecting rooms with opulent moire silk curtains matching the pale yellow walls. Padded Louis XV style chairs, chandeliers and gilt-framed portraits add to the formally elegant atmosphere. Internationally-experienced owner-chef Michael Fleming serves a classical French menu with snails, sweetbread terrine and foie gras among the starters, and elaborate main courses like chicken breast filled with mango mousse wrapped in pastry, fillet steak in red wine with a confit of garlic and shallots, or salmon mousseline with trout in a champagne sauce. There are four spacious bedrooms with bathroom en suite and television, decorated in a similarly elegant style with antique furniture, brocade bedspreads and tasselled brocade curtains matching the skirted bedside tables. Ask about the special "dine and stay" rate, which at press time was a very competitive £50 per head.

Cork City Restaurants

Moderate: £13-£20 for a 3-course meal, excluding drinks and service.

THE OYSTER TAVERN

Market Lane, Patrick St. Tel. 021/272716. Open 12-3 and 6-12 midnight, Mon.-Sat. Reservations advised. Fully licensed. Credit Cards: Visa, Access, Amex, Diners.

This is a Cork institution that has been serving hearty meals for over 200 years, and is still a favourite for business lunches and family celebrations. The 1989 refurbishment added a piano to the front bar, which regulars are still getting used to. The main attraction of the Oyster is its old fashioned atmosphere, reminiscent of a Victorian gentleman's club, with dark woodwork, plush upholstery, original 18th century mirrors and black and white uniformed waitresses. It is best known for its char-grilled steaks, roast duckling, Dover sole on the bone, and home-smoked salmon.

JACQUES

9 Phoenix St. Tel. 021/277387. Open 9AM-12 midnight, dinner from 6PM. Booking advisable PM. Wine licence only. Credit Cards: Visa, Access, Amex, Diners.

Jacques is in a small side street off the street that runs down the side of the Imperial hotel to the GPO.

In the daytime this is a rather ordinary self-service place; at night it transforms itself into a romantic 35-seater restaurant with an interesting menu closely supervised by the female co-owner and chef. The candle-lit decor is reminiscent of an Italian trattoria with rough cast walls, hung with framed modern prints, and a choice of low-backed four-seater booths or round tables with stick-back chairs. The menu is eclectic and tempting - for example, oven-baked quail marinated in sesame oil, soya and garlic, or organic goat stuffed with a duxelle of walnuts on puy lentils with bordelaise sauce.

O'KEEFFE'S OF CORK

23 Washington St. Tel. 021/275645. Open from 6.30 Mon.-Sat.; lunch by arrangement. Booking advisable PM. Wine licence only. Credit Cards: Visa, Access, Amex, Diners.

A small shop has been converted into a 33-seater restaurant, and is run by a husband and wife team, Marie being the chef. The O'Keeffes have built up a good reputation since taking it over in 1990. Heavy pine-green curtains in the window cut it off from the street outside; the walls are dove grey, and the tables are set with linen cloths and fresh flowers. The cooking is stylish and imaginative: Brazilian salad with fresh prawns and crab claws is a typical starter. Main courses might include rack of lamb with a mashed potato and pesto crust, or fresh scallops with olive oil and garlic.

Cork City Restaurants

Inexpensive: under £13 per head for a 3-course meal, excluding drinks.

BALLYMALOE AT THE CRAWFORD

Crawford Art Gallery, Emmet Place. Tel. 021/274415. Open 10-5 Mon.-Sat.; lunch 12-2.30; dinner 6.30-9.30 Weds.-Fri. Wine licence only. Credit Cards: Visa, Access.

The restaurant is in a room that was previously part of the gallery, and still has a couple of large statues. Tables are well-spaced, and it is so popular that there is often a queue at lunchtime. The reason for this is that the food, prepared by a team from the famous country house hotel, Ballymaloe, is superb. There is a good selection of unusual open sandwiches at lunchtime, and the seafood is freshly caught daily in Ballycotton. Their cakes and puddings are also renowned. A proper three-course dinner here will take you into the Moderate price bracket, but still represents good value. In between meals it is a good place to observe Cork's more artistic souls indulging in animated gossip.

BULLY'S
14 Paul St. Tel. 021/273555. Open 12-12 midnight, Mon.-Sat., 5-12 Suns. Wine licence only.

This well-established restaurant is in a long, narrow room with a good buzzy atmosphere, in the fashionable pedestrianised area parallel to Patrick Street. The menu is mainly Italian, featuring pizzas, pastas, including vegetarian options, fresh seafood and grills. Their home-made cannelloni, with meat or spinach filling, is especially recommended.

DELHI PALACE
6 Washington St. Tel. 021/276227. Open 12.30-2.30 Thurs.-Sat. and 5.30-12.30AM Mon.-Sun. Wine licence only. Credit Cards: Visa, Access.

This rather smart tandoori restaurant is separated from the busy street outside by a wooden screen. Black lacquer Louis XV type chairs are placed at tables set with practical pale peach paper cloths and over-mats. There is an authentic range of Indian food including sizzling tandoori specials, rogan josh, paratha, chappatis and complimentary poppadums. Late-night opening is unusual in Cork, making this a very useful place to know about.

HALPIN'S
14 Cook St. Tel. 021/277853. Open 9-12 midnight, Mon.-Sat.; 12-12 Suns. Full licence. Credit Cards: Visa, Access.

In the daytime this is a busy self-service restaurant offering generous salads, home-made pizzas and curries, a selection of hot daily specials and a good range of patisserie. At night it changes into a more intimate restaurant with waiter service. There is a labyrinth of interconnecting rooms furnished with variations on a theme of old pine - you can choose between large or small refectory tables or private booth-type seating with old church pews. The food is not wildly exciting, but it is reasonably priced, and comes in portions large enough to satisfy most appetites.

THE HUGUENOT
French Church St. Tel. 021/273357. Open 12.30-2.30 Mon.-Sat.; 6-10.30 Mon.-Fri., 6-11 Sat. Wine licence only. Credit Cards: Visa, Access.

Situated in one of the pedestrianised lanes running between Patrick Street and Paul Street, this restaurant is in an unusual high ceilinged room which is dominated by an elaborate carved mahogany fireplace on one side and a bar on the other. A gallery runs around the top of the room and has extra tables for busy nights or private parties. It looks the sort of place that will be rather expensive, but surprisingly it is not, with a very accessible bistro-style menu offering dishes like lamb cutlets in red wine sauce, seafood pasta or seafood pancake, chicken Kiev, stir-fried pork with bean sprouts, and, at the expensive end of the menu, a 10oz. sirloin steak. There is usually a special value pre-theatre menu available between 6 and 7.30.

QUAY CO-OP
24 Sullivan's Quay. Tel. 021/967660. Open 10-6 Mon.-Sat., 6.30-10.30 Weds.-Sat. Wine licence only. Credit Cards: Visa, Access.

This is Cork's leading vegetarian restaurant, but you need have no fear of the proverbial dry nut cutlet here; the menu is most imaginative, and the chefs are not afraid to make generous use of seasonings. It is easy to find from the Tourist Information Office in Grand Parade; first cross the street, then cross the pedestrian bridge over the river. The restaurant is in two interconnecting rooms above the Co-

Op's wholefood shop. In the day-time it is self-service and is patronised by the kind of anxious-looking committed vegetarians that you find wherever there is a whole-food shop; at night the room with the food counter is divided off by a dark-wood bead curtain, there is waitress service and a rather more congenial crowd of diners. The walls of the old house are painted in peach with dark blue woodwork, and there are polished wood floors. A large marble fireplace lined with potted plants gives the place a certain elegance. The menu borrows vegetarian dishes from a wide variety of ethnic cuisines and invents some variations of its own - baba gounosh, an aubergine puree dip, is usually one of the starters, cannelloni are served with cauli-flower and blue cheese filling, or how about tofu and broccoli in coconut chile sauce?

Cork City Accommodation
Very Expensive - bed and breakfast over £50 per person sharing.
THE IMPERIAL
South Mall. Tel. 021/274040. Closed Dec.25-26. Credit Cards: Visa, Access, Amex, Diners.

The Imperial, in the heart of Cork's banking and legal district, and three minutes' walk from its main shopping streets, is the grand old man of Cork hotels. It has been here since 1816, and its 101 rooms (all with en suite bathrooms) are constantly being refurbished. If you enjoy nostalgia, ask for one of their old style rooms with antique furniture and velvet curtains; otherwise you can choose from various styles of modern decor. The bars and restaurants and meeting rooms are made great use of by the natives, so it is livelier than many hotels of similar age and status.

JURY'S
Western Rd. Tel. 021/276622. Closed Dec.25-26.Credit Cards: Visa, Access, Amex, Diners.

One of a small chain of four modern hotels, the 185-room Cork Jury's is an eye-catching smoked glass and steel structure on the banks of the River Lee about 5 minutes' walk from the city centre. Its leisure centre - gym, sauna, tennis, squash and indoor-outdoor pool - and Cork's Bar make it a popular meeting place with afflu-ent young locals. The best rooms overlook the interior patio garden and pool, but they are all relatively spacious and furnished in an unremarkable modern style with quilted bedspreads, small sofas or sitting chairs and floor-to-ceiling picture win-dows.

MORRISON'S ISLAND HOTEL
Morrison's Quay. Tel. 021/275858. Credit Cards: Visa, Access, Amex, Diners.

Cork's newest luxury hotel opened in the summer of 1991 in an excellent central location a stone's throw from the Imperial. It is the city's only "suites only" hotel, with 36 suites and 4 penthouses. Each suite has a sitting room, dining area, fitted kitchen and bathroom with one or two separate bedrooms. They are also equipped with radio, TV, direct dial phone, fax point and radio alarm. Although designed primarily for business travellers, they are also ideal for holiday-makers who hate hotels, as the rooms feel more like luxury apartments than hotel rooms. They are all beautifully designed in a clean-lined modern style, and the penthouses have picture windows opening on to small terraces overlooking the river. The light-wood fittings and furni-ture are hand-made by Jim O'Donnell in Skibbereen, who also made the hand-paint-ed furniture for the bar and restaurant. These are on the raised ground floor over-looking the river, and are fast becoming a popular meeting place for the local busi-ness community. They are most attractively furnished with polished Irish marble floors and warm coral-coloured walls. The bar food menu offers light, slightly differ-ent choices like smoked haddock and potato pie or chicken fricassee. A set dinner menu is served in the pretty but unfussy-looking restaurant.

FITZPATRICK SILVER SPRINGS
Tivoli. Tel. 021/507533. Closed Dec.25. Credit Cards: Visa, Access, Amex, Diners.

Businessmen and tour bus groups make up the majority of clients at this 1960s glass and concrete hotel. It overlooks the River Lee 10 minutes' drive from the city centre on the main Dublin/Waterford road. There are 110 bedrooms in various wings, the fanciest of which are done up in a kind of French boudoir style with much pink and grey plush. It has the biggest and newest leisure centre in town: gym, jacuzzi, steam room, indoor pool, squash, tennis, bowling and 9-hole golf.

Expensive - Bed and breakfast £36-£50 per person sharing

ARBUTUS LODGE

Middle Glanmire Rd. Tel. 021/501237. Closed 24-29 Dec. Credit Cards: Visa, Access, Amex, Diners.

This is the country-house style option, a two-storey Victorian villa on a hill overlooking the River Lee and the city. It is clearly signposted uphill from the junction of MacCurtain Street and the Lower Glanmire road, near the railway station on the main N22. The house is beautifully decorated with antique furniture and original Irish paintings. There are 20 rooms, divided into suites, superior and ordinary, the latter two being in this category. They are all large and airy, some with a more modern aspect, others with covetable antiques such as the carved four-poster bed, and one with a large bay window on to the amazing view. Discerning Americans form a regular core of guests; it seems that many others assume that the rooms at the Arbutus will be far more expensive than they actually are.

THE METROPOLE

MacCurtain St. Tel. 021/508122. Credit Cards: Visa, Access, Amex, Diners.

The Metropole is a large and long-established city centre hotel. Recent refurbishment successfully emphasises the solid art deco aspects of its interior, a period which seems to suit the hotel though it is in fact well over 100 years old. Long ocean-liner-like corridors lead to the 91 bedrooms, some of which overlook the River Lee. They are solidly furnished and decorated in neutral shades of beige, with nice details like deflected wall-lights. The Metropole really comes into its own during Cork's jazz festival and the folk festival, when it is the official Festival Club and hosts innumerable gigs, scheduled and unscheduled. The Riverview restaurant is a pleasant spot overlooking the river.

Moderate - Bed and breakfast £22-£36 per person sharing.

MOORE'S

Morrison's Island. Tel. 021/271291. Credit Cards: Visa, Access, Amex, Diners.

In spite of its romantic address, this is a city centre hotel with a relentlessly urban outlook. It is very central, across the road and around the corner from the Imperial. All 35 rooms have TV and direct dial phone, and the rates are very reasonable. It consists of 3 old town houses that have been knocked into one, resulting in long twisty corridors and oddly-shaped, rather small rooms. It looks sadly run-down next to its swanky new neighbour, the Morrison's Island Hotel, but people consistently praise the friendliness of the staff here. Try to get a room with a river view.

ASHBOURNE HOUSE HOTEL

Glounthaune. Tel. 021/353310. Credit Cards: Visa, Access. Amex, Diners.

Cork city is not greatly endowed with hotels in this price range, so I have cheated a little and included this one which is about 6 miles outside the city on the main N25 Waterford road. You might also consider options covered in Chapters Two, Three, Four and Eight under Cobh, Crosshaven, Douglas, Glanmire, Blarney and Kinsale. Ashbourne House was built in the early 19th century, and is mainly remarkable for its beautiful grounds, which would not disgrace a far more expensive and luxurious hotel. They have some fine camellias, magnolias, roses, bamboos, yucca and other exotic shrubs amid mature pines and beech trees. The 29 rooms all have en suite bathrooms, TV and direct dial phone, and are simply furnished with white candlewick bedspreads and modern fitted units. Much of the ground floor of the house has oak wainscotting, although the dining room is in a discreet modern extension. There is an outdoor pool, tennis court and horse riding on the premises, as well as lovely woodland walks.

Inexpensive - Bed and breakfast under £22 per person sharing.

GABRIEL HOUSE
Summerhill, St. Luke's. Tel. 021/500333. Wine licence. Credit Cards: Visa, Access, Amex.
This large Victorian guest house is a five minute walk from the railway station and about eight minutes from the bus station. There are 20 rooms, all with bathroom en suite, TV and direct dial phone. The rooms are small, but have good views over the city and are simply furnished with matching duvets and curtains. There is a comfortable lounge where tea and coffee are served, and a restaurant serving simple evening meals.

GLENVERA HOUSE
Wellington Rd. Tel. 021/502030. Credit Cards: Access, Amex.
Two Victorian red brick terraced houses north of the River Lee in a road parallel to MacCurtain Street have been combined to make this 34-room guesthouse. The rooms are plain with padded headboards and light cotton bedspreads and curtains, and all have TV, direct dial phone and bathrooms en suite. The Glenvera has a bar, but there is no restaurant.

LOTAMORE HOUSE
Tivoli. Tel.021/822344. Credit Cards: Visa, Access, Amex.
The entrance is on the left hand side of the dual carriageway between Silver Springs Hotel and the Dublin/Waterford roundabout. This is a Georgian manor in its own grounds on top of a hill overlooking the River Lee and Blackrock Castle. There is a large sitting room with a coal fire and velvet wing back chairs, and the entrance lobby has an impressive marble-topped side table with an ornate gilt mirror above. All 20 rooms have TV and direct dial phone, and are pleasantly decorated with mohair bedspreads, tweed curtains and reproduction mahogany furniture. The front rooms have large windows overlooking the river. If you do not mind the absence of a bar and restaurant, and have your own transport, this place offers a very good level of comfort in its price range.

VICTORIA LODGE
Victoria Cross. Tel. 021/542233. Credit Cards: Visa, Access.
This guesthouse was, until quite recently, a Capuchin monastery, and the good monks seem to have left a very special, peaceful atmosphere behind. It is in the western suburbs of the city, a 10-minute bus ride from the centre on the N71 West Cork road. It is in its own grounds set back slightly from the main road. Breakfast is served in the old wood-panelled refectory and the common room is now a sitting room and library.

ISAAC'S
MacCurtain St.. Tel. 021/500011. Credit Cards: Visa, Access.
Isaac's is a combination of hostel and budget hotel. It is in a stylishly converted warehouse on MacCurtain street, handy for both bus and rail stations. There are 200 beds, some of them dormitory-style in bunk-beds with 4-14 people per room, and the rest in hotel style double and single rooms. Continental breakfast is included in the price, and Isaac's also have a rent-a-bike concession. To be sure of private accommodation book in advance. (The restaurant under the hotel is re-opening in May 1992 under separate management, and is well worth checking out as it is a big, cheerful warehouse conversion, and in its first incarnation quickly gained a reputation for its lively atmosphere and live jazz sessions.)

Cork City Bed and Breakfast
There are about 50 Irish Tourist Board registered private houses offering Bed and Breakfast accommodation in Cork city and suburbs at prices ranging from £10 to

£18, the more expensive ones offering rooms with private bathrooms. These can be booked through the Tourist Information Office, Tourist House, Grand Parade. Tel. 021/273251.

Self-Catering, Caravan and Camping, Hostels: - See INSIDE INFORMATION, Page 8.

Cork City Shopping

Cork's shopping centre is so compact that all the visitor needs are the following basic pointers. Most shops open from 9-5.30 with the larger ones opening until 8 on Fridays. Some places close for a half day on Saturday, with a few small specialist places closing all day Monday, and from about 1-2. Friday is the busiest day of the week, being the traditional shopping day for out-of-towners.

Patrick Street is the location of the main department stores, the up-market Cash's, and the more popular Roches Stores. In the **Merchant's Quay Shopping Centre** beside Patrick's Bridge you will find **Marks & Spencer, Dunnes Stores, Laura Ashley, Sock and Knicker Shops,** and a good selection of fashion boutiques aimed at the younger market. For the rest, it is pretty much a normal high street, with clothes shops, shoe shops, record shops, newsagents and fast food joints. Between Patrick Street and the South Mall and parallel to both is **Oliver Plunkett Street**, which has several fashionable and expensive ladies' clothes shops, some good lingerie shops, card shops, several jewellers and a couple of interesting antique shops. At the Parnell Place end is **Hickey's**, a useful hardware store and general builders' supplier.

On the other side of Patrick Street is the **Paul Street** shopping area with a good range of small specialist shops selling well-designed stuff for the home (**House of James**), books (**The Collins Bookshop**), Donegal tweed and country clothing (**The House of Donegal**), lighting, kitchenware, high fashion (**Monica John**) eccentric fashion (**Red Square**), health food (**Paul Street Health Food Shop**), and much more. There are also several tea shops with very good cakes. In the City Centre Car Park you will find a large branch of the **Quinnsworth Supermarket**, and there are several antique shops in the lane beside it, with another opposite the Crawford Gallery. Another good hunting ground for antiques is MacCurtain Street on the north side of Patrick's Bridge.

2 | **CHAPTER TWO**

Cork Harbour East

This chapter explores the east of Cork harbour, from Cobh to Roches Point. Cork Harbour is the second largest in the world, after Sydney, and the ideal way to explore it is by boat. Failing that, a car is really essential to follow all the routes, but without one, you can cover the most interesting part of the east harbour by taking one of the trains from Kent Railway Station in Cork to Fota Island and on to Cobh (about 25 minutes journey time). Travelling by car you can return to the mainland and then head back for the water's edge to drive through Rostellan woods past the Trabolgan Holiday Centre to the light house at Roches Point.

The railway line to Cobh, designed by the great Victorian engineer Isambard Kingdom Brunel, provides a far more scenic approach than the main road, and if you are based in Cork it is worth abandoning the car for a day and setting off by rail. *(Tel. 021/503399 for train times).* Otherwise, it is about half an hour's drive to Cobh, leaving Cork on the main N25 Waterford road.

You might like to take a detour just beyond the roundabout to visit **Dunkathel House** *(Tel. 021/821014. Admission £1.50. Open Weds.-Sun. 2-6. May-Sept. and by appointment).* It is signposted to the left. The Georgian house has well-proportioned rooms, two of them with Adam fireplaces, and the front hall has early 19th-century Italian painted decoration. Its centrepiece is a gracefully balustraded staircase of Bath stone. The furniture and mirrors are mainly Irish Georgian, and there is a collection of watercolours by Beatrice Gubbins. There is also an antique shop on the premises.

The turning for Cobh and Fota is clearly signposted about 6 miles beyond the roundabout. The road crosses Fota Island by means of two causeways. The gates of the Fota Estate are well signposted on the right about 20 minutes after leaving Cork. The walls alongside the road mark the boundaries of the 900-acre Fota Estate. Until recently it was owned by University College Cork who used part of it as an experimental farm. Previously the land belonged to the Barrymore family, and the centrepiece of the estate is their shooting lodge, Fota House. It was enlarged in 1820 to a neo-classical design by Sir Richard Morrison. It is surrounded by a mature arboretum, one of the best in the country, with many mature exotic trees interplanted with native shrubs. At the time of writing neither house nor arboretum are open to the public, as they have been acquired by a property developing company who intend to put a luxury hotel, time-share chalets and two golf courses on the island, proposals which have met with considerable local opposition. It is hoped that public access to the arboretum will eventually be restored - ask for up-to-date information at the Cork TIO (Tel. 021/273251).

Also on the estate is **Fota Wildlife Park** *(Tel. 021/812678. Admission: £2.20 , children and senior citizens £1.10. Open daily 17 March to 10 Sept, 10-5.15; 11-5.15 Suns.; Sat. and Sun. only to 30 Oct. Closed winter.)* which was created by the Royal Zoological Society of Ireland with the aim of breeding selected groups of animals that are endangered in the wild. Giraffes, zebras, ostrich and antelope range freely in 40 acres of grassland; there are also cheetahs, kangaroos, lemurs, peafowl, macaws, pelicans, flamingos and penguins. There is a special children's corner and playground, and wheelchair facilities are provided.

The road past Fota crosses Belvelly Bridge on to Great Island. On the island side of the bridge is the ruin of the 16th-century **Belvelly Castle** which once guarded the landing place of the ferry from the mainland. Next to it is a Martello tower, one of several erected around Cork Harbour in the early 19th century when there were fears of an invasion by Napoleonic forces.

The main road runs down the west, or seaward, side of the island past the former

Verolme ship yard and the tall stacks of the NET fertiliser plant. There is some heavy industry in Cork Harbour, but rather than ruining the outlook, it adds a certain character, especially at night when the installations are dramatically illuminated. The road enters Cobh through the prosperous Victorian suburb of **Rushbrooke** which consists of large detached and semi-detached Victorian villas looking out to sea.

Cobh, pronounced Cove, recalls Cobh's earlier name, "The Cove of Cork". From Queen Victoria's visit in 1849 until 1922 it was known as Queenstown. It is unusual among Irish ports in that it was not originally a Viking settlement, but only grew in importance at the time of the American Civil War, when the British Navy recognised its value as a natural harbour. Cobh has always thrived in times of adversity, and it grew and prospered during the Napoleonic Wars. In the peaceful years following 1815 local entrepreneurs decided to promote Cobh as a health resort. Most of its buildings date from 1820 to 1900.

The town was built on the side of a steep hill overlooking the sea, and by the 20th century its Gothic cathedral with its tall delicate spires beneath terraces of brightly painted houses, had become a familiar sight to generations of emigrants and returning sailors. Cobh's links with emigration began in the mid-19th century when convicts were assembled on Spike Island to await their passage to Australia. In the century following the Great Famine of 1847 over a million emigrants left Cobh for America and Australia. It went on to become an important point of call for transatlantic liners, an activity which only ceased in the late 1960s. The Cork ship, *Sirius*, the first steamship to cross the Atlantic, sailed from Cobh on 1 April 1838. Cobh was the last port of call of the *Titanic* in 1912, and it was to Cobh that most of the bodies from the sinking of the *Lusitania* in 1915 were brought. The passenger liner was torpedoed by a German submarine off the Old Head of Kinsale in 1915, over 1500 people drowned and the USA joined World War One. The people of Cobh have a long tradition of sea-faring, as can be seen from the names of old Cobh families: Verling, Stromso, Rasmussen, Carlos, Patchkey. Seafarers, it seems, are accepted more easily than land-lubbers, who, if not born on Great Island, are referred to as "across-the-bridgers" for the first few generations.

Many of Cobh's wonderful Victorian buildings are sadly run-down at the time of writing, but the town's fortunes could be about to take an up-turn with the opening of a £3 million visitor attraction to be known as **"The Queenstown Project"**. Its first phase, a heritage centre illustrating Cobh's links with emigration, is based in the baggage buildings and emigration halls beside the railway station. But even in its run-down state, Cobh is an interesting and highly atmospheric town to explore, very much a working port, used by some 1000 boats a week, but also a good recreational centre with facilities for sailing, golf, tennis and riding and some excellent walks. (See below for details).

The Tourist Office (*Westbourne House. Tel. 021/811391*) is on the left as you enter the town. This is a good starting place for a WALK around Cobh. (*If you would like to join a guided walking tour, ask about the schedule by phoning the Tourist Office in advance.*) Opposite the Tourist Office is a small Scots Presbyterian church which was in use from 1854 to the 1960s. It is now the **Cobh Museum** (*Open Suns. 3-6, also Weds. 3-6 May-Sept.*), which has a collection of items of maritime and local historical interest. From the museum follow Spy Hill which climbs uphill to Bishop's Road, giving good views of the harbour. Immediately ahead, as you look out to sea, is **Haulbowline Island**, an Irish naval base which also has a steel works, whose crashing noises can be heard at times in Cobh. There are some fine late 18th century buildings on its docks, but it is not accessible to the public. The lower, greener island is **Spike Island**, behind which is the harbour mouth and the open sea. The fort on Spike Island was one of three built by the British to defend Cork Harbour, and handed back to the Irish Government in 1938. Since 1984 it has been in use as a prison. This is scheduled to open in March, 1993, Tel: 021/813591 for details.

Turn right at the top of Bishop's Road, and look down the steep terrace of houses beloved of photographers, known officially as **West View**, and unofficially as "the pack of cards", presumably from the sensation that one little push would send all the houses tumbling down the hill. Cut across to Cathedral Place which is visible ahead. This short cut is named **The Khyber Pass**, a sample of the well-travelled local sense of humour.

St. Colman's Cathedral was built between 1868 and 1915, and belongs to the Catholic diocese of Cloyne. The large Gothic-revival church was designed by E. W. Pugin and G. C. Ashlin. The exterior is of Dalkey granite with dressings of Mallow limestone. The interior is worth a visit; a multi-lingual leaflet on the cathedral is available inside. Its spire has the biggest carillon in Ireland consisting of 47 bells covering a range of four octaves. Carillon recitals are advertised locally, but Westminster chimes ring out all day in Cobh, and a hymn is played on the bells at 9, 12 noon, 4 and 6 daily. There is another excellent panorama of the harbour from the terrace of the Cathedral. From here, looking towards the harbour mouth, you will see the oil refinery at Whitegate, and the electricity station at Aghada (distinguished by its tall striped shaft) which is fuelled by natural gas from the Celtic Sea nearby.

If you want to extend the WALK, turn right out of the cathedral gates and walk up the hill to the area known as **The Top o' the Hill**. The road is soon out into open countryside, and after about half a mile you will reach **The Old Church Graveyard** on the left. It is here that some of the victims of the Lusitania were buried in mass graves which are clearly marked. Time spent reading some of the other gravestones will give you a vivid insight into the human cost of Cobh's maritime past.

For a shorter WALK, continue downhill along Cathedral place and Harbour Hill, turning sharp right at the bottom of the latter and emerging on the seafront at **East Beach**. Walk back along the seafront, past the quays and the main pier. If you fancy a boat tour of the harbour, check the schedule of **Marine Transport** who run daily one-hour harbour tours, subject to weather and demand. *(Tel. 021/811485. Cost: £3 adults, £1.50 children. 12 noon and 2.30 May-Sept.).*

Just beyond the main pier, in Casement Square on the opposite side of the road, is a monument by the sculptor Jerome O'Connor (1876-1943) to the memory of the Lusitania victims. Just below your starting point is a waterside Italianate villa. It was built in 1854 as the headquarters of the Royal Cork Yacht Club, the oldest yacht club in the world, and was its home until 1969 when the RCYC moved to Crosshaven, and it was left derelict. It has now been restored on local initiative, and renamed **The Sirius Centre**. It should be open as an arts centre and coffee shop. If it is, its well worth taking a look at its elegant interior and its waterfront views.

Great Island, perhaps because it is well off the main road, and over-shadowed by its only town, Cobh, tends to be rather neglected by visitors. It is four miles long by about two wide, and the only village is the small inland one of Ballymore, leaving a long, unspoilt coastline to explore.

There is a good WALK from Cobh to a small shingly cove at **Cuskinny** which is also a good picnic spot with safe swimming. Simply follow the main road out of town to the west for about a mile. You can come back by an inland route by taking the lane to the left behind Cuskinny. A left turn at the first cross roads will bring you back to the seafront in Cobh.

Drive out to **Marlogue Wood** which is about four miles from the centre of Cobh, and well signposted. Here there are nature trails and picnic areas with access to the shingly beach. There are good WALKS on this corner of the island with views across the narrow channel to the picturesque little church at East Ferry on the mainland. The ferry no longer exists, but there is a new yacht marina on the Great Island side, and there is always the chance that you might get a lift across to the pub.

The **Back of the Island** or **Rossleague**, as it is properly known, looks across a narrow channel to the mainland, with a distant view of Midleton in clear weather.

There is a very pleasant waterside WALK which is best approached by turning left instead of right when you arrive on to the island at Belvelly. Park the car as soon as the road reaches the water, and you can walk along beside it for about 3 miles. The Martello tower at Rossleague is being developed as an amenity centre. If you are good for a 5-mile WALK, there is an inner ring which you can follow from the Martello tower by turning right and heading inland, turning left after about a mile at the top of the hill, right at the next T junction, left fork in the village of Ballymore, and left after the road to Marlogue Woods, returning along the water's edge.

If the views from Cobh have aroused your curiosity about the eastern shore of Cork harbour, the following short scenic drive with good optional walks will satisfy it. The end of the road, Roches Point light house, is about an hour from Cork city, and about half an hour from Midleton, (on the main N25 4 miles beyond the turn-off for Cobh) which is the starting point.

Take the R629 heading south out of Midleton, and after about a mile follow the right hand fork on to the R630 for another two miles, looking out for a signpost on the right to **East Ferry**. The road detours along the water's edge of a pretty lightly-wooded peninsula, and across the narrow channel you can see Great Island. Turn right at the main road, and continue for about three miles until you see the entrance to **Rostellan Woods** on the right. The woods cover an area of about 4 square miles, and one side of them is on the water's edge. The lake at the entrance to the inland woods is a wildfowl refuge with interesting bird life. If you take a WALK here, look out for the folly on the foreshore known as **Siddons Tower**. A Lord Inchquin, whose family had a castle and house on this site (now in ruins), had it built in the 18th century to express his admiration for the actress, Sarah Siddons. It can also be seen from **Aghada**, which is the next little village on the road, and is chiefly distinguished by its power station which generates electricity from natural gas piped in from the off-shore gas field.

About two and a half miles beyond Aghada, at **Whitegate**, the road turns inland and continues to the gates of the **Trabolgan Holiday Centre**. If you feel like a good breath of air, leave the car here, and WALK the next two miles along the relatively traffic-free cliff-top road to **Roches Point Light House**. At close quarters it can be seen that Roches Point was once a little village with two terraces of houses, some of which are still inhabited. The ruins of an older light house stand on the land above the existing structure, which is smaller and much lower down the rocks than most light houses.

Special Events
Cobh International Folk Dance Festival takes place in July. *Cobh's People's Regatta* is in August.

Sports Facilities
Golf: *Cork Golf Club*, Little Island. Tel. 021/353451. 18- holes. Green fees Mon.-Fri. *Harbour Point Golf Club*, Clash Rd. Little Island. Tel. 021/353094. 18-holes. Green fees 7 days but book in advance. *Cobh Golf Club*, Great Island. Tel. 021/353451. 18- holes. Green fees Mon.-Fri., weekends after 2.30. **Tennis**: *Mount Crozier*, Back Road, Cobh. Tel. 021/811391. **Horse Riding**: *Rock Farm Equestrian Centre*, Little Island. Tel. 021/353024. *Ballywilliam Riding Centre*, Nr. Cobh. Tel. 021/811908. **Indoor Swimming**: *Trabolgan Holiday Centre* offers day tickets including use of the indoor pool complex for £7 adult, £4 child, 9AM-9PM. **Boat Hire**: Sailing dinghies, windsurfers, canoes and fishing: *International Sailing School - Eddie English*, East Beach, Cobh. Tel. 021/811237. **Sea angling boats, rods and tackle**: Ted Geary, Cobh. Tel. 021/353089; John Conroy, Cobh. Tel. 021/508847; Tom Conway, Tel. 021/812167. **Cobh Sea Angling Club**, competitions monthly May-Sept., visitors welcome. Tel. 021/812167.

PUBS, RESTAURANTS, SHOPS AND ACCOMMODATION
(Price Categories are explained in HOW TO USE THIS BOOK)

COBH
Bar
THE ROTUNDA
14 Casement Sq. Tel. 021/811631.
This is a nice old-fashioned bar on the seafront with dark curtains on wooden poles in the windows and converted oil lamps hanging above them. The bar itself is an unusual double-curved shape, which gives a lot of character to the small, cosy interior. There are interesting photographs of shipping on the walls, whose significance will be explained to you if you ask.

MANSWORTH'S
Top-of-the-Hill. Tel. 021/811965.
Mansworth's is in the part of Cobh known as "the top of the town", which starts just above the Cathedral, and is about a block uphill from the Cathedral's doors. It claims to be the oldest pub in Cobh, and was bought from Murphy's Brewery by the great-grand aunt of the present owner in 1895, when Cobh had over 100 pubs. (Now there are 30 plus two hotels). It still has the original bar counter installed by Murphy's, and the walls are laden with old photographs and advertising material. The owner, John Mansworth, is the Chairman of Cobh Regatta, so there is a strong nautical trend to his collection of pictures, and his other hobby, owning and breeding racehorses, is also represented. It is a popular shore base with visiting seamen, including members of the U.S. Navy, to whom John gives an especially warm welcome.

Bar/Music
THE ROARING DONKEY
Top of the Hill. Tel. 021/811739.
This memorably named bar is even further up the hill than Mansworth's, and is the place to go for traditional music, but if that is your main interest then phone in advance to be sure that there is something on.

Bar/Restaurant
CLIPPERS
17 Westbourne Place. Tel. 021/813099. Bar Food 12.30-3 and 6.30-9; restaurant open 7.30-9.30; no food Suns. Credit Cards: Visa, Access. Bar food: Inexpensive; Restaurant; Moderate.
This bar has the only restaurant in Cobh which has any pretensions to up-market elegance. It has a wonderful location down on the waterfront almost opposite the Commodore Hotel, and the bar has French windows opening on to a lawn which has tables in summer. The bar food is fairly average - steaks, fish, lasagna, curry - and the restaurant has a rather fancier a la carte menu featuring steaks, lobster, roast duckling and the like. The room is attractively decorated in a grey and pink theme with stylised modern chairs and candle-lit tables.

Bar/Restaurant/B & B
ATLANTIC INN
West Beach. Tel. 021/811489. Lunch and dinner menus 12.30-2 and 6.30-9.30 in bar or cafe; light snacks available 11.30-9.30; restaurant open from 7PM. Credit Cards: Visa, Access. Inexpensive; Restaurant: Moderate.
The Atlantic Inn is a tall, narrow house in the line of shops along the seafront. The front room is a snack bar with low-backed booths, which has a well-varied all-day menu with main courses like chicken Kiev, deep fried scampi or stuffed pork steak, and also serves tea, coffee and cakes. This is supplemented by daily specials at

lunch and dinner time which can also be eaten in the bar. The bar is behind the cafe, and has oriental rugs on the bare floorboards. It is sparsely furnished with tables and chairs of dark wood, and a snooker table in the middle. The result is highly atmospheric, perhaps because it is so far back from the street that it feels like a secret hideaway. The restaurant is on the first floor, and has views of the shipping coming and going from the town quay. There is a small bar off it, and the main room has dark blue walls and small tables set with pink napery. It is dominated by a large oil painting of a Victorian gentleman. There is a set menu or a la carte, and the emphasis, especially in summer, is on seafood: poached fillet of brill on a bed of noodles, for example, or, as a starter, warm smoked salmon with mussel and chive sauce. There are six rooms up the narrow, skewy staircase, which share bathrooms on the landings. The top ones, under the eaves, have attractive dormer windows overlooking the harbour. They all have TV and phone, floral duvets and curtains, plain walls and carpets and modern fitted furniture.

Hotel
THE COMMODORE
Tel. 021/811277. Bar food 12-6. Credit Cards: Visa, Access, Amex, Diners. Moderate.

This is a large four-storey Victorian seafront hotel. It is a busy place with a strong local trade which gives it a certain buzz. The bar has interesting photos of Cobh at the turn of the century, and serves large portions of food. In summer the indoor pool is open. A rather half-hearted effort is made to retain a sense of the hotel's past, with antiques dotted around the place and classically draped velvet curtains at the tall windows, but it is marred by plastic hanging plants and unconvincing chandeliers. (Maybe they were just dusty but they looked kind of...plastic). There are 36 rooms with bathrooms en suite, TV and direct dial phone, beige colour schemes and modern furniture. Nineteen of them overlook the sea, and have wonderful views, especially at night.

B & B
BELLAVISTA
Bishop's Rd. Spy Hill. Tel. 021/812450. Closed 15 Jan.-15 Dec. Inexpensive.

The vista is undeniably bella, even though it is seen through modern aluminium plate glass windows which ill-suit this imposing Victorian villa. The best way to find it is to take the left-hand fork between the Tourist Office and the museum at the entrance to the town, and keep following the curve. The windows are not the fault of the kindly owner, Peggy O'Rourke, who only opened her B & B in 1991, and is doing her best to restore the dauntingly large house appropriately. There are 4 rooms en suite, 3 with views of the Cathedral spire, Spike Island and the mouth of the harbour. They all have TV and direct dial phone, and tea and coffee making facilities are available on request, as are extra beds for families. They are prettily decorated with floral quilts and curtains, and the one without a view has splendid antique furniture by way of compensation. There is a large TV lounge downstairs with its original marble fireplace and a piano, plump sofas and armchairs. Breakfast is served at separate tables in an adjoining room.

EAST FERRY

Bar/Music
MURPH'S
Tel.021/652676. Sandwiches, tea and coffee.

This is an unassuming little bar in a lovely waterside location above the quay at East Ferry, with good views from its windows across the channel to Great Island. In summer there are tables outside. There is music every Sunday night, described as "a sing along", and golden oldies every second Friday.

ROSTELLAN
Restaurant
THE REEF RESTAURANT

Tel.021/66104. Lounge menu 12 noon - 10PM; dinner from 6.30; Sunday lunch; open 7 days. Booking advisable Sunday lunch and dinner at weekends. Wine Licence. Credit Cards: Visa, Access, Amex. Moderate.

Just outside the village of Rostellan look out for flags on your right hand side announcing The Reef. The restaurant is in a modern one-storey building on its own quay with views of Cobh and East Ferry, and of water breaking on the reef of rocks that give the place its name. An all-day menu featuring dishes such as quiche, burgers and seafood cocktail is served in the lounge, and at outside tables in summer. The separate dining room is an elegant, relaxing room with pale green carpet, white and peach napery and paper table napkins, fresh flowers on the tables and large windows overlooking the sea. There is a set menu for dinner containing six choices of starters and six main courses, with Ballycotton seafood platter and pears with tarragon among the starters. Fillet of pork with herbs and apple, or rainbow trout with almonds are typical main courses. On Saturday nights a pianist entertains. In summer it's a popular spot with holiday-makers from nearby Trabolgan.

3 | **CHAPTER THREE**

CORK HARBOUR WEST

This chapter explores the western shores of Cork harbour. The west of the harbour is less interesting historically than the east, much of it disappearing under encroaching suburbs, but there are good views all along the way, some good beaches and some surprisingly pleasant walks to be discovered. Non-drivers can take the regular bus service from Cork city to Crosshaven and Fountainstown. Travelling by car, choose a walk or a beach as your main destination, and work out an interesting route to or from it.

Leave Cork City by the South Ring Road, and follow the signposts for Douglas. This is now a suburb, laid out in the mid-20th century, but the road takes you through the original village which is just beyond the shopping centre and supermarket. In the 18th and 19th centuries, Douglas was an industrial centre with flax and woollen mills, and an important sail-making centre.

Follow signposts for Rochestown and Passage West. The road runs parallel to the **Douglas River** which joins the river Lee in a wide expanse of water bordered by Blackrock Castle, Little Island, Fota Island and Great Island, known as **Lough Mahon**.

A blue signpost on the left hand side of the Rochestown road, just before the Rochestown Inn, leads to a small car park beside a quay. There is an excellent WALK here on a footpath that runs along the edge of Lough Mahon then crosses the Douglas river by a disused railway bridge - about a mile in all. Either return the same way, or turn right and take the first left which crosses open land for about a mile before emerging in Mahon. A right hand turn past the cemetery and another half mile will bring you to **Ring Mahon Point** opposite Little Island, where there are interesting wading birds to see at low tide.

The main road continues on through **Passage West**, a decayed town once famous for its dockyards. Another blue sign-post just before the town leads to a coastal WALK which follows a disused railway line for about two miles to **Monkstown**. This stretch of the road runs beside a narrow channel, with Great Island forming the other bank, before it emerges into the waters of outer Cork Harbour. A ferry previously connected Glenbrook, on the west, with Carrigaloe on Great Island, and there are plans to reintroduce a car ferry at this point, which would greatly reduce travelling time from west Cork to Cobh and Fota. *(For the latest information contact Cork TIO, tel. 021/273251).*

Monkstown developed in the 19th century, when there were steamers connecting it with Cork, as a prosperous suburb consisting of large Victorian villas built on a steep hill with good views of the outer harbour. The ruins of a fortified house, known as **Monsktown Castle**, dating from 1639, now form part of the clubhouse of Monkstown Golf Course. The story goes that the woman who built it, Anastasia Gould, made a condition that the workmen should buy all their provisions from her during the course of construction, and when she weighed the profit on these sales against the cost of the building, the castle had cost her only a groat - or about four pence.

If you are interested in seeing **Ringaskiddy**, it is well signposted from Monkstown, and involves a 5-mile detour on the way to Carrigaline (which is also well-signposted from Ringaskiddy). Ringaskiddy is the point of arrival for ferries from Swansea and Brittany and consists of a small village with an expanding industrial estate on a flat and rather desolate stretch of land. The nicest thing about Ringaskiddy is the view of Cobh and its cathedral across the harbour - a view which ferry passengers will already have enjoyed on their way up Cork harbour. At points the view is obscured by the backside of the Irish Steel Works on Haulbowline Island which is connected to Ringaskiddy by a causeway.

The only building of interest in Ringaskiddy is a tiny chapel directly opposite the entrance to the ferry port. Beside it is a life-size plaster statue of Christ carrying the cross and showing His Sacred Heart. There is a plaster statue of the Virgin in a similar naive style over the chapel door which is supported by two plain pillars. The chapel dates from 1923 and is known as "The Oratory". The interior is of a touching simplicity with 11 short pews and a painted wood-hipped ceiling. Mass is said there at 9AM every Sunday thanks to the initiative of a local priest, having been closed to worshippers for many years previously.

Carrigaline is just over 4 miles from Monkstown on the direct route. Thirty years ago this was a rural village with a population of about 300. Today it is a thriving dormitory suburb with over 11,000 inhabitants. Its main historical interest lies in the ruins of **Carrigaline Castle** which is on a high limestone bluff about a mile outside town, just beyond the Church of Ireland. They are on the north bank of the **Owenabue River**; take the road to the left beside the Catholic church at the entrance to the town. The castle was built soon after the Norman occupation of Cork in 1171 by either a De Cogan or a De Prendergast. The present ruins consist of a typical Norman tower, another, probably later, building with a pointed roof and several outhouses, one of which is used by the farmer who works the land around it.

If you are interested in a very attractive WALK continue down the Coolmore road following signposts for about 4 miles to **Currabinny Wood**. These largely deciduous woods are sensational in the autumn, but make a pleasant, undemanding outing for all age groups at any time of year. They originally belonged to a private house, and there is a gazebo in the centre where the owners used to take tea. At the highest point in the woods is a pre-historic burial cairn in rather bad condition, known locally as the Giant's Cave. The forest trails here are unusual in that they were originally laid out for horse and carriage so that they are wide and airy, with none of the enclosed feeling that dense woodland can produce. They are situated on a peninsula which looks across the water to Crosshaven, only a few hundred yards away. In the distance on the other side is Spike Island, and beyond it Cobh and its cathedral. It takes about 45 minutes to make a circuit of the woods.

Crosshaven is approached via Carrigaline or the new by-pass, and is clearly signposted. The road runs along beside the Owenabue River for 4 miles. After about 2 miles it opens into a pool, known as **Drake's Pool**. This is reputedly the spot where Sir Francis Drake took shelter from pursuing Spaniards in 1587, successfully shaking them off his tail by disappearing from Cork harbour into the Owenabue. The story first emerged in Smith's *History of Cork* in 1750, and is believed by many to be apocryphal. Whether it is Drake's Pool or not, it is an exceptionally pretty, well-sheltered anchorage with wooded banks on either side.

Crosshaven is a pleasant little village with most of its buildings dating from the late 19th and early 20th century. The town is built on parallel roads on a sloping hillside, and looks best from a distance. The large Catholic church at the top of the town was designed in the Gothic style by E. W. Pugin, the son of William Pugin, and its foundation stone laid in 1869. Pugin is not responsible for the ill-proportioned spire which is a later addition. The arrival of the railway from Cork via Monkstown and Carrigaline in 1904 did much to promote Crosshaven by making it accessible as a cheap day trip for city visitors. Previous to this both Crosshaven and Currabinny were linked to the city by steamer. The railway line was closed in 1932, being uneconomical, an ironic decision in view of the subsequent popularity of the area with commuters. The Royal Cork Yacht Club, founded in Cobh in 1720, moved to its present location in Crosshaven in 1969.

Since the departure of the British Army, which had a large base here at Fort Camden, the main local activities have been boat-building and tourist related enterprises. The boat-yard is still flourishing, and among the many boats built here were Sir Francis Chichester's *Gypsy Moth IV*, and the *St. Brendan*, a skin-covered replica of the sort of boat that St. Brendan the Navigator used for his journey across the Atlantic in the 7th century A.D.. It was subsequently sailed to America by the writer and explorer, Tim Severin. The internationally famous Ron Holland team of yacht designers are also based in the area. For generations of Cork children an outing to the "Merries" at Crosshaven, with rides on the chairoplanes and dodgem cars followed by a bag of chips, was the highlight of the holidays. The "Merries" are still with us, but the Majorca Ballroom beside them has long been up for sale. Today many visitors choose Crosshaven as a holiday destination to enjoy its excellent deep sea fishing facilities.

In the flat centre of Crosshaven, opposite the bus stop, **Crosshaven House** can be seen, a 3-storey Georgian house built in 1759 to an interesting design which separates the two wings from the main body of the house. The Hayes family, who built it, farmed the estate until 1972. It is now a community centre with a pitch and putt course in the grounds. Cronin's Pub, also near the bus stop, was built originally as the Railway Hotel.

Cronin's is the starting point for several excellent WALKS in the area. For a short orientation (about 30 minutes), turn left as you face the pub and walk along past the boat yard, the "Merries", and a little seaside garden, and turn up the narrow road lined by small, sea-facing houses and fuchsia hedges. Just after the place which marks the limit of car access, a steep climb on your right will bring you out at **Fort Camden**, which has views of **Fort Carlisle** on the other side of the harbour, and a good prospect of Roches Point light house and the mouth of Cork Harbour. On the left is Spike Island and Cobh. Fort Camden, one of 3 forts built by the British in the late 18th century to guard the harbour, all of which are visible from this point, (the third one being on Spike Island) is derelict at the moment, but there are plans to restore it as a military museum. For the time being, if you are lucky, you might spot a rabbit or even a fox in its deep, overgrown moats. Over the last few summers, shoals of dolphins have been seen swimming in the harbour between Forts Camden and Carlisle. The Forts were renamed after Irish patriots when the British handed them back in 1938, but the new names - Meagher (Camden), Davis (Carlisle), and Mitchell (Spike) have not caught on.

From Fort Camden you can return to Cronin's by a road parallel to the one you came up which runs directly downhill from the fort. The circuit takes about 40 minutes.

A more adventurous and dramatic approach to Fort Camden, strictly for able-bodied adults and carefully supervised children, can be had by walking up the road beside Cronin's (signposted Fort Camden) and taking the first turning on the right which runs steeply uphill. This leads across the peninsula on a little-used road lined by pre-war holiday chalets typical of many a modest sea-side town, some of them unbelievably small, some almost derelict, others lovingly cared-for, and most of them delightfully eccentric. Follow the road until it ends above the rocks at Weaver's Point - a good picnic and swimming place with views of Roches Point. Up to this point the road is accessible by car, but the walk continues along a footpath. There are signs warning of "Dangerous Cliff Path", so you are at your own risk. Common sense is essential. The path runs above a series of little rocky coves, sandy at low tide, and then heads inland across country, emerging in a large new car park which is just behind Fort Camden. Look for the road running closest to the sea by following a little track downhill to the left of the fort. The round trip takes under an hour, and is a grade A walk in terms of variety, scenery, magnificent views, and the sea air.

Another very popular WALK takes the road to **Church Bay**, a popular fishing and swimming beach about a mile out of town, and leaves Cronin's Pub on the narrow road immediately to the left of Crosshaven House. As the road emerges at the top of the hill there is a fine view of Roches Point and the outer harbour. The first left will take you past Weaver's Point, the Bull Rock and ends at the Helm Hotel (cul de sac) about a mile further on. The second left leads down to Church Bay strand, which can be seen below. An interesting round trip of about 2 miles can be made by turning right after the road to the strand and heading uphill through the field to **Templebreedy Church** and graveyard. The church is now ruined, but dates from 1778. Just beyond the church is a stile leading to a footpath on the right which goes down through **Cruchan Woods** to the grounds of Crosshaven House.

Beyond Crosshaven on the outer shores of Cork harbour there are several popular swimming and picnicking places. Follow the signposts in Crosshaven for **Myrtleville**, a small village swelled by its commuter population, where the road appears to end by running into the sea. In fact it turns to the left and right just before the water.

For a good cliff-top WALK leave the car here and follow the right hand road which emerges about a mile later in **Fountainstown**, a good sandy beach on **Ringabella Bay**. You can head back for Myrtleville by turning inland and taking 3 right hand-turns, but it is probably more tempting to do the cliff path in the opposite direction, enjoying a different set of views.

There is a network of small roads between Ringabella Bay and Oysterhaven Creek. The next place on the coast is **Robert's Cove**, a popular day trip destination with city people which has several sandy beaches, best visited at low tide, and a safe anchorage. To reach it you must travel inland to Minane Bridge and pick up the signposts. From Robert's Cove you can return to the main Cork-Kinsale road through the pretty stone-built village, **Nohoval**.

Signposted off this road about two miles outside Robert's Cove is another popular beach, known as **Rocky Cove**. There is a cliff WALK of about a mile and half from Rocky Cove to Robert's Cove, around a very rocky headland which is especially impressive in stormy (but not *too* stormy) weather.

Two miles beyond Nohoval, a left hand turn at **Ballinaclashet Cross** (beside a restaurant called The Oystercatcher) will take you to **Oysterhaven**, a sheltered harbour with a thriving wind-surfing centre, but no proper village. The large ruined house that can be seen from the cross-roads is **Mount Long Castle**. It can be reached by going straight over the crossroads and turning left after a sharp right hand bend about half a mile on. Turn right at the T-junction and left almost immediately. (These are very narrow roads; ideally park near the cross and WALK). The castle was built in 1631 as a defensive mansion rather like Kanturk Castle (See Chapter Five) and Coppinger's Court (Chapter Eleven). Large towers are attached to each corner of an impressively large central main block. Mount Long has loopholes for small arms fire and machicolations at its extreme corners. John Long, who built the castle, lost his lands and was hanged in Cork in 1653 following the Cromwellian Wars. His lands were given to a Cromwellian soldier, Giles Busteed, and his family lived there until 1830. It appears to have been derelict ever since, and is, understandably, in a pretty bad state, although, oddly enough, the towers facing the sea are in a better condition than the landward ones. Much of the fine cut stone has been stolen, as have the oak lintels, and there are fears that it might collapse.

The main road is reached at **Ringanane Bridge** beside Kinsale Golf Club, by following signs for Kinsale. Kinsale is two miles to the left; Cork city is about 16 miles to the right.

Sports Facilities

Cork Harbour West

Golf: *Douglas Golf Club*, Douglas. Tel. 021/895297. 18-hole. Green fees Mon.-Fri. *Monsktown Golf Club*, Parkgarriffe, Monkstown. Tel. 021/841376. 18-hole. Green fees Mon.-Fri. *Frankfield Golf Club and Driving Range*, Douglas. Tel. 021/363124. 9-hole. Green fees Mon.-Fri. *Raffeen Creek Golf Club*, Ringaskiddy. Tel. 021/378430. 9-hole. Green fees Mon.-Fri,, after 2.30 weekends. **Tennis**. *Crosshaven Tennis Club*, Community Centre. *Fountainstown Tennis Club*, Fountainstown. *Oysterhaven*

Boardsailing Centre, Oysterhaven. Tel. 021/770738. **Horse Riding**. *Hitchmough Riding School*, Monkstown. Tel. 021/371267. *Hop Island Riding Centre*, Rochestown. Tel. 021/361277. *Knock na Mana Riding Stables*, Minane Bridge. Tel. 021/887111. **Bicycle Hire**: *Curra Cycles*, Main St. Carrigaline. Tel.021/371845. *Amazonia*, Coast Rd. Fountainstown. Tel.021/831115. **Boat Hire**: *Oysterhaven Centre*, (Canoeing, windsurfing and dayboats, also tuition), Oysterhaven. Tel. 021/770738. *Crosshaven Sea Angling Club*, The Pier. Tel. 021/371956. *Whispering Pines*, Crosshaven. Tel. 021/831843. **Fishing**: *Deep Sea*: see Boat Hire above. The Owenabue River between Ballinhassig, Carrigaline and Crosshaven is primarily a sea trout fishery. Fishing is strictly with permission of various owners: enquire on the spot.

PUBS, RESTAURANTS, SHOPS AND ACCOMMODATION
(Price Categories are explained in HOW TO USE THIS BOOK)
CARRIGALINE

ROSIE'S
Main St. Tel. 021/372262.
    A plain two-storey white building in the middle of the village, opposite the turning for Crosshaven, Rosie's has been at the centre of Carrigaline life since it was founded in about 1835. Inside, this aristocrat among Carrigaline's bars is dimly lit with a Liscannor slate floor beneath the low roof. The bar is lined with comfortable tall stools with backs, upholstered in a tapestry fabric to match the surrounding banquettes. The decor has a horsey theme expressed in historic prints, paintings and photographs as Rosie's is the unofficial headquarters of the South Union Hunt who meet here at least three times a year.

Bar Food
THE STABLE
Tel.021/372051. Bar food 12.30-2.30 Mon - Sat.
    The home-cooked lunches available at this hostelry, a few doors away from Rosie's, have proved so popular that the lounge has recently been extended and is now a large, well furnished room with green tweed seating and mahogany tables beneath a pair of large art nouveau chandeliers. The original narrow lounge bar at the entrance was indeed once a stable, and horse collars, metal hay baskets and bridles hang from the walls in memory of the former occupants. The proprietor's wife, Anne McLaughlin, is personally responsible for the daily menu which always includes at least 3 hot specials including a joint of the day, and home cooked dishes using local produce.

Restaurant
PEW'S BISTRO
Main St. Tel. 021/371512. Open from 7PM Tues.- Sun. and Sun.lunch, closed Sun. dinner winter. Credit Cards: Visa, Access. Booking advisable weekends. Wine licence only. Expensive.
    A shop has been cleverly converted to make this small but stylish restaurant. Diners sit on stripped-pine pews at tables which are set relatively formally with white napery and upstanding fanned napkins. The dark green walls are decorated with framed menus from restaurants where the young owner chef, Barry O'Connor, worked before opening here in 1990. These include Peter Langan's, Odin's, Maxime de Paris and Le Gavroche, names which will whet the appetite of serious foodies. His menu should not disappoint. Starters include fish soup, and a saute of escargots in puff pastry. Among the main courses on my autumn visit was a warm salad of char grilled goose with pink grapefruit and raspberry vinegar, poached breast of chicken stuffed with a mussel and coriander mousse and grilled saddle of lamb with a lemon and thyme crust. There is always at least one vegetarian special.

B & B
BEAVER LODGE
Tel. 021/372595. Inexpensive. Credit Cards: Visa, Access.

Coming from Cork or Ringaskiddy, Beaver Lodge is clearly signposted on the right hand side just beyond Cogan's Garage and the Allied Irish Bank. It is a large two-storey Victorian villa on about an acre of mature grounds beside a little stream. It is only about 100 yards off the main road, but gets hardly any traffic noise. The closeness to Ringaskiddy makes it a convenient stopping place for travellers heading to or from the ferry. There is a delightful Victorian-furnished entrance hall dominated by a large stag's head, and a large, comfortable guest lounge with TV and piano. There are 6 rooms, 4 with bathroom en suite and all with TV, direct dial phone, and tea and coffee making facilities. They are simply decorated with duvets and old but not quite antique furniture.

CROSSHAVEN

Bar Food
CRONIN'S BAR.
Tel: 021/831207 Bar food Mon-Sat 12.00-2.30, till 7pm or later in summer. Inexpensive.

This large pub is situated in the centre of the flat part of town beside the bus stop and the public car park - not surprisingly, because it was the Railway Hotel during the short life of the Crosshaven branch line. Nowadays it is a characterful Victorian bar with a welcoming open fire surrounded by its original Victorian tiles. You get real home-cooking here as all the bar food is prepared by Thecla Cronin, who also bakes her own brown bread. There is a standard menu, including a very popular home-made burger, a daily special such as steak and kidney pie or seafood pie, and open sandwiches on brown bread. The walls are crammed with memorabilia reflecting the owner, Sean Cronin's, two interests: boxing and Crosshaven's maritime past, which are well worth studying. This is a comfortable, friendly, well-run bar, the perfect haven after a brisk walk up to Fort Camden and the headland.

Bar Food/Music/Hotel
THE HELM
Weaver's Point, Church Bay. Tel.021/831400. Credit Cards: Visa, Access, Amex, Diners. Inexpensive.

Take the road to Church Bay behind Cronin's, turn left at the top and the hotel is at the end of the road - about a mile in all. At the time of writing it is the only hotel in Crosshaven, which once had three. This fact, and its location, perched on top of a cliff overlooking Fort Carlisle and Roches Point are the main reasons for mentioning it. The decor will delight lovers of accidental kitsch; others may be put off by its exuberance. The bar has spectacular views of Roches Point and the shipping activity in the mouth of Cork harbour from its 3 bay windows. It also has a red tiled floor, dark blue floral wallpaper, mosaic topped coffee tables and black and red plastic chairs, plus nautical bric-a-brac including a brass and mahogany ship's compass. In summer you can drink out in the cliff top garden which has a large goldfish pond. The bar food features plaice, sausage or chicken with chips. The 19 bedrooms have direct dial phones, are basically furnished, and share bathrooms on the corridor. If you can get one with a bay window overlooking the sea you could have an amazingly romantic night at a bargain price. There is music in their large function room (no cover charge) on Saturday and Sunday nights all year round, and nightly in the summer, described by the owner Catherine Middleton as "middle of the road country rock and folk".

Guesthouse
WHISPERING PINES
Tel. 021/831448. Wine Licence (meals for residents only). Credit Cards: Visa, Access, Amex, Diners. Inexpensive.

Soon after entering Crosshaven you will see a large sign on the right hand side indicating this guest house which is situated on a slope overlooking the river. It is a plain but comfortable place to stay, a modern purpose-built two-storey extension to a bungalow, much frequented by deep sea fishermen on package tours from Holland, France, Belgium and the UK, and the deep sea fishing facilities offered by the hosts are the main reason for staying here. All 15 rooms are plainly decorated and have fully tiled bathrooms en suite and direct dial phone. The best views are from the upstairs ones.

B&B
BEN BULBEN
Upper Rd. Tel. 021/831436. Inexpensive.

Follow the signpost for Myrtleville off the main road in Crosshaven and you will find this large Victorian semi-detached house about 100 yards up it. There are 6 well-proportioned rooms, 3 with bathrooms en suite. Try to get the one with a bay window overlooking the harbour. They all have stripped pine doors and plain, homely furniture. There is a TV lounge downstairs, and breakfast is served at one large table.

DOUGLAS

Bar Food
MICHAEL BARRY'S
Douglas East. Tel:021/891370. Bar food 12.30-2. Inexpensive.

Behind the traditional facade at the traffic lights of Douglas Village is a large lounge bar where green leatherette seating surrounds formica topped tables and plastic foliage hangs from the ceiling. Barry's has been in business since 1773, and Michael and Rose Barry are the fourth generation to run the establishment. Rose and her son Eamon are responsible for the home-cooked bar food, which includes soup served with soda bread, a choice of hot dishes, lasagne, quiche, and cold meat platters. Their freshly-made sandwiches are generously filled.

Bar Food/Restaurant
LOVETT'S
Churchyard Lane, off Well Rd. Tel:021/294909. Restaurant open 12.30-2.15 and 7-10 Mon-Fri; 7-10 Sat. Credit Cards: Visa, Access, Amex. Diners. Booking advisable. Closed Sundays and 24-31 Dec. Bar food lunch and dinner, Inexpensive; restaurant Moderate (lunch); Expensive (dinner).

This excellent restaurant is situated in a detached Victorian villa in its own grounds in a quiet suburban road about 10 minutes' drive from the centre of Cork City. Follow signposts for Blackrock or Douglas then pick up the restaurant's own signposting. It is well worth the effort. There are two bars to choose from on the ground floor: the intimate Boat Bar with an open fire in its tiled Victorian fireplace, or the larger front bar with a bay window overlooking the grounds and pictures of Cork's breweries and distilleries. There is an adventurous bar food menu displayed on a blackboard featuring dishes such as squid cassoulet, chicken stir fry and seafood pasta. The restaurant, also in a ground floor room with a large bay window, has large, well-spaced tables covered in beige linen, and is hung with Victorian portraits. The set menus at both lunch (3-course) and dinner (5-course) offer good value and plenty of choice, featuring dishes from the a la carte such as breast of chicken burgundy or poached brill with sorrel sauce. Vegetarians are well catered for. The wine list, personally selected by your hosts Margaret and Dermot Lovett, is famed for its wide choice of "Wild Geese" wines - wines from Chateaux founded by exiled Irishmen:

Lynch Bages, Chateau Mac-Carty, Chateau Dillon, Chateau Kirwan. You may well be tempted to finish your meal with the most famous of all Wild Geese products, Hennessy Brandy.

There are also 9 exceptionally well-equipped self-catering homes in the grounds.

Restaurant
BULLY'S RESTAURANT AND WINE BAR
7 Douglas Village. Tel.021/892415. Open 12 - 11.30 Mon-Sat, 5-11 Sun. Wine licence only. No Credit Cards Inexpensive.

This is a branch of the popular Paul Street Bully's (See Cork City) with a similar menu offering a wide selection of pizzas and pastas, with budget specials at lunchtime.

Bar Food/Restaurant/Hotel
ROCHESTOWN PARK
Rochestown Rd. Tel.021/892233. Credit Cards: Visa, Access, Amex, Diners. Open all year. Expensive. Carvery lunch, 12.30 -2.30 Inexpensive.

This is one of Cork's newest luxury hotels which opened in June 1989. It is based in and around a Victorian mansion in its own mature grounds on the banks of Lough Mahon. The spacious, naturally lit lobby, a modern extension tiled in white marble, is furnished with plump sofas. The 39 bedrooms are all modern with cotton spreads, wool carpets, light oak fittings and fully tiled bathrooms, and all have direct dial phone, multi-channel television, tea and coffee making facilities, hair dryer and trouser press. Most of the rooms overlook Lough Mahon. The Windsor Restaurant is a fairly formal room with a good choice of seafood and meat entrées. The self-service carvery lunch is available daily in the Douglas Tavern, and is proving very popular with locals. It offers a better than average menu with hearty main courses such as boiled collar of bacon with parsley sauce or roast rib of beef with horseradish sauce, plus a choice of starters and desserts. The mahogany and brass-trimmed bar is dimly lit in spite of an enormous Tiffany lamp; it is far more pleasant to sit in its front conservatory-type extension which has bamboo sofas and light oak tables.

MONKSTOWN
Bar/Music
MONKSTOWN INN
The Glen Rd. Tel:021/841541 Bar food in summer. Music at weekends.

This place is signposted off the main road through Monkstown. It faces a small park about 200 yards inland which is reached by crossing an iron footbridge which runs over a swift stream. There are picnic tables, children's rides, and swings and slides are about to be added. Inside it is a pleasant country style bar with a low beamed ceiling, quarry tiles in the bar area, some exposed brick walls, and tapestry-upholstered seating. The live music at weekends ranges from traditional Irish to blues and country rock. A limited selection of bar food - sandwiches and burgers - is available in the summer.

Bar Food/Restaurant
THE BOSUN
Monkstown. Tel.021/842172. Bar food 12 - 2.30, bar snacks all day; restaurant 12-2.30 Mon-Sat, 7-9.30 (last orders) Tues-Sat.Credit Cards: Visa, Access. Booking advisable weekends and summer. Bar Food Inexpensive, Restaurant Moderate.

The Bosun has a waterfront location, but unfortunately there is no view from the restaurant, a narrow cosy room separated from the bar by a huge ship's wheel and a tropical fish tank. Red velvet banquettes line the wall, and there is pink napery and fresh flowers on the tables. The menu features an abundance of seafood - fresh prawn cocktail, baked plaice stuffed with crab, baked mussels in garlic - as well as chicken, duckling and a selection of steaks. In the bar there is a choice of four or five hot dishes every day as well as home made soup, chowder, and oysters in season. In the summer there are tables outside where you can enjoy the view which is not really marred by thc heavy industry at Rushbrooke on Great Island across the narrow channel.

MYRTLEVILLE
Bar/Restaurant/B & B
BUNNYCONNELLAN
Myrtleville. Tel.021/831213. Restaurant open from 7pm Weds-Sat; Fri, Sat only Oct. to May, and Sunday lunch. Credit Cards: Visa, Access. Moderate.

The road in Myrtleville ends at the sea, and the gates of Bunnyconnellan are on the right hand side just before the strand. An avenue winds along the cliff top until you arrive at the strange turreted building (which in fact dates from 1830) and the extensions which form the bar and restaurant. The bar is the sort of local that people dream about having, a spacious yet intimate bar that positively oozes character. Its amazing cliff-top location makes it an idyllic drinking spot on a summer's day, and there are labyrinthine cliff gardens to enjoy besides a generously furnished patio. But it is even better on a dark winter night when you can hear but maybe not see the waves pounding on the rocks beneath, and the foghorn groaning from Roches Point across the harbour mouth. Inside there is a stone fireplace with miniature cannons on either side, a quarry tiled floor, rough hewn table tops and all manner of brass bric-a-brac hanging from the ceilings. The restaurant, a large room also overlooking the sea, has a more genteel ambience, with dusty pink floral wallpaper above an eau de nil dado. The menu offers no surprises - prawn cocktail, melon, followed by dishes like grilled black sole on the bone, duckling, steaks and veal, and there is always a vegetarian special. There are 3 good-sized bedrooms with en suite bathrooms and a sea view, and a few smaller ones that can be made available on demand. As for that name, I discovered that I am not the only person under the illusion that the place was run by a person called Bunny, when the O'Brien family, who have run it for the last 16 years, told me that they regularly get phone calls asking for Mr. Bunny Connellan. They suspect it might have been called after a Mayo village, Bunnyconlon, though there are numerous other speculations on its origins.

RINGASKIDDY
Pub/Restaurant
RINGASKIDDY INN
Middle House. Tel. 021/378298. Restaurant open 7.30-10; 12.30-2 and 7-10 (nightly in summer, Thurs.-Sat. only winter). Credit Cards: Visa, Access, Amex, Diners. Inexpensive.

You will find this pub on your left hand side almost immediately on leaving the ferryport if you're desperate for a real pint of stout. It stands slightly back from the road and has a black and white timbered front, and a conservatory extension which houses the restaurant. The long-established bar is smallish with an open fire. The separate restaurant, which opened only in the autumn of 1991, is far prettier, with natural light from all sides in the daytime and pretty floral drapes against dusty pink walls at night. The modern black wood tables are set with place mats and fresh flowers. All soup, most desserts and the brown bread are home made. There is an all day snack menu with choices like smoked salmon platter, ploughman's lunch and stuffed baked potatoes. The chef's daily special at lunchtime is usually a roast joint. In the evening there is a four course set menu.

TRACTON

THE OVERDRAUGHT

Tracton/Ballyfeard road. Tel.021/887177. Dinner from 7PM, last order 10.30, closed for dinner Mon. Off-season phone to confirm hours. Credit Cards: Visa, Access. Booking advisable. Moderate.

This attractive stone-built country pub is well-signposted on the roads from Cork and Carrigaline. It was one of the first "theme decorated" pubs in the area, and is certainly one of the most successful. The bar, labelled "The Cashier", was once a counter in the Allied Irish Bank in Cork, and the ceilings are clad in mahogany panelling taken from the lifts in the old Munster Arcade. In winter there is a welcoming log fire. Outside there is a pretty beer garden beside a stream. They have won several awards for bar food, which is served either on place mats at a table in the bar area, or in a separate dining room. This is bar food for serious eaters - fillet steaks are wrapped in bacon or stuffed with garlic; also popular is black sole on the bone in lemon and butter, or prawn and smoked salmon salad. There is a full range of starters and puddings.

4 | CHAPTER FOUR

EAST CORK

This chapter explores the coast of Cork to the east of the main N25 Waterford road. The tour starts at Carrigtwohill with its well preserved castle, then passes through Midleton and detours to the cathedral and round tower in Cloyne. From Cloyne we head for the coast at Ballycotton and Garryvoe via Shanagarry, returning to the main road at Castlemartyr and travelling on through Killeagh, with its beautiful forest walks, to Youghal on the estuary of the Blackwater river. The area can easily be explored in a relaxed day trip, as it covers only about 50 miles including detours, but there are many tempting stopping places along the way including Ballymaloe House (buffet lunch at 1PM), as well as numerous sandy beaches.

Barryscourt Castle is clearly signposted on the right (coming from Cork) in the unprepossessing village of **Carrigtwohill**. It is about half a mile off the main road, and freely accessible. The castle is in ruins, but the ruins are extensive and well-preserved, and were opened to the public in 1990.

The remains of the castle keep are surrounded by fragments of the western bawn wall of an earlier castle built between 1207 and 1234. The tower is about 60 feet high. The remains of a great hall can be seen, its window seats and large windows clearly defined. It was the principle residence of the Barry family for over 400 years. Its strategic importance lay in its location on the Cork-Waterford route, overlooking the ferry access to Great Island. The castle was attacked by Sir Walter Raleigh in 1580 during the Elizabethan Wars, and needed major repairs after. A date on the fireplace indicates that these took place between 1582 and 1588.

Return to the main road, which turns into a dual-carriageway at this point, and by-passes **Midleton**. To visit the town centre, follow signs to the left. Midleton is a prosperous market town 15 miles from Cork at the head of the Owenacurra Estuary. The first recorded settlement in Midleton was a Cistercian monastery in the 12th century. The monastery was destroyed in the time of Henry VIII. The present town was founded by the Brodericks, later Earls of Midleton, in about 1670.

Midleton is best known for its distillery, which produces most of Ireland's whiskey, vodka and gin. It still has many of its 19th century features including a large water wheel in working order, an 1825 beam steam engine and the world's biggest pot still, with a capacity of more than 30,000 gallons in gleaming copper. **The Jameson Heritage Centre** (Open May-Oct, daily 10-4, otherwise by arrangement. Tours 3.30PM Mon.-Fri. year round) covers 11 acres of grounds, and includes some fine examples of industrial architecture. Visitors are warned to allow 2 hours for the full tour.

The commercial premises on the main street of Midleton are mainly Victorian, and above the often incongruous modern facades you will find some interesting buildings. One of the finest is an attractive 3-storey stone house with Gothic windows, one half of which is now Rosie's Bar. It was designed originally as two houses by Augustus Pugin in 1851 for Lord Midleton, and has been used as an inn since the late 19th century. Just near this is a bridge over the River Owenacurra, and a small public park called **The Baby's Walk**. Directly across the bridge is **Midleton House**, a large Georgian town house which makes an attractive focal point to the street. The Baby's Walk lead to another restored Georgian house which is used as council offices, and a picnic area beside the old distillery.

Leave Midleton through **Ballinacurra**, by following signposts for **Cloyne**, a small cathedral town about 6 miles to the south. Now only a village of about 600 people, Cloyne is the seat of an ancient bishopric founded by St. Colman in the 6th century, now absorbed into the Protestant diocese of Cork, Cloyne and Ross. Its most famous bishop, from 1734, was the philosopher George Berkeley (1685-1753).

Cloyne Cathedral is a small, plain, 13th-century building, which has lost much of its character through successive restorations. There are some interesting carvings on the small north door, representing pagan symbols of life. The 100-foot tall **Round Tower**, opposite the cathedral, is the only relic of the 10th-century monastery which succeeded St. Colman's settlement. Instead of the usual conical top, this one has castellations, which were added in the 18th century after it was struck by lightning. It is one of the few in the country whose interior is accessible, and it is worth the effort of climbing to the top, from where there are good views of the surrounding countryside and coast. If it is unattended, collect the key from the Cathedral Cottage beside it. Like most round towers, it probably served a variety of purposes: as a belfry, a look-out post and a refuge against Viking attacks or warring local tribes. In such an event, the monks would carry their valuables into the tower with them, raise the ladder (which leads to the only entrance about 15 feet above the ground) and hope - or rather pray- for the best.

From Cloyne follow signposts 5 miles to the south east to reach **Shanagarry**. The famous **Ballymaloe House** hotel, on the edge of the village, incorporates the remains of a 15th-century Geraldine castle. Ivan Allen, who farms the adjacent land, is one of a small community of Quakers associated with the area, another being the father of Stephen Pearce, owner of the **Stephen Pearce Pottery** in the village (well worth a visit- see below for details). The most famous Shanagarry Quaker was the first one, William Penn, the founder of Pennsylvania. It was while living at Shanagarry in 1666, managing his father's estates, that he attended a meeting in Cork and became a Quaker. He did not return from his American sojourn until 1698, but Penn descendants held the Shanagarry estate until 1903. They lived at Shanagarry House in the village which is still a private residence.

Ballycotton is clearly signposted from Shanagarry, about 3 miles south. This pretty fishing port consists of a line of white-washed cottages strung out along the top of a curving headland with an island and a lighthouse just off-shore. There are excellent cliff WALKS to the west of the village, and it is renowned for its sea birds. There are three bird sanctuaries in the area, on **Ballycotton Island**, **Capel Island**, and **Ladysbridge**. Landing on the islands is not encouraged as there are colonies of nesting sea birds, but ask about boat trips around the islands at the pier.

Return to Shanagarry, and turn right for **Garryvoe**, a long sandy beach which was awarded a blue flag for general excellence in 1991. There are several other sandy beaches between here and Knockadoon Head in the east. We turn inland for **Castlemartyr**, rejoining the main N25 about 5 miles inland.

The castle which gave this little market town its name is now part of the Carmelite College, but parts of their once remarkable landscaped grounds are incorporated into **Castlemartyr Wood**, whose entrance is about a mile west of the town on the main road (so turn left when joining the main road and back-track a mile if you want to get there from Garryvoe). There are easy-going WALKS in the woods along forest trails.

An even better spot for woodland WALKS is **Glenbower Woods** in **Killeagh**, a village about 5 miles east on the N25. In the woods you will find nature trails and an ornamental lake. This was previously the demesne of **Aghadoe**, and was known until 1932 as the "maiden estate" as it had remained in the Capell family for almost 700 years.

From Killeagh it is about 8 miles to **Youghal** along a good stretch of main road. If you are looking for its sandy blue flag beach, turn sharp right before entering the town, as soon as the wide estuary of the River Blackwater comes into view. This is the fun end of Youghal with amusement arcades, fun fair and a long promenade above the beach. Apart from excellent swimming, the five mile-long stretch of firm sand is also a good place for WALKS.

Follow signs for Waterford to reach the town centre, which is the flat area around the quays and the **Clock Tower**. In this direction the main road actually passes under the Clock Tower, a wide-arched four-storey building topped by a cupola and weather vane. This is the starting point of a short but steep walk around Youghal, today a market town and fishing port town with a population of about 5800. At first sight it looks run-down, verging on the seedy, but in fact, within the area of the old walled town there are several interesting buildings.

Youghal, pronounced "yawl", comes from *Eochaill* which means "yew wood" in Irish. It is assumed, because of its important strategic position with a sheltered harbour at the mouth of the Blackwater, that Youghal was originally a Viking settlement. The town was founded by the Anglo-Normans in the 13th century, and in 1275 Edward 1 of England levied a tax to build a stone wall around it. The original building on the Clock Tower site was one of several gates in these walls. At the Plantation of Munster in the reign of Queen Elizabeth I, Youghal was included in a vast grant of land given to Sir Walter Raleigh. In 1602 he sold out to Richard Boyle, who later became the first Earl of Cork (1566-1643). Boyle was almost penniless when he landed in Ireland, and was probably the richest man in the country when he died. Throughout the county we will come across towns which he founded. During the 1641-53 war he strengthened Youghal's defences, and it became one of the most important English bases in Munster. In 1649 the English garrison at Youghal went over to the Parliamentarian side, and Cromwell and his army wintered there.

The Clock Tower itself dates from relatively modern times - 1776 - and was originally built as a gaol. The walled town of Youghal was a "closed borough", totally dominated by Protestants. Catholic merchants were not permitted to become "freemen" of the town, and at the time the Clock Tower was built, the Penal Laws were still in existence, depriving Catholics of religious, political and civil rights. The new gaol was built to deal with rebels in the area, and quickly became a symbol of cruelty and tyranny. Prisoners were regularly tortured here; some were flogged and immediately deported; other were publicly hanged from the windows of the tower. A plaque, which was added to the tower in the mid-sixties, gives details of the deaths of two priests, killed in Youghal in 1580 and 1602. Inside there is a small local history museum.

A set of steps beside the Clock Tower on North Main Street leads, up several steep flights, to a well-preserved stretch of the old town walls. From here there is a spectacular panorama of the town, allowing you to appreciate its layout and its position on the estuary of the Blackwater. Having looked at the walls and the view, I suggest coming down again to Beau Street, which runs parallel to the walls and North Main Street midway between them. Beyond the Catholic church the road is named Nelson Place, a suitably nautical name for a road which contains many fine houses overlooking the bay, well-suited to retired sea captains.

At the end of the road on the left is New College House, built in the late 18th century, and recently restored. Beside it is **St. Mary's Collegiate Church**, one of the largest and most interesting Church of Ireland churches in the county. (If it is closed the key can be found with Mr. Collins in the Church Lodge). It was built around 1250 on the site of an earlier building. The most recent restoration stripped Victorian plastering from the interior walls to reveal the original stone, and the structure of the nave roof. The East window dates from 1498, and the stained glass, which was inserted later, shows the coats of arms of local families. In the nave is a 14th-century font, which has an old oak cover with a carved dove. Among many interesting effigies, the most conspicuous is the enormous and colourful tomb of Richard Boyle, the Earl of Cork (see above) with his 3 wives and 16 children. (There is another "Boyle Monument" in St. Patrick's Cathedral, Dublin, ordered because he travelled a lot, and could not be sure whether he would die in Youghal or Dublin). The children lying down are the ones who died in infancy. As the colours are well-preserved, it is an interesting guide to the dress of the times. The less ostentatious graves outside the church cover a wide time span, and tell many an interesting story.

Next door to the gates of the church is **Myrtle Grove**, once, it is claimed, the residence of Sir Walter Raleigh. *(Tel. 024/92274. Admission £2, £1 children and senior citizens. Unsuitable for disabled people. Guided tours only. 2.30 and 4, Tues. Thurs. and Sat. 1 May-30 Sept.).* It is a triple-gabled 3-storey building which dates from pre-1600, and is one of the oldest unfortified houses in Ireland. The main rooms are on the first floor, and have low ceilings, dark oak panelling and an ornately carved mantelpiece, retaining much of their original character. All non-local authorities that I have consulted agree that Sir Walter Raleigh spent very little time in Youghal, (his duties as Mayor in 1588-9 were carried out by a deputy), and he neither built nor lived in Myrtle Grove. Youghal's historians make other claims; not only did he live there, but he planted the first potatoes in Ireland in his garden. And it was while sitting under a yew tree at Myrtle Grove, smoking a pipe, that a servant threw a bucket of water over him, believing that his lordship was on fire. There is already a Potato Festival in Youghal in early July; I wonder are there any plans to introduce a Tobacco Festival?

Return to North Main Street down the lane beside Myrtle Grove. On the corner is a row of Elizabethan almshouses dating from 1601. A plaque announces that the Earl of Cork built these almshouses and bequeathed £5 per year "for each of ye six old decayed soldiers or Alms Men forever". They have recently been attractively restored.

Returning to the Clock Tower along Main Street, look out on the right for an unusual example of a Dutch town house, built about 1710 for the Uniacke family. A cut through the plaza on the left of the Clock Tower will take you down to the quays for a look at Youghal's trawlers.

Seasonal Events
Youghal Potato Festival - July - contact 024/92213.

Sporting Facilities
Golf: *Youghal Golf Club*, Knockaverry. Tel. 024/92590. 18-hole. Green fees Mon.-Fri., after 3PM Sat. and Sun. **Horse Riding**: *Monatrea Equestrian Centre*, The Farmhouse, Kinsalebeg. Tel. 024/94214. **Boats for Hire: Deep Sea Fishing:** *East Cork Angling Centre*, Loughcarrig House, Ballinacurra, Midleton. Tel. 021/631952. *Dietmar Scharf*, Kilderrig, Cloyne. Tel. 021/646056. *Sea Angling Centre*, Market Quay, Youghal. (No tel.) **Fishing gear and tackle, and local information on salmon and sea trout and coarse fishing:** *Evelyn Pratt*, The Arcade Stores, Youghal. Tel. 024/92386.

PUBS, RESTAURANTS, SHOPS AND ACCOMMODATION
(Price Categories are explained in HOW TO USE THIS BOOK)
CARRIGTWOHILL

Cafe/Craft Shop
BARRYSCOURT CASTLE
Tel. 021/883864. Open 9.30-6.15; Oct.-Apr. 10-5.30. Inexpensive.
The 18th-century farmhouse adjoining the castle has been carefully converted into a small two-storey tea room and craft shop. There are simple pine tables with stick back chairs on a Liscannor slate floor, with a spiral staircase leading to further displays. The menu includes open sandwiches and a home-made soup of the day, but concentrates on home-made cakes with a choice of up to 16 different kinds on busy summer weekends. Robert Williams, who buys all the crafts, likes to concentrate on local producers, and apart from Jerpoint Glass, everything is Cork-made. He has plenty of choice in the less expensive range, including reproductions of old posters and handbills, dried flowers, honey, chutneys and Shanagarry pottery. There are

also some unusual ceramics by Tony Breslin and Caroline Couchman, and a selection of sweaters from the Youghal knitting Co-op.

CASTLEMARTYR

B&B

KILNAMUCKEY HOUSE

Tel.021/667266. Open 1 May to 1 Oct. High tea or evening meal by arrangement. Inexpensive.

The house is signposted on the left hand side as you enter the village coming from Cork, and the entrance gates are about a mile down this road on the right-hand side. The driveway leads you past the 140-acre dairy and beef farm to a modest symmetrical two-storey whitewashed farmhouse which is about 150 years old. It was originally built for the daughter of the Rector of Castlemartyr, and now has a pretty flower garden in the front leading to the orchard. Its off-the-road location gives it a particularly peaceful quality, something that you might appreciate after spending a day on the popular nearby sandy beaches. The low-ceilinged rooms are enhanced by antique furniture and hunting prints. There are three double rooms with stripped pine doors and large comfortable old furniture. Guests share a large mahogany table in the dining room where the sideboard is laden with Mr. de Cogan's cattle-breeding trophies. There is a quiet residents' lounge: the TV is in the back breakfast room for children, who are usually the only ones who want it.

CLOYNE

Restaurant/Hotel

KILCRONE HOUSE

Tel.021/652444. Restaurant open daily lunch and dinner May-Aug.; off season Thurs. Fri. Sat. from 7PM and Sunday lunch. Advance booking advisable. Fully licensed. Credit Cards: Visa, Access. Moderate; Inexpensive without bathroom.

Follow the signpost in Cloyne and keep straight on for about a mile, ignoring a left hand fork. The large secluded brown and cream Georgian house stands at the end of a sweeping gravel drive in 14 acres of grounds. The front porch, which I suspect is a Victorian addition, gives the facade an unclassical, rather raffish air. Inside the atmosphere is more like a relaxed country home than a hotel, with an open log fire in the antique-filled sitting room. The owners also sell antiques, large and small, which are discreetly displayed about the place. It is popular with families in high summer, and some budget-minded Americans stay here and eat the occasional meal at Ballymaloe. Marguerite Farrane, who took over the hotel two years ago, is still re-doing the bedrooms, which are individually decorated with large antique furniture, duvets or handmade quilts, and Laura Ashley curtains. Beds in all ten rooms have electric blankets (in addition to central heating), and five of them have bathrooms en suite, ingeniously built into corners. The first floor rooms have tall ceilings, while those on the top floor are under the eaves and have curious small waist-high sash-windows. The dining room is in an elegant front room and has a large marble fireplace and two pine dressers, with windows on two sides overlooking the secluded grounds. Organically grown produce, free-range chicken and wild salmon feature in a home-cooked menu that includes dishes such as coq au vin and salmon poached in white wine sauce.

KILLEAGH

Bar Food

THE OLD THATCH

Tel.024/95116. Lunch 12.30-2.30; evening meal 5.30-7.30; hot snacks all day. Inexpensive.

This long, low and, of course, thatched building is on the left hand side in the village coming from Cork. There are outdoor tables under the overhanging eaves, and the entrance to the lounge bar is at the side. It is packed with pine tables and stick-backed chairs. There are daily hot specials at lunch such as corned beef or beef stew, and a selections of grills in the early evening.

Restaurant/B&B
BALLYMAKEIGH HOUSE
Tel.024/95184. Open all year. Dinner from 7PM; advance booking essential for non-residents; Nov.-Mar.: dinner by previous arrangement for groups of six or more. Wine licence only. Credit card policy unconfirmed. Moderate.

The farmhouse is five miles from Youghal and one mile outside Killeagh, signposted off the main N25 beside the Old Thatch Bar. It is set in the midst of a 180-acre dairy farm which supports 180 cows. Mrs. Margaret Browne was Calor Housewife of the Year in 1990, and the standards of comfort, decor and cleanliness are exceptionally high. There is a large lawn with flowerbeds in front of the house, a pretty patio at the rear and a hard tennis court. Pre-dinner drinks are served in the sitting room from the mahogany sideboard. There is also a TV and games room, with snooker and table tennis, and a conservatory with a collection of books and magazines for guests. The bedrooms are named after local rivers, and are low-ceilinged, like the sitting room, as this part of the house is over 250 years old. All five rooms have bathrooms en suite stocked with a lovely selection of fluffy towels. They are individually styled, with duvets, pretty floral curtains and attractive antique furniture. The top floor rooms are under the eaves with dormer windows overlooking the gardens.

All the food is prepared personally by Margaret Browne, using only fresh ingredients and herbs from her own garden. There is a five course set menu and your preferences must be discussed beforehand. When I called she was preparing the following helped only by her elderly mother and a small daughter: filo pastry basket with mushrooms, pineapple and cream on passion fruit puree, potato, leek and tomato soup, raspberry and sweet geranium sorbet, rosemary scented rack of lamb with mustard sauce and redcurrant puree, a selection of fresh vegetables, with a choice of home made ice cream, meringue gateau or apple and blackberry crumble for pudding. Not, as you may gather, the average farmhouse evening meal! The dining room has pine green and red decor with an open fire in the original cast-iron grate, reproduction Chippendale chairs and large tables set with white napery, with a candle floating in a bowl of fresh flowers on each one.

MIDLETON

Bar Food
O'DONOVAN'S
58 Main St. Tel.021/631255. Bar food from 12 noon; evening menu from 6-9. Bookings accepted for evening. Inexpensive.

This bar is on the right hand side of the main street just before the bridge. It claims to be the oldest pub in Midleton, and three years ago it was very sympathetically renovated in Victorian/art nouveau style with lots of mahogany, and etched glass partitions. There is an old cast iron fireplace, and an overhead skylight gives natural light to the bar area. In the evening food is served only in the back area of this small L-shaped bar, thus allowing the front to function as a regular local. The lunch menu includes dishes such as lamb casserole, chicken and mushroom quiche, and toasted or open sandwiches, plus some very tempting puddings. In the evenings the choices include chicken Kiev, grilled black sole on the bone, or sirloin steak with green pepper sauce. The wine list has six choices, all under £9.50.

Bar Food/Restaurant
FININ'S
75 Main St. Tel. 021/631878. Bar food from 12 noon; restaurant open from 7 Mon-Sat. Credit Cards: Visa, Access, Amex, Diners. Inexpensive. Restaurant Moderate.

Finin's have won several awards for bar catering in the past. It is a small, rather dark bar in the centre of the main street, with red velvet banquettes and photographs of old Midleton on the walls. Seafood platter, plaice and chips and daily specials such as Irish stew feature on the lunch menu. The restaurant has a good reputation for seafood. It is in a small upstairs room with dark turquoise walls and wood panelling, tweed seated chairs with place mats and linen table napkins set on dark wood tables. There is a choice of set menu or a la carte.

Deli/Restaurant
THE FARM GATE
Coolbawn. Tel. 021/632771. Deli open 9.30-6 Mon.-Sat. Restaurant open Fri., Sat. 7.30-9.30. Full licence. Credit Cards: Visa, Access. Moderate.

Take the right hand turn off the main street just after the large Quinnsworth supermrket. The delicatessen sells the best local produce, and is an ideal place to make up a picnic, with home made pates from various sources, a selection of Irish farmhouse cheeses, and bread and cakes baked on the premises. The restaurant has a good local reputation for imaginative treatment of fresh local produce, including the catch of the day from nearby Ballycotton. There is a set menu or a la carte, displaying an eclectic variety of influences including oriental and Mediterranean.

Hotel
MIDLETON PARK
Tel.021/631767. Carvery lunch in bar 12.30-2.30 Mon.-Sat.; Restaurant 12.30-2.30 and 7-9.30 7 days a week. Restaurant Moderate; Accommodation Expensive.

The newest luxury hotel in the area is on the main road between the by pass and the town centre. Its second phase opened in 1991. It is an attractive modern building, cream painted with a slated roof and distinctive red window frames. Already their three function rooms are attracting a busy local trade, which makes the place feel like an integrated part of the scene, rather than an insulated capsule for wealthy travellers. The large, well-lit bar has split levels and an art nouveau style interior with stained glass, mahogany and brass, and overlooks the road. The restaurant also has split levels, and is divided by stained and etched glass partitions. The 40 spacious rooms in the three-storey bedroom block are much as you would expect in a new luxury hotel, with mahogany fitted furniture, brass bedside lamps, large bathrooms, direct dial phone, TV, hair dryer and trouser press.

Shops and Galleries
CORABBEY LTD.
Presentation Convent. Tel. 021/63842. Open 8.45-4.30, Mon.-Fri.

For many years the Presentation Convent has been known for its fine Irish linen, hand-made lace and hand crochet.

SHANAGARRY

Restaurant/Hotel
BALLYMALOE HOUSE
Tel. 021/652531. Lunch 1PM (hot buffet); dinner 7-9.30. Hotel closed to non-residents from 3.30 until pre-dinner drinks. Booking advisable. Fully licensed. Credit Cards: Visa, Access, Amex, Diners. Expensive.

Ballymaloe (pronounced Ballymaloo) is probably the most famous country house hotel in Ireland, the one that sets the standards for ambience, decor and cuisine. You will find it well-signposted, two miles outside Cloyne on the Ballycotton road. Originally the home of farmer, Ivan Allen, and his wife Myrtle, the restaurant (which was the start of it all) and the hotel have expanded into a business with some 30 bedrooms and a restaurant seating 120. It is still managed personally by various members of the Allen family.

The house itself is a traditional creeper-clad two-storey building with a large fan-light over the front door, which has been rebuilt and modernised down the centuries. It was built on to an old Geraldine castle, whose 14th-century keep still stands. The emphasis here is on providing a relaxing interlude from the stresses of modern life for their guests, hence the decision to close the house to non-residents during the afternoon. (See above). The house is surrounded by well-tended gardens, with a croquet lawn, tennis court and outdoor heated pool, and adjoins the family's 400 acre dairy farm.

Inside, the "reception desk" consists of one simple table beside the main stair-case and is devoid of the usual bustle and ceremony of the luxury hotel. Off the entrance hall is a large drawing room with vast sofas in shades of beige, and a big open fire. Ballymaloe attracts its share of celebrities, and is a fashionable hideaway for actors and other media folk from the U.K.

The bedrooms are all individually decorated to the highest standard with attractive antique furniture, and small sitting areas near the windows. The whole house has lovely aromas of pot pourri and wood fires. Because of the age and development of the house the rooms are all different shapes and sizes, with differing themes of decor along traditional country house lines. The Allens are proud of the fact that none of the 13 rooms in the main house have locks on the doors, in true country house style.

The restaurant consists of a series of inter-connecting dining rooms, some of which are reserved for non-smokers. An interesting collection of modern Irish paint-ing, including works by Jack B. Yeats, hang on the dark red walls. The table linen is heavy white damask, the cutlery is by David Mellor. Myrtle Allen has developed her own style of country house cooking, combining the best of traditional Irish and French techniques in order to bring out the freshness of the ingredients. The menu is always based on the best fresh ingredients available, with vegetables and salads picked the same afternoon, locally raised meat and game, and fish fresh off the Ballycotton boats. The 5-course set menu (£27 in 1991) - there is a separate one for vegetarians - offers a choice of three soups or a salad plate followed by six starters such as Ballycotton fish mousse with shrimp butter sauce or hot buttered oysters on toast, and 6 main courses such as baked brill with carrot and chive sauce, escal-lops of baby beef with Irish mustard sauce or rack of Cloyne lamb with redcurrant sauce.

Shops and Galleries
BALLYMALOE SHOP
Tel.021/652032. Open 9AM-8PM in summer; 9-1 & 2-6.30 in winter, 7 days a week. Credit Cards: Visa, Access, Amex, Diners.

The shop is situated in a converted stone-built outhouse in the car park of the hotel. The front part of it is dedicated to Irish-made crafts; in the back is a specialist cook's shop. Both are among the best of their kind in the Cork area. The crafts include all the usual ranges of sweaters, mohair, tweed clothing, caps, scarves etc. plus local products like Ardmore Angora sweaters, Fermoy waxed coats, ceramic and silver jewelery, home-made jams and relish, kites, mobiles and hammocks. They also sell Irish Georgian Society place mats and coasters. The kitchen equip-ment includes Italian stainless steel saucepans, Danish cast iron pots, Italian cafetieres, French white porcelain, and all manner of classic kitchen equipment from forcing bags to cooks' knives, thermometers and whisks.

STEPHEN PEARCE POTTERY
Tel.021/646807. Open 8-5.30 Mon.-Fri; 10-5.30 Sat., 2-5 Sun. Credit Cards: Visa, Access.

The pottery is signposted to the right (coming from Cloyne) in the village, and is about 50 yards down the lane. Before going shopping you can watch the craftsmen at work using locally dug clay to form Stephen Pearce's distinctive chunky, serviceable pots. This part of the visit makes a good outing for children, who are invited to participate and given their own ball of clay to take home. Schools are welcome by previous appointment. There are basically three ranges to choose from in the attractively laid-out showroom, - the familiar brown and cream, a newer white and blue line and the original Shanagarry black and white. You can buy separate pieces or order a complete dinner service. There is also a good range of seconds which usually include some of the larger jugs and bowls at considerable savings.

YOUGHAL

Bar Food
THE MOBY DICK
Market Square. Tel.024/92756.
There are two reasons for liking this bar: for its location, on the quay where the local trawlers land and sell their catch, and for its associations with John Huston's film of Moby Dick. The interior is fairly basic, and soup and sandwiches, as well as tea and coffee are available all day. It is visible from the main N25, and makes a handy quick stop if passing through Youghal. Don't forget to have a look at the pictures of the filming of Moby Dick, with the pub and its location strongly featured, which you will find along the walls.

Bar Food/Restaurant/B & B
AHERNE'S
Tel.024/92424. Open: bar food: 10.30-10.30; restaurant: 12.30-2.15 and 6.30-10. Credit Cards: Visa, Access. Reservations advised weekends and summer. Bar food: Inexpensive; Restaurant and accommodation: Expensive.
People travel for many miles to eat at this acclaimed seafood bar and restaurant. Internationally trained chef David Fitzgibbon (whose mother was an Aherne) is the third generation of the family to be closely involved in the business. Their seafood, which is renowned for its freshness, has won many awards at home and abroad. The bar food is absolutely outstanding. You can eat either in the informal front bar, where you can chat to the locals dropping in for their pints, or in the more secluded wood-panelled cocktail bar. Their hearty portions of seafood pie or seafood tagliatelle are both well-recommended, or choose from various styles of mussels, oysters or smoked salmon. There are also a few non-seafood choices, a selection of soup and sandwiches, and a far above average choice of house wine by the glass.
The separate restaurant is in a relaxing pastel-toned back room, with local landscape paintings (most of them for sale) on the walls. The generously-sized tables are set with linen napery and good heavy cutlery and have fully upholstered spoonback chairs. There is a four course set menu at £17.50 and a large selection of seafood on the a la carte. Starters may include hot crab with rosemary, or prawns cooked in garlic butter; typical main courses might be poached brill with prawns in a Chablis sauce, hot seafood selection with two sauces, or gratin of sole, prawns and mussels. The wine list is chosen with seafood in mind: of the 70 on it, 50 are white. The luxurious en suite bedrooms are in a separate block at the back of the bar, and will be open by Easter 1992.

Bar Food/Hotel
THE DEVONSHIRE ARMS
Pearse Square. Tel.024/92827. Bar food 12.30-2.30 and 6-8. Credit Cards: Visa, Access, Amex, Diners. Bar food: Inexpensive; Accommodation: Moderate.
The Dev, as it is known locally, is on the left-hand side as you come into the town from Cork on the N25. It is a handsomely proportioned, symmetrical two-storey building dating from 1896. It feels as if it has been there forever. Its position on the

main road with easy parking makes it a good stopping place if passing through Youghal. You can have coffee in the sitting room just off the lobby if you don't fancy sitting in a bar, a fact which women travelling alone will appreciate. The public rooms have a pleasantly old-fashioned atmosphere, with lots of chintz and large pieces of Victorian furniture. Its large bar has been renovated with red upholstery, polished wood and stained glass, and has a separate entrance from the street on the right of the main hotel door. The bedrooms have bland modern decor, but are all equipped with en suite bathroom, TV and direct dial phone.

B & B

AVONMORE HOUSE
South Abbey. Tel.024/92617. Credit Cards: Visa, Access, Amex. Inexpensive.

This is a Georgian house set back from the main N25 just before the corner that leads to the Devonshire Arms. It is a respectable budget choice in a town which, to judge by my own efforts to find a single room there one October night, contains some highly eccentric, possibly insalubrious establishments with misleading notices outside. All 8 rooms at Avonmore have a shower closet and a washbasin, but only one has its own toilet. The rooms are spacious with sensible charcoal grey blankets instead of bedspreads, and no frills. Downstairs there is a TV lounge with comfortable sofas and chairs, and a breakfast room with individual tables. There is off-the-road parking in the front yard, which has a pretty flower garden.

5 **CHAPTER FIVE**

TO THE BLACKWATER VALLEY

This chapter follows the main Dublin road (N8) north from Cork as far as Fermoy on the river Blackwater, with a detour to the east to Castlelyons. From Fermoy the Killarney road follows the Blackwater river to the west. We take a detour to visit the pretty village of Glanworth, its castle and the nearby pre-historic wedge-tomb, Labbacallee. The road continues to Castletownroche, location of the magnificent Annesgrove Gardens, and on to the famous 18th-century spa town, Mallow. We head south beyond Banteer to Millstreet, best-known for its annual horse show. Millstreet is situated at the head of a valley between the Derrynasaggart and the Boggeragh mountains. (Kanturk and the rest of area to the north of the Blackwater are covered in Chapter Six).

Fermoy is about half an hour's drive from Cork (23 miles). If starting from Youghal, the tour can be joined in Castlelyons by taking the R634 Tallow road and the R628 via Conna Castle, a pleasant cross-country drive of about 45 minutes. The Blackwater valley drive is also a good alternative route to Killarney, which is about an hour west of Mallow.

The main attraction of the area is the excellent fishing on the Blackwater, salmon and trout in season, and good stocks of roach, dace, perch and pike. Fermoy and Mallow are not obviously attractive at first sight, but a little exploration will reveal hidden charms. The rich agricultural land around the Blackwater provides good scenery and walks. The Blackwater area has many large country houses, some of which can be seen from the road, most of which are still private residences.

The N8 leaves Cork city by passing through the village of Glanmire at the time of writing, but a by-pass is under construction. **Glanmire** is an extremely pretty wooded glen with the trees reflected in a wide creek. A half-mile detour off the main road (4 miles from the city) signposted on the right hand side just beyond the village leads to **Riverstown House** *(Tel.021/821025. Admission £1.50. Open 2-6 Thurs.-Sat., May-Sept. or by appointment).* This was originally built in the late 17th century and remodelled in the mid-18th. The exterior was left unadorned, with all resources being dedicated to the plasterwork of the interior. The Francini brothers, who had worked at Castletown in Co. Kildare, decorated walls and ceilings with ornate stucco work which was recently restored by the current owners with the help of the Irish Georgian Society.

The main road continues up a long hill through **Watergrasshill**, where a restaurant named after Father Prout recalls the 19th-century Cork wit, Father Mahony (see Shandon Steeple in Chapter One). He borrowed his pseudonym from a recently deceased parish priest of Watergrasshill, and has no other connection with the place.

If you keep an eye on the right-hand side of the road about seven miles after Watergrasshill, just before the village of Rathcormac, you will see **Kilshannig House**, an impressive 18th-century country house situated in mature parkland. It has been in the family of the Lords Fermoy, who are related to the Princess of Wales, since 1837.

There is a choice of two detours to the right in **Rathcormac**, both leading to ruined castles. The R628 Tallow road leads, after about 7 miles, to **Conna Castle**, a large square tower on top of a limestone bluff surrounded by mature trees. Its position on a high rock overlooking a valley makes it especially imposing. Its northern aspect overlooks the river Bride and a wide stretch of richly wooded country. It was built by the Fitzgeralds in the late 16th century. Less than a hundred years later, having changed hands several times and been pounded in several battles, it was destroyed in a fire in which the three daughters of the steward were burnt to death.

Efforts were made to restore it in the 19th century, but all that remain now are the four walls, its basement, and a winding internal staircase. However, it is an impressive building at about 80 foot tall, and its site is well-cared for by local initiative. A garderobe and numerous windows give some clues to its original five-storey lay-out. Its site and its size, and the fact that it has survived over 3 centuries of dereliction, will please all castle-fanciers.

From Conna it is about 5 miles across country to **Castlelyons**. From the N8, follow the signs in Rathcormac for about 3 miles. The extensive remains of the **Barrymore Castle** (also known as Castle Lyons) can be seen from the road as you enter the village, in a field beside the river Bride. (Not easily accessible). The original castle, dating from about 1204, was enlarged in Tudor times, and eventually made into the Jacobean manor house whose tall chimneys and great square windows stand out on the skyline. The Earls of Barrymore, much given to drinking, gambling and hunting, were not very popular locally, which might explain why no great efforts were made to extinguish the fire which started in the roof of the richly furnished mansion on 22 July, 1771. Verbal records passed down from that time recall that the building smouldered for two whole months. The Earls of Barrymore are buried in a mausoleum in the cemetery of St. Nicholas church in the village.

The main street of Castlelyons was designed as a grand avenue for the Barrymore house. In its centre are the ruins of a **Dominican Friary**, now cared for by the Office of Public Works *(Freely accessible)*. It was founded in 1307 by John de Barry for the Carmelite Friars, and the Franciscans have also been associated with it. The present ruins probably date from the 15th century, and include the nave and chancel of a church with a fine west doorway and window. There is a spiral staircase in the tower dividing nave and chancel. The monastic community died out in the mid-18th century, but it continued to be used as a "hedge school", where Catholics, subjected to penal laws, could seek a proscribed education.

Return to the main N8 and turn right. Up ahead on the left-hand side is a wooded hill with a cross on top. This is **Corrin Hill**. The cross was erected in the 1952 Marian year and is the site of an annual pilgrimage. A left-hand turn, signposted to the Golf Club, will bring you to the entrance to the forest after about half a mile. There is a well-surfaced path through the woods to the summit, a WALK of about 20 minutes. The remains of a ring fort can be traced in the woods, and on its summit is a cairn, reputedly the burial place of a legendary druid, Mog Ruith. It is a local custom to carry a stone with you up the hill and place it on the cairn.

Fermoy, which is just a mile from Corrin Hill,is a market town on the Blackwater (pop.5000), which has, alas, seen better days. Although the Irish Army has a base in nearby Kilworth, the town never really recovered from the departure of the British Army. Elizabeth Bowen's novel, *"The Last September",* gives a fascinating glimpse of the social life of the town's officer class in those days.

The army was invited there by the town's founder, a Scottish merchant, John Anderson, who bought the land in 1791 and laid out the town, providing a hotel, business premises, houses and a mail coach service between Cork and Dublin. He then persuaded the government to contract him to build military barracks on the north bank, and by 1800 Fermoy was up and running. Before Anderson's arrival, the little village was all on the south of the river, and the saying "All on one side, like Fermoy" is still used around county Cork.

In fact, it is still a bit all on one side, and if you want to explore it, the best place to park is on the south bank of the river beside the Grand Hotel. The 13-arched stone bridge dates from 1689, and there is a weir on either side of it. This is the start of a short but attractive WALK which follows the Blackwater upstream for about half a mile. There is a rich wild life for a spot so close to a town centre, including several herons and otters.

Leaving the river at your back, walk up to the traffic lights and turn left up Patrick Street. Keep going until the shops start petering out and you will come to **Fermoy**

Courthouse, a classical building dating from 1808. The main street, with its predominantly plastic and neon shop fascias defacing the interesting 18th and 19th century buildings, is depressing. You may prefer to take a right on your way back and walk along the side of the river. Some shops on the other side of Market Square have reverted to traditional wooden hand-painted signs and look much better.

Leave Fermoy on the Mallow/Killarney road by crossing the bridge and taking the first left. The road passes the gates and demesne wall of **Castle Hyde**, an 18th-century house on the banks of the Blackwater which is not open to the public. A detour to the right shortly after leaving Fermoy will bring you to **Glanworth**, a pretty village where a 13-arch stone bridge dating from the 15th century crosses the River Funcheon. There is a pretty waterfall on either side of the bridge, and a good view of the recently restored limestone shell of **Glanworth Castle**. It is a good example of an early Norman fortress with a large rectangular area surrounded by massive curtain walls with a defensive rounded tower at each corner. Within the walls is a central keep about 30ft. by 40ft. Built in the 12th century, it was in the hands of the influential Roche family until it was destroyed by artillery in 1649. The druid's daughter, Cliona, is said to have lived in an earlier fort on this site. She married an O'Keefe chieftain, having turned his original choice, her sister, into a white cat. The old stone-built mill below the castle has also been restored recently. Originally a flour mill, it was converted into a woollen mill at the turn of the century.

In Glanworth there is a signpost to the minor road near which is **Labbacallee**, one of Ireland's best preserved wedge-tombs, a burial chamber about 3500 years old, whose name translates as the hag's bed. Such tombs were usually surrounded by a cairn of loose stones which were probably used as a ramp to haul the huge capstone into position. Tradition has it that the woman buried here was the mother of Cliona (see Glanworth Castle above), the Queen of the Munster fairies, and when it was excavated in 1934 a headless female skeleton was found in the inner chamber. There are several standing stones in the Glanworth area, and the remains of a ring fort, suggesting that this river-crossing was a place of some importance in pre-historic times.

Return to the main road and carry on to **Ballyhooly**. The village is signposted off the main road and is about half a mile to the left. The name, incidentally, which often raises a smile, translates quite respectably as "the place of the ford of the apple tree". If you look back across the Blackwater after crossing the bridge you will see the remains of **Ballyhooly Castle**, which was built as a fortress of the Roche family in 1314. It is partly obscured by a large house dating from 1922. The builders used what remained of the bawn walls as the foundation of the new house. About half a mile outside the village on the right hand side of the road is **Castleblagh Wood**. Paths are marked on a map at the entrance, and an uphill WALK will be rewarded with good views of the Blackwater valley.

Return to the main road and carry on to **Castletownroche**. As you enter the village you will see that an old rustic bridge has been built beside a mill over the meeting place of the rivers Awbeg and Blackwater. This was the inspiration for the song "The Old Rustic Bridge by the Mill" which was written in the 19th century by Thomas P. Keenan who is buried in the churchyard above the road bridge. Castletownroche is an attractive, well-cared for village.

Annes Grove Gardens (*Tel. 022/26145. Admission £2, children and senior citizens £1. Open 10-6 Mon.-Fri.; 1-6 Sat. and Sun., Easter-Sept.*) are signposted in the village. The house, built in the 1740s (which is not open to the public) and gardens have been in the Annesley family since the late 18th century.

The gardens were created by the late Richard Grove Annesley in the first half of this century, and were inspired by the ideas of William Robinson, a 19th-century gardener who favoured the interplanting of native and exotic species in a natural setting with the minimum of formality. Beyond the walled garden is an extensive riverside garden featuring a huge collection of rhododendrons, a steeply sloping rock garden, and an extensive wild water garden which has an almost tropical lushness in high summer. Its features are re-created in miniature in one part of the walled garden. The woodland garden peaks in the late spring; the river walk, rockery and walled garden are at their most interesting in the summer. Allow at least an hour to see everything, although keen gardeners will want more time here.

Mallow (population 6550) is about 6 miles west of Castletownroche on the main N78, a more attractive approach than that of the N20 from Cork on which the town is hidden by a large bright blue factory which is its sugar refinery. Between October and December large beet lorries can be a considerable hazard on all approaches to Mallow.

The N20, which is the main Cork-Limerick road, by-passes Mallow (which is 21 miles from Cork). The **Mallow Racecourse** is about a mile outside town on the N72. Many visitors do not bother making the small detour to visit the town centre, which is a pity. In the 18th century Mallow was a fashionable spa, often spoken of in the same breath as Bath, though it is hard to believe today.

Its main street looks a bit run down, but beneath the peeling paint are some interesting Victorian and Georgian buildings, many with overhanging bay windows some of which are at fairly crazy angles. Park at the top of the street near the nicely restored Hibernian Hotel and walk down towards the castle to appreciate them more fully. The Cork and Limerick Savings Bank, for example, has an elaborate bay window surrounded by decorative plasterwork. Half way down the street on the right, set slightly back from the road is St. Mary's Catholic Church, built in a modest Romanesque style and featuring the "streaky bacon" combination of limestone and sandstone so popular in the region. The English novelist, Anthony Trollope (1815-1882) lived at no.139 for a time, and hunted regularly with the Duhallow, an experience he made good use of in his novels. **The Clock House**, a half-timbered building dating from 1855, looks almost derelict, but in fact its ground floor is in use as an accountants' office. It is on the site of the "Rakes of Mallow Club", the headquarters of the notorious gamblers, drinkers and fortune-hunters of 18th- century Mallow.

The **Tourist Office** (Bridge St. Tel. 022/42222) is to the right of the castle gates. Only the ruined **Mallow Castle**, in the grounds of a newer one, is open to the public. It was built in the late 16th century on the site of an earlier Desmond castle, captured by Cromwell in 1650, and burned by the Jacobites in 1689. The stables were then converted into the house beside the castle, which was enlarged again in 1837. From here you can view the white fallow deer which are unique to Mallow, having been originally presented by Elizabeth I as a wedding present.

Turn right out of the castle and walk along the river to have a look at the **Spa House**, a Tudor-style building dating from 1828, now privately owned.

Leave Mallow and head west on the Killarney road. At the turning for **Longueville House** (now a hotel - see below) the castle on the opposite banks of the Blackwater is **Dromaneen Castle**, a ruined 17th-century fortified house with square mullioned windows and gables that rises from a steep escarpment on the river bank. Both Longueville and Dromaneen belonged to the O'Callaghan family, and each can be seen from the other across the intervening river.

The N72 leaves the river to the south beyond the Banteer-Kanturk crossroads, and reaches the Kerry border at Rathmore. A left turn about four miles beyond that junction takes you over the river to **Millstreet**, famous for its annual horse show. It is at the foot of the Claragh Mountain near the entrance to the pass between the **Derrynasaggart** and the **Boggeragh Mountains**. The mountains are rich in megalithic remains: cairns, dolmens and stone circles. **Knocknakilla Stone Circle**, about a mile south-east of the town is worth a visit, both for its archaeological interest (five stones remain standing) and a fine hill-top panorama. The R582 runs through a scenic, sparsely populated valley between the Derrynasaggart and the Boggeragh Mountains, emerging in Macroom about 45 minutes' drive from Cork.

Seasonal Events
Horse Racing: For details of fixtures at *Mallow Racecourse*, Navigation Rd., Tel. 022/21338. **Show Jumping**: For details of Millstreet International Horse Show (late July) and Indoor International Horse Show (Sept. or Oct.) contact Noel Duggan, tel. 029/70039.

Sporting Facilities
Golf: *Fermoy Golf Club*, Corrin Hill. Tel. 025/31472. 18-hole. Green fees Mon.-Fri., book in advance weekends. *Mallow Golf Club*, Ballyellis. Tel. 022/21145. 18-hole. Green fees Mon.-Fri., after 3PM weekends. **Tennis**: *Mallow Golf Club* (see above). **Horse Riding**: *Beech Park Riding Centre*, Rathcormac. Tel. 025/36277. *Marie Whelan*, Glanworth. Tel. 025/38138. *Clonmeen Lodge*, Banteer. Tel.029/56238. **Bicycle Hire**: *Shortcastle Cycles*, Shortcastle St Mallow. Tel. 022/21843. **Clay Pigeon Shooting**: Contact Pat Hayes, Mallow Pet Centre, The Spa. Tel. 022/20121. **Fishing**: The Blackwater valley abounds in opportunities for salmon and trout angling and coarse angling (primarily a roach and dace fishery with some small pike and perch). Contact the following for detailed local information: In *Fermoy* area: *Salmon Angler's Association*, Liam McGarry, Moorepark, Fermoy. Tel. 025/31422(day); *Coarse Angling*: Teresa Lawlor, Corrin View, Fermoy. Tel. 025/32074. Coarse fish bait: Jack O'Sullivan, 4 Patrick St. Fermoy. Tel. 025/31110 In *Mallow* Area: Dick Willis, Bridge House Bar. Tel. 022/21057; Pat Hayes, Pet Centre, The Spa. Tel. 022/20121. 022/20121.

PUBS, RESTAURANTS, SHOPS AND ACCOMMODATION
(Price Categories are explained in HOW TO USE THIS BOOK)
BALLYHOOLY
Bar Food/Music/B&B
CASTLE TAVERN
Tel. 025/39206. Open all year. Inexpensive.
   The tavern is on the south side of a bridge over the Blackwater, and is well sign-posted about half a mile off the main Fermoy-Mallow road on the Fermoy side of Castletownroche. The B&B has a separate entrance at the back of the pub. Here everything is modern, functional but pretty, with plain white walls, light pine Habitat-style furniture, pastel coloured duvets and a total absence of clutter. The 12 rooms have gas central heating, washbasins with hot and cold water and shared bath-rooms, and look out on to the river across a field. They are in a converted outhouse which has been very nicely finished on the outside with traditional slated walls above the old stonework. However, even the owners, Roy and Sue Walters, original-ly from Reading, admit that the pub side of their business needs smartening up. It is so different from the B & B that you could be in another establishment altogether. The front bar is very basic, and mainly patronized by TV-watching locals; on the other side is a quiet but rather shabby lounge bar with two tall Victorian windows overlooking the Blackwater and Ballyhooly Castle, a piano, and gothicky alcoves with upholstered banquettes. The bar food is limited to soup and sandwiches, and the live music consists of old time country music - for the dancing of waltzes and quicksteps - on Sunday evenings, Bank Holidays and church holidays.

BANTEER
Restaurant/Guesthouse
CLONMEEN LODGE
Tel.029/56090. Closed for the month of October. Advance booking essential for dinner. Wine licence only. Credit cards: Visa, Access, Diners. Moderate.

This modest Georgian house is two miles outside the village of Banteer at the western end of the Blackwater valley (clearly signposted from the R579). It is surrounded by a 230-acre farm and has a riding stable attached which offers all levels of riding from tuition for beginners to hunting with the Duhallow. It is run by a German, Dagmar Ott, and there is a continental feel to the interior, the solid dark wood furniture contrasting with stripped pine doors. The dining room has a grandfather clock and an open fire, with good quality crochet mats beneath the hunting prints at each place setting. There is a choice of five main courses at the set dinner which vary according to season, and there is a special German dish daily. The seven bedrooms are well-maintained and individually decorated with large antique furniture and pleasant colour schemes. All have private bathroom, direct dial phone and television. Some even have their original wooden shutters. Additional bedrooms in a new house across the road will be available by the summer of 1992. There is also a self-catering family apartment with its own entrance available by the week. There is also access to one and a half miles of trout and salmon fishing. The proximity to Banteer railway station (direct line to Killarney and Cork) makes it a good choice for car-less travellers seeking a rural base.

CASTLELYONS

Restaurant/B & B
BALLYVOLANE HOUSE
Tel.025/36349. Advance booking essential for both accommodation and dinner - preferably at least 24 hours in advance. Wine licence. Private fishing. Credit cards: Visa, Access, Amex. Diners. Moderate, dinner Expensive.

Although the nearest town is Castlelyons, the best way to find Ballyvolane is to follow the sign post for it on the right hand side of the N8 Cork-Fermoy road on the outskirts of Rathcormac, and continue following the signs for about 4 miles. This large country house was built in 1728 on the site of an earlier house and modified 120 years later in the early Italian style. Jeremy Green runs a cattle farm on 100 acres of adjoining land while his wife, Merry, manages the house. The symmetrical stone mansion is surrounded by extensive gardens including a woodland shrubbery, walled vegetable and herbaceous gardens and woodland walks. The emphasis here is on family-style hospitality and a true country house atmosphere. The spacious reception rooms and pillared entrance hall are genuinely lived-in, and comfortably furnished with a family's accumulation of porcelain and paintings (rather than an interior decorator's fantasy), and open fires. Books, magazines and board games are left around for your entertainment.

All five bedrooms have large bathrooms, one of which, with a raised Victorian bath with brass taps enclosed by wood panelling reached by two wooden steps, is a showpiece in its own right. They are all luxuriously appointed, with oriental rugs as well as carpets, interesting antique furniture, generous sitting areas, and heavy velvet or damask curtains. There is one ground floor bedroom suitable for the elderly or disabled.

Most guests choose to sit at the large central table in the dining room, house-party style, although there are smaller tables if you prefer privacy. The dining room has 3 large windows opposite a black marble fireplace, and is restrainedly elegant with white napery and silver candelabra. There is no choice on the four-course menu, which usually features a main course of local beef or lamb, but any special requirements can be sorted out when you book.

FERMOY

Bar Food
THE GRAND HOTEL
Tel.025/31444. Bar lunch 12.30-2.30. Inexpensive.
Turn left just before crossing the bridge over the Blackwater (coming from Cork), and you'll find an unexciting but substantial carvery lunch in the hotel's red-carpeted lounge bar. Choose from home-made soup, the roast of the day, fried plaice and chips or daily specials such as lasagne or beef curry. Unfortunately there is no view of the pretty weir on the Blackwater from inside the bar, but there are some good photographs of local heroes, Dawn Run and Jonjo O'Neill, on the walls.

Restaurant/B & B
AVONMORE HOUSE
Mallow Road. Tel.025/32568. Advance booking for dinner essential for non-residents. Wine licence. Credit cards: Visa, Access, Amex. Moderate.
Cross the bridge over the Blackwater and take the left hand turning on to the N72 Mallow road, and you will find the entrance gates on the left hand side after about half a mile. It is a modest Victorian villa set in 7 acres of riverside grounds with private fishing. Hunting and shooting can also be arranged. The Californian owner, Constance Ramirez, has furnished the house in an appropriately Victorian style, from the massive carved-wood-framed 3-piece suite in the sitting room right down to the lace curtains. The large first floor bedrooms are all individually styled, and rather sparsely furnished by Irish standards, with interesting antiques, and oriental rugs on the floorboards. All 5 bedrooms have bathrooms en suite with bath or shower; an open fire can be lit in the original Victorian fireplaces on request and satellite TV is also available on request.

There is a three quarter-size billiard table in one of the downstairs rooms. The dining room has a bay window looking out across the gardens to the river, and a small conservatory that is used in the summer. Constance, who trained in the food side of the catering business, cooks and serves an interesting set menu which she describes as "Californian-European eclectic". House specialties include Oysters a la Ramirez - oysters baked with herbs and Tabasco, and oak and apple-wood smoked lamb. Seasonal dishes include Blackwater salmon, pheasant and venison, and in summer there are barbecues in the garden.

Shops and Galleries
DAVE PRICKETT - SUE PRICKETT
Sir Henry's House, Castlehyde. Tel.025/31924. Open: 9-5, later in Summer.
Dave Prickett specialises in making made-to-measure solid wood kitchens, while his wife, Sue, deals in antiques and restoration. They live in the dower house of Castle Hyde, and their workshops and showrooms are in the old stable yard beside it. You will see their sign on the left-hand side of the Mallow road (N72) about 3 miles outside Fermoy. Visitors are asked to park at the roadside and walk up the 100 yards or so to find them. Sue scours the country for characterful pieces of furniture, and is more interested in their visual appeal than their age or provenance. As her speciality is wood restoration some of the chairs she sells will need re-upholstering, but she can arrange for this to be done in Cork to the buyer's specifications. All her stock is restored in such a way as to let its age contribute to its charm, rather than over-restoring so that it looks as good as new. She is a good source of sought after items such as Victorian chaises longues and canopied beds. Much of her furniture is pine, with a pine chest selling for £45, a particularly attractive pine washstand for £100 and a nicely proportioned pine dresser for £475.

GLANMIRE

Bar Food

JOHN BARLEYCORN

Riverstown. Tel.021/821499. Bar lunch 12-2.30, Mon-Sat. Inexpensive.

This rambling old coaching inn is signposted to the right (coming from Cork) about 500 yards off the main Cork-Dublin road. There is a business-like bar to the left of the hotel lobby. The bar area is tiled, and the front room, with views over a meadow, has Turkey red carpet and red banquettes with Tiffany lamps and interesting old bar trade point-of-sale advertisements. The menu typically includes items such as home-made burgers, cold meat platter, stuffed mussels and brown bread, and Chinese vegetarian spring rolls.

Bar/Restaurant/Hotel

VIENNA WOODS

Tel.021/821146. Restaurant open daily 7-9.30 and Sunday lunch. Booking advisable. Credit Cards: Visa, Access, Amex, Diners. Moderate.

Don't be put off by the garish green and white sign indicating this hotel on your left-hand side about a mile after joining the main Cork-Dublin (N8) road. The well-tarmacked driveway sweeps uphill through over-hanging trees to emerge beside a charming late-18th century villa, designed by the same architect as Fota House. The front door is on the far side of its focal point, a two-storey rounded bay flanked by a Victorian canopy. A large modern extension which caters mainly for weddings is mercifully hidden at the side. The reception rooms have wonderful ornate stucco ceilings and appropriately grand carved and gilded furniture. The dark mahogany bar is in a quiet room with 3 tall windows looking on to the trees beyond the car park.

The 18 bedrooms all have TV, direct dial phone, tea and coffee facilities and en suite bathrooms. Most of them have tall ceilings and small sitting areas with views over the tree tops. They have modern fitted furniture in dark wood, duvets and wool berber carpets.

Even if you are not planning to eat here, it is worth having a look at the restaurant, the Austrian Oak Room, which was the display piece of the original house. The ceiling consists of a massive piece of intricately carved Austrian oak incorporating several skylights, and there is a raised alcove with carved surround in matching style. It was originally a library, then a billiard room. Nowadays it has nicely spaced tables set with place mats depicting hunting scenes and tall-backed upholstered dining chairs. The cooking is traditional Irish hotel style, with a choice of a la carte or a more economic set menu.

MALLOW

Bar

THE NOGGIN BAR

Tel.022/21588. Chapel lane.

Tucked away behind Keppler's Restaurant in a small lane half way down the main street, this bar is a compendium of salvaged materials from all over the county which have been moulded together again to create a uniquely atmospheric drinking place. Much of the pine came from the West Cork Railway station in Cork; the Gothic window in the rear bar is from the old church at Ballyclough, the timber settles are from the Wesley Chapel, Patrick Street Cork, and the cast iron supports come from the old Butter Market. Its well worth the price of a drink just to have a look at the way its all put together.

Restaurant

KEPPLER'S

Bank Place. Tel.022/21946. Open 7 days, from 12 noon. Fully licensed. Credit Cards: Visa, Access, Amex. Lunch: Inexpensive; Dinner: Moderate.

The restaurant entrance is down the area steps of a tall Victorian house. It has a pleasant interior of the rough-hewn kind with exposed stone walls, chunky beams, an open fire and a choice of seating in alcoves or open areas. There are daily specials at lunchtime for under £5 - dishes like fricassee of chicken and ham, or roast lamb - and an afternoon menu of hot snacks including curries and home-made burgers. The dinner menu features more elaborate dishes like noisettes of lamb florentine, or fresh trout stuffed with celery, walnuts, almonds and prawns.

Bar/Restaurant/Hotel
THE HIBERNIAN

Tel.022/21588. Lunch 12-3, dinner 9-9.30. Open all year. Credit Cards: Visa, Access, Amex. Moderate.

Halfway down the main street on the left-hand side, this hotel dates from 1770, and has recently been given a new lease of life by a tasteful and imaginative refurbishment which could serve as an example to the average dreary, unkempt, town-centre hotel. The facade, panelled in dark green with gold lettering and ornate coach lamps opens on to a light-hearted Victorian-style interior which is full of pleasant surprises. The Cloister Coffee Dock, immediately inside the front door, is a handy place for the traveller in search of quick sustenance in reviving surroundings. The interior (obviously by the same hand as the Noggin Bar - see above) is constructed from materials salvaged from a local mill, and is heavy on the pine: mortice and tenon-jointed pine beams, chunky pine tables, some of them large refectory-style ones to stimulate conversation among diners, a stripped pine floor, pine choir stalls and sturdy pine kitchen chairs. This is complemented by red and green Tiffany lamps and hanging plants. The coffee is real, and there is an all-day menu available at the self-service counter with hot and cold dishes. The dinner menu is waitress-service. The restaurant-proper is separated off by a wall of stained glass, and is an exceptionally pretty room with soft lighting, an open fire and a large pine overmantel opposite a tall grandfather clock. The rest of the hotel is decorated in Victorian repro, with painted dados and panels dividing the walls, softened by pretty floral wallpapers. All 28 bedrooms have co-ordinated colour schemes with matching floral duvets and curtains, pretty but not overdone, and all have en suite bathrooms, TV and direct dial phone.

Restaurant/Hotel
LONGUEVILLE HOUSE

Tel.022/47165. Open 1 March-20 Dec. Lunch 1-2; dinner 7-9.30. Booking advisable. Credit cards: Visa, Access. Very Expensive.

Longueville is 5km west of Mallow on the main Killarney road (N72). This magnificent Georgian manor flanked by a large Victorian conservatory is a sophisticated retreat for grown-up people, the sort of place politicians and jaded captains of industry would choose for a relaxing weekend. It is set in a 500-acre estate overlooking the Blackwater valley, and has 5km of its own trout and salmon waters. There is a high-ceilinged drawing room with large gilt-framed mirrors and oil paintings where you can relax by the fire with a pre-dinner drink. The small bar, behind it, is about as discreet as a bar can get. In the basement is a games room with a full size billiard table and a tennis table to while away wet afternoons. Alternately, you can help yourself to books and magazines from the vast piles left in wicker baskets on the staircase landing. The 16 bedrooms are all close to perfection: luxuriously carpeted, generously curtained, individually furnished with myriad varieties of attractive, solid antiques, supplied with enormous televisions, top quality bathroom fittings, hairdryers etc.

The dining room has a small ante-room for smokers in what used to be the library, a carpeted room with plush chairs lined on two sides by floor to ceiling mahogany breakfront bookcases. Non-smokers are seated in the President's Dining Room, where portraits of Irish presidents look down from the walls. This is a much larger space with a red pine floor, salmon pink moire walls beneath the elaborate plaster ceiling, formal curtains on the tall windows, and an Adam mantelpiece in Italian marble. In mild weather the conservatory offers a further option.

William O'Callaghan, son of the host family, a professional chef who has survived the heat of Raymond Blanc's kitchen at Le Manoir aux Quat' Saisons, is in charge of the kitchen. Typical main courses include lightly spiced monkfish with saffron and mussel sauce; roasted rack of suckling pig with garden parsnips and apples; breast of farmyard duck with a prune and sage sauce. Many of the herbs and vegetables come from Longueville's own walled kitchen garden, and they also have a vineyard which produces very palatable wine.

WATERGRASSHILL

Restaurant
FATHER PROUT
Bishop's Island. Tel. 021/889217. Open: 12-2.30 Mon, Tues; 12-2.30 lunch, last orders 9.30 Weds-Sat. Closed Sun, Bank Holidays. Full restaurant licence. Credit Cards: Visa, Access, Amex, Diners. Tourist Menu. Inexpensive (lunch), Moderate (dinner).

This large one-storey building has been a landmark on the left hand side of the main Cork-Dublin road since 1979. It is owned and managed by Louis and Stella Murphy, and Stella, who trained with Trust House Forte in England, is also the chef. They take the cliche of "fresh local produce" to new extremes by growing nearly all their own vegetables in a field behind the restaurant. The spacious interior consists of one large barn-like room with red brick walls dominated by a big grey stone fireplace and open fire at one end. The diamond-paned windows are filled with thriving house plants. Brown and beige tweed place mats are set on plain wooden tables, each with a posy of flowers, and the chairs are rustic ladder-backed style. There is a wide selection of steaks - T bone or Steak Diane (flambed in brandy) as well as variations on fillet and sirloin, salmon or trout, seafood Mornay and a good selection of home-made puddings - for example, chocolate and brandy trifle, lemon souffle. There is a choice of set menu or a la carte at lunch and dinner, and a la carte only for the hours in between.

6 | **CHAPTER SIX**

NORTH CORK

This chapter covers the area north of the Blackwater and south of the county's borders with Tipperary, Limerick and Kerry (with the exception of Annes Grove Gardens and Glanworth which were visited in Chapter Four).

This is predominantly rich farming country supplying the two major creameries at Mitchelstown and Charleville, bisected by the main roads from Cork to Dublin and Limerick. Today it is a quiet corner of the world, with no major towns, but its past importance is indicated by the number of substantial 16th and 17th century buildings, mostly in ruins, which include Kilcolman Castle where the poet Spenser lived until 1598, and the magnificent Elizabethan castle at Kanturk which was never actually completed. It is not an area generally frequented by tourists, lacking (until the restoration of the 18th century Doneraile House is completed) any major attraction, but, once away from the main roads, you are truly "off the beaten track" which will be, for many, attraction enough in itself.

We start by taking the N8 from Fermoy to Mitchelstown, which is about ten miles north. After about three miles there is a sign for Kilworth on the right. Before the building of Fermoy in the late 18th century, Kilworth was on the main Cork-Dublin road, and was the most important town hereabouts.

The ruins of **Cloghlea Castle** can be seen from the main road beside the turning for Kilworth. It is a late 15th-century Norman tower of seven storeys; it was repaired in the late 19th century, but is not at the moment, accessible to the public, as the surrounding land, known as Moore Park, is used by the Mitchelstown Co-Op who have a pig-rearing station on the site of the "Big House".

Kilworth is a quiet little place about a mile off the main road, with an attractive village centre which includes a recently-restored Market House, now used as a craft centre, and an 18th-century Church of Ireland which is sometimes used for exhibitions. If you follow the road from Kilworth for about 3 miles to the east, you will come to Araglin Bridge, the starting point for a WALK or a drive along the lovely wild, wooded valley of the **Araglin River**. The village itself, at the head of the valley, is on the borders of Cork, Waterford and Tipperary.

From Kilworth return to the main road and head north again. There is a large Irish Army camp on the left, and around this point, from the top of the **Kilworth Mountains**, there are wonderful views of **The Galtees**, up ahead to the east in county Tipperary, the peak of **Galtymore** rising above them. The **Ballyhoura Mountains** can be seen in the west.

Mitchelstown (32 miles form Cork) is an old-fashioned market town which is much enhanced by the glimpses of the surrounding mountains which can be had from its wide main street. Arthur Young, who visited the town in 1776, said it has "a situation worthy of any capital in Europe". Thursday is **Market Day** in the main square, a practical, no-frills country market, where large bags of spuds labelled "Balls o' flour" and bunches of green-topped carrots are the stars of the show. The **Market Square** itself is a good example of 19th-century town-planning. On the pavement to the south of the statue of John Mandeville are three crosses commemorating three men who were shot dead by the police during a Land League meeting in 1887. An "eternal light" burns to their memory in the wall of a nearby shop.

To find the other town square, **College Square**, walk or drive down (north) to the traffic lights and turn left (it can also be reached from the west corner of the main square). The square is named after **Kingston College**, a range of almshouses built and handsomely endowed in the early 19th century by the Kingston family of Mitchelstown Castle "for the use of decayed Protestant gentlefolk". They are used for the same purpose today, and have recently been renovated. The cut stone around the doors and windows, the tall chimneys and the walled front gardens echo the style of Mitchelstown Castle, an immense Regency-Gothic castle, modelled on Windsor Castle. It was completed in 1823 to the design of George Richard Pain for the then Earl of Kingston. He had built it in anticipation of a visit by King George I of England which never took place. From the square you can see a large, turquoise building, part of **Dairygold Co-Op** which stands on the site of the ill-fated mansion, and still has its cellars below. The cost of the castle encumbered subsequent generations of the Kingston family with debt, and it was burnt down by Republican forces in 1922.

An unpaved track on the left inside the creamery gates leads to what remains of **Mitchelstown Castle Gardens** *(No tel. Freely accessible, but donations towards shrubs and plants are appreciated)*. Timmy White, who now owns the land, lives in what was once the Head Gardener's House in one of the two walled gardens. Four years ago they were both a wilderness. Now there is a herb garden by the house, a rose garden, a pear alley and 50-foot pergola, and a large lawn, with herbaceous borders taking shape according to Gertrude Jekyll's planting schemes. At the far end of the garden a collection of old farm machinery is being assembled and renovated. The second walled garden has been laid out as a pitch and putt course to generate funds for further restoration work, and should be open in May 1992.

Leave Mitchelstown on the N73 **Kildorrery** road. It is about six miles to this mainly Victorian village whose little two-storey houses contain some well-preserved shop fronts. Less than a mile further on, just past a bridge across the little Farahy river, is **Farahy Church**, which stands near the site of Bowen's Court, the home of the novelist Elizabeth Bowen (1899-1973). After her husband's death, Elizabeth Bowen reluctantly gave up the struggle to keep on the house, which had been in her family since it was built in 1776, and sold it to a local farmer. He removed the roof to avoid rates (the death-knell of many an Irish house in those days) and it was demolished in 1960. The house, and previous buildings on the site, are nevertheless preserved in her book *"Bowen's Court"*, which besides being a most unusual family history, is a lively account of the social life in this area in the 18th and 19th centuries.

The church is a short WALK from the road along a narrow, high-walled footpath. An interesting feature of this small, Protestant church is the adjoining charity school "Erected in 1721 by Elizabeth Bridge of the City of London for the Christian instruction of the poor children of Farrahy", an unprecedented and far-sighted gesture at the time. The Bowen family graves are at the top of the churchyard opposite the main door. There are rumours of a plan to open an Elizabeth Bowen museum in the church, but this is unconfirmed at press time.

Beyond Farahy is a turning for Annes Grove Gardens (see Chapter Five) which leads after about 3 miles to **Castle Curious**, an amusing mid-19th century folly set in woodlands near the **Awbeg River**. It is also known as Johnny Roche's Tower, and was built single-handedly by a local eccentric of that name. He was also an accomplished tailor and maker of musical instruments, and was much in demand as a maker of false teeth, which he fashioned from cow's hooves. The strange circular design of his tower has all the hallmarks of a true individualist.

Return to the N73 and continue to the west. Look out for the sign to **Doneraile**. It was to the church in this attractive little village that two men raced across country on horseback from Buttevant in 1757, using the steeple to guide them in the first recorded "steeplechase".

You will need to take a left in the village to reach **Doneraile Forest Park** *(Admission free. Open 11-7 daily, to sunset in summer)*. This 400-acre park on the banks of the Awbeg River offers great scope for WALKS. It belonged to the neighbouring house, Doneraile Court, which backs on to it, and that is why it is so beautifully landscaped. It has wonderful vistas combining water, woodland and meadow. The park has been designated a wildlife sanctuary, and among its residents is a herd of Irish red deer. It is said that when the 7th Viscount of Doneraile died at the house in 1956, the doctor found the herd of red deer gathered in a semi-circle facing the door.

The St.Leger family bought the property (with an earlier house on it) from the son of the poet Edmund Spenser in 1627. **Doneraile Court** *(Tel. 022/24310. Tea room open 2-6 Suns; groups by arrangement at other times)* is a fine Queen Anne style house with large bow windows dating from 1725. In 1976 it looked as if this beautiful house would become derelict. It was rescued just in time by the Irish Georgian Society, and its restoration is now nearing completion. It is hoped that the hall, boudoir and library, with a photographic exhibition, will be open to the public by the summer of 1992, but phone in advance to confirm.

The house is best known for an incident which led to the first, and only, woman being initiated into the rites of Freemasonry. In 1712 Elizabeth Aldworth, daughter of the 1st Viscount Doneraile, hid in the library (some say inside a clock) during a Masonic meeting. When she was discovered, the enraged masons decided that the only way to ensure her silence was to enrol her in their Lodge. There is a plaque to her memory beside the pulpit in St. Finbarre's Cathedral, Cork.

From Doneraile Court return to the R522 and turn left for Buttevant to look at the ruins of **Ballybeg Abbey**, which are on the main road just south of the village. Although known as an abbey, this was in fact an Augustinian priory founded in the 13th century. The church was built shortly after, and the remains of two fine west windows can be seen. There are also some cloisters, and a central tower with an interior staircase which is a 15th-century addition. The most attractive feature here is the dove-cot to the south east of the church, which is one of the best-preserved in the country.

Buttevant, a large village or small town on the main Cork-Limerick road, was founded by the Anglo-Norman de Barrys in the 12th century. Its unusual name comes from the word *botavant*, the Norman-French name for a defensive outwork, and not, as many people believe, from the Barry war-cry *"Boutez-en-avant"*. Nowadays the town is best known for its old-fashioned horse-fair, **The Cahirmee Fair**, which is held in the streets every year on or around July 12, and has been for as long as anyone can remember. This is real old-fashioned horse trading, and always attracts a big crowd. It is a festive occasion, with plenty of entertainment on the side.

The best way to find **Kilcolman Castle** is to drive north of Buttevant on the main road for about three miles, and take the second right hand turn which is signposted Doneraile/Kildorrery/Mitchelstown. (The castle can also be reached from Doneraile, where it is signposted, but for some time now the *second* signpost has been missing, sending hapless visitors around in circles. You have been warned). All that is left of the castle is a single small tower about 40 feet tall, covered in ivy. It is on a small rocky hill overlooking a reedy lake about half a mile from the road. However, it still attracts visitors because it was here that the poet Edmund Spenser (1552-1599) lived for 11 years from 1587. He was awarded 3028 acres of land in 1586 in the course of the Protestant Planation of Munster. Sir Walter Raleigh visited him here in 1589, and brought his long, allegorical poem *"The Faerie Queen"* to the attention of Queen Elizabeth. From the castle you can see the Ballyhoura mountains, which Spenser wrote about as the Mountains of Mole, and nearby is the Awbeg river which he called "the gentle Mulla". Although he undoubtedly loved the Irish scenery, he held harsh views of the native people, so harsh that his report, *View of the Present State of Ireland*, was never published by the English government. During the rebellions which followed the efforts to "plant" Munster with English Protestants, Kilcolman was attacked by rebels and burnt. Spenser and his wife survived the incident (some say Spenser was away at the time), but it is said that their baby son perished in the fire.

Also in Kilcolman is the **Kilcolman Wildfowl Refuge** *(Open by appointment in* *winter, tel. 022/24200, Mrs. Ridgeway)* which has a hide and an observatory on the unique alkaline **Kilcolman Bog**. It is a winter destination for Hooper and Bewick swans, ducks and other waterfowl. In January 1992 they had over 800 duck of 7 species.

Return to the main road, and either turn right to look at **Charleville**, or **Rathluirc**, a 19th century market town near the border with LImerick, or turn left to Buttevant and take the R522, a right hand turn heading southwest, for **Liscarroll Castle**. The castle ruins dominate the tiny village, and are signposted up a footpath. It is one of the largest medieval castles in the country, and conforms in size and design to the archetypal idea of a fortified castle. The fact that it is built on an enormous limestone rock adds to its impressiveness. The massive curtain walls rise from the rock in the form of a rectangle which is about 200 by 150 feet. It has six towers, including two round ones. It was built by the de Barry family in the 13th century and modified in the 15th century. It saw action during the Confederate Wars in 1642 when it was held for a time by a force of 7000 Irish. An artillery attack by the Parliamentarians in 1650 resulted in damage to the square towers and a gap in the west wall, the latter recently restored. The south tower is the largest, and contained the entry gate beneath the arch, which was defended by heavy doors and a portcullis. Above the arch is a "murder-hole", similar to the one that can be seen at Blarney Castle which was used to deter invaders (in the days before guns, by pouring boiling oil on them). It is possible to climb the 60-foot tall south tower to the parapet, an extremely dangerous undertaking, and for this reason the tower is usually locked. The key can be obtained from O'Brien's bar in the village. Traces of the old chambers can be seen inside the tower.

From Liscarroll head west for the R579 by following signposts to **Kanturk**. The road runs parallel to the **River Allow**, which meets the **River Dalua** in the town. Kanturk has a somewhat run-down aspect, but is in many ways a pleasant little back-water with its river bridge and some good Victorian shop facades.

Outside the town, on the R579 Banteer road is **Kanturk Castle** which has a car park beside it. It is a large rectangular building with massive square towers at each corner. There are four storeys in the main block, and five in the towers. It is an interesting combination of the traditional Irish tower-house architecture with pointed arches, and the new Tudor architecture with Renaissance doorways and mullioned windows. There are a remarkable number of well-preserved stone fireplaces, with an especially fine one on the south wall of the third floor. It was built by a local MacDonagh MacCarthy chieftain around 1601. English settlers complained to the Privy Council that the house was "much too large for a subject" (i.e. an Irishman), and the Council forbade the completion of the work. The enraged MacCarthy subsequently smashed every single one of the blue glass tiles that he had ordered for the roof, and the house was never completed.

About three miles beyond Kanturk Castle the road joins the N72 which runs west to Killarney and east to Mallow.

Special Events
Cahirmee Horse Fair, Buttevant. On or around 12 July. Tel. 022/23395.

Sporting Facilities
Golf: *Charleville Golf Club*, Tel. 063/81257. 18-hole. Green fees Mon.-Sat. *Doneraile Golf Club*, Tel. 022/24137. 9-hole.Green fees Mon.-Fri. *Mitchelstown Golf club*, Tel. 025/24072. *Rockmills Golf Driving Range*, Kildorrery. Tel. 022/25222. **Horse Riding**: *Foley's Riding School and Trekking Centre*, Killowen, Newmarket. Tel. 029/60048. **Fishing**: For angling permits on the rivers Dallua and Allow contact *Kanturk and District Trout Anglers*, c/o John Sullivan, Sports Trophies, Strand House, Kanturk. Tel. 029/50257. For angling permits on the river Funcheon contact *Glanworth, Kildorrery, Kilworth and Mitchelstown Trout Anglers*, c/o Peter Collins,

Kildorrery. Tel. 022/25205.

PUBS, RESTAURANTS, SHOPS AND ACCOMMODATION
(Price Categories are explained in HOW TO USE THIS BOOK)

BUTTEVANT
Bar Food
THE HORSE AND JOCKEY
Lunch menu 12.30-2.30; light snacks all day.
A large mural on the gable end of the bar as you enter Buttevant announces this establishment. It is a welcome sight if driving up from Cork city, as the diversion of Mallow and the re-routing of the main road means that there is a dearth of stopping places between Blarney and here. Avoid the cavernous lounge bar and head straight for the front one which has been converted into a farmhouse-style restaurant with oilcloth table cloths laid with wicker mats, a pretty pine dresser and stripped wood floor. At lunch there are hearty plates of daily specials like lamb casserole or half roast chicken, and lighter options such as scampi. Each dish comes with a generous portion of vegetables and potatoes, and there is no extra charge for the chips which are offered as well. Scones, toasted sandwiches and soup are available for the rest of the day.

CHARLEVILLE/RATH LUIRC
Cafe
THE COFFEE POT
Tel.063/81203. Main St. Open 9-5.30. No wine licence. Inexpensive.
This shop in the middle of Charleville's main drag - which is also the main Cork-Limerick road - has been there since the mid-19th century according to the dates on its pompous marble-pillared facade. To reach the self-service restaurant at the back you must run a unique gauntlet of temptations - the alcoholic beverages of the off licence on one side, the cream cake-laden patisserie counter on the other. The simple restaurant has three rows of plain wooden tables beneath soft lighting. As well as hot daily dishes there is a selection of pates, quiche, pizza and salad, and those award-winning cream cakes for afters.

Shops and Galleries
FORTLANDS ANTIQUES
Tel.063/81295. Open 9-6, 7 days a week; evenings by appointment.
Fortlands is well signposted to the left on the outskirts of Charleville coming from the Cork direction. The showroom is in a converted cow byre (though you'd never guess) behind Carol O'Connor's large detached house. She specialises in Georgian furniture, particularly tables. This is serious period furniture, all fully restored, and her prices reflect its rarity, with an eight-seater dining table averaging about £2000. When I visited she also had a small inlaid Georgian chest-of-drawers - much sought after because of their compactness - for the same price. She usually has a good selection of wall clocks from around £380 all in guaranteed working order. Among the smaller items is a small selection of good quality jewellery, brass fenders and fire dogs - all guaranteed Victorian or Georgian - and a good collection of Victorian and Georgian door furniture - or knobs and knockers if you prefer.

MITCHELSTOWN
Bar Food
CLONGIBBON HOUSE
Market Square. Tel.025/24116. Bar lunch 12.30-2.30. Credit Cards: Visa, Access.
If you absolutely must have bar food in Mitchelstown, then the Clongibbon is the

best of an uninspired lot. Its location on the main square ensures a busy local trade and a busy turnover. Food is served in the lounge bar on the left as you go in the door, a long narrow windowless room with a nice old mahogany bar and comfortable banquettes. The owner-manager is usually there in person to take your order, thus ensuring prompt and pleasant service. The menu is of the more old fashioned kind featuring substantial dishes such as minute steak and onions, roast rib of beef, and, on the lighter side, smoked salmon platter. The place is regularly patronised by the clergy.

Restaurant/Deli
O'CALLAGHAN'S
19 Lower Cork St. Tel.025/24657.Open 9-6 Mon.-Sat.; lunch 12.30-2.30. Credit Cards: Visa, Amex. Wine licence only. Inexpensive.

O'Callaghan's is about 20 yards north of the main square on the right hand side of the main road. The delicate aroma of freshly baked bread, herbs and spices tells you straight away that the food here is more sophisticated than that on offer in the other local hostelries. Beyond the self-service delicatessen counter is a narrow but pleasantly relaxing room with plain wooden tables, stick back chairs, plain grey carpet and dark blue floral drapes. There is a regular all-day menu with dishes like seafood terrine, savory quiche, salad plates, shepherd's pie and roast chicken, and varying lunchtime specials, for example, chicken and mushroom vol au vents or chicken tandoori with baked potato. All bread, jam and cakes are home-made and are also on sale in the front of the shop. This is the only place I could find in town that sold whole farmhouse cheeses - although, if you so wish, you can buy enormous blocks of Mitchesltown Cheddar (factory produced) in the local supermarkets. Here they have a selection of whole or cut farmhouse cheeses that includes Glen O'Sheen, (red cheddar) Bay Lough from the Vee Gap, gouda-type Knockanore and a good selection of continental cheeses. Their bread is most appetising - french sticks, Viennas, skulls and scones as well as wholemeal and soda bread. There is also the usual range of wholefood products, teas, coffees and herbs and spices.

DONERAILE

Restaurant/Guest House
SPRINGFORT HALL
Twopothouse. Tel.022/21278. Dinner only, from 7PM. booking advisable. Fully licensed. Credit cards: Visa, Access. Moderate.

Situated on the R581 Doneraile road (signposted to the right off the N20 Cork-Limerick road after Mallow in Twopothouse) this is a large white bow-fronted Georgian manor in a lightly wooded setting. The interior fails to live up to the promise of its elegant facade, with a plain and charmless bar behind a sitting room stuffed with nondescript sofas and armchairs. The front dining room is by far the nicest room in the house, with three tall windows overlooking the lawns and white plaster mouldings picked out against Wedgwood blue walls. There is a plain marble fireplace, long red curtains and heavy white damask table linen. The a la carte menu features a big choice of steaks, including an unusual version of turf 'n' surf - fillet steak stuffed with prawns served with a red wine and beurre blanc sauce. There is also a big choice of chicken and fish, and pheasant in season. The back dining room is darker and altogether less attractive.

Upstairs, floorboards creak atmospherically under fitted carpets. There are eight bedrooms in all, plainly furnished, five of them extremely spacious with large bow windows. All have direct dial phone, television, and basic en suite bathrooms of a certain age with vinyl flooring. This may not be the height of luxury, but why complain, when their rates are approximately half those of most other places with such imposing architecture and secluded grounds?

KANTURK

Bar Food
THE VINTAGE
O'Brien St. Tel.029/50549. Lunch 12.30-2; evening meals 6-9.
This is a small off licence and bar on the Newmarket road just across from the river. You will find a better than average cup of coffee here, as well as a very good selection of hot dishes, including steaks. The interior is small and cosy with exposed stone walls and a well-worn, quarry tiled floor. Most eaters sit on wooden-backed bar stools at tall pine tables.

Restaurant/Guest House
ASSOLAS COUNTRY HOUSE
Tel.029/50795. Dinner only - advance booking essential. Open 15 Mar.-15 Oct.; dinner for parties of 8 and over by arrangement rest of year. Fully licensed. Minimum stay 2 nights. Credit cards: Visa, Access, Amex, Diners. Very Expensive.
Assolas is the real thing - a luxurious, family-run country house, where, provided you have at least minimal delusions of grandeur, you will quickly start to feel at home. It is not hard to find - provided all the signposts are in place, which they were not on my visit (due to no fault of the owners). From Kanturk follow the Mallow sign-post and turn left at the grotto, the first Assolas sign. Two more signs and about 4 miles later you should be there. The symmetrical, creeper-clad Queen Anne facade is architecturally misleading. From the side of the house you will see that the bow-fronted wings with their distinctive cantilevered roofs were added to a 16th- century tower house, which still forms the core of the building today. The front rooms over-look the lawn tennis court, croquet lawn, rose beds and a large pond - complete with swans - which has been created by damming a stream. There are about ten acres of gardens, with woodland walks beyond the flowerbeds. Salmon fishing is available for two rods on the nearby Blackwater. There is no bar as such, but drinks are provided by tray service in the drawing room, a spacious, airy room with plump beige and chintz armchairs and sofas, yellow walls and curtains, an open fire and large gilt mirrors.
The nine bedrooms are all individually decorated with soothing carpets and cur-tains, and modest antique or simply old furniture. "Superior" (i.e. more expensive) rooms are larger with generous sitting areas and luxurious bathrooms, including his and hers washbasins. Three of the rooms are outside in the courtyard behind the main house in a converted stone-built outbuilding, each with its separate entrance. They are, in their own way, just as attractive as anything in the main house, and even quieter.
The dining room has large windows on three sides, and dark red walls with the plasterwork picked out in white. The antique mahogany tables are set with leaded glass, family silver and a heavy damask napkin on each place mat. Mrs. Bourke has been opening the house to guests for 26 years, and recently her daughter-in-law, Hazel, an internationally trained chef, took over the kitchen. There is a daily set menu, which can be varied by choosing one or more courses from the options on the seasonal dinner menu. All herbs, soft fruits and unusual vegetables come from the Assolas walled kitchen garden, and the menu is determined by the seasonal produce available. Typical main courses would be oven baked fillet of brill with a golden crust of garden herbs and a beurre blanc, or breast of duck with a Cassis and blackcurrant sauce.

7 **CHAPTER SEVEN**

THE LEE VALLEY & THE GAELTACHT

This chapter leaves Cork city on the N22 which is the main Cork-Killarney road, and follows it, and the valley of the River Lee, west to the Derrynasaggart Mountains on the Cork-Kerry border, pointing out interesting places to visit both on and off the main road. The most famous of these is Blarney Castle, which is a mere ten minute's drive from Cork. Later we pass the site where Michael Collins, a leader of Sinn Fein was ambushed and killed in 1922, and continue to Macroom, a small market town which marks the entrance to the Irish-speaking area of west Cork. Less than an hour after leaving the suburb of Ballincollig you are among rugged low mountains in sparsely populated countryside in the midst of which is the Gougane Barra National Park. Within the 1000-acre park is the site of St. Finbar's early Christian hermitage. It can all be seen in a day, although you may prefer to drive directly to Gougane Barra and spend your time in the nearby mountains which have been marked out with a series of scenic trails providing long or short woodland WALKS.

Do not leave Cork on the road signposted Blarney, which is not a very attractive route and gets very congested in summer; instead follow the N22 Killarney signs which will take you out of town past the County Hall along a stretch of road known, for obvious reasons, as the **Carrigrohane Straight Road**. Note the rather witty bronze statue outside County Hall of two men, one in a cloth cap, staring up in wonder at the tall modern building. At 17 storeys, it is the tallest building in Ireland, and the closest Cork has to a skyscraper. On the opposite side of the road is a small park beside the River Lee. The Blarney road, which crosses the River Lee, is signposted to the right at the end of the straight stretch. (If you are not planning to visit Blarney, stay on the main road at this point, and skip to Ballincollig Regional Park, below).

Blarney is about 4 miles up this road, with all the turnings clearly signposted. At the centre of the village is its square green, with the castle on the opposite side of the main road. There is a large car park beside the castle, and another adjoining the Blarney Woollen Mills on the right just beyond the village square.

Blarney Castle, and the tradition of seeking the gift of eloquence by kissing the **Blarney Stone**, have made this little village one of Ireland's busiest tourist centres. There is a tendency today to take a rather condescending attitude towards the crowds who flock to Blarney in order to climb the castle and kiss the stone. Perhaps we natives are simply jaded. Most of us have kissed the stone at least once as a child, and made the outing again innumerable times with visitors, often lurking in the car park, the pub or the craft shops, while our guests "do" the castle. In fact, as long as you know what to expect - many visitors do not realise that the world-famous castle is a ruined shell - Blarney makes a good half-day outing. The castle itself is impressively big, and attractively located. As it is the best-preserved castle interior accessible to the public in the county, the visit can also be an education which will stand to you when visiting less complete castles, and castles from other periods.

It is situated in an estate of 1130 acres, 400 of which are laid out as parklands and gardens, and are especially attractive in the early spring, when the naturalised daffodils are out, and again in high summer. It is also an exciting outing, provided you do it properly and climb the 120 inner steps of the castle, up to its battlemented top. For those with a fear of heights it is almost too exciting; you need very strong nerves indeed to lean out backwards over the top-floor wall and kiss the stone. On my last visit I noticed that one party had brought a flashlight, which is a great help in exploring the dark inner chambers, and securing your footing on the steep spiral stairs. Wear comfortable rubber-soled shoes. Allow about two hours to climb the castle, walk in the grounds and explore the village, and another half hour if Blarney

House is also open.

The village itself has an English look to it, with its snug little houses grouped around a central village green. In fact it was laid out by an Englishman, General Sir James Jeffreys, who bought the property in 1703, and whose family still own it. (The MacCarthys left Ireland in 1691 in the "Flight of the Earls" that followed the Battle of the Boyne - see Chapter Nine). The main business here, until the arrival of mass tourism, was the manufacture of wool. The mills, large stone buildings now occupied by a craft shop and hotel, date from 1750, and used the water of the adjacent **Shornagh River** for power. By the 1890s they were employing 750 people, and were in use until the mid-1970s. There are some interesting old photographs of the mills in the bar and lobby of **Christy's Hotel**.

Blarney Castle *(Tel. 021/385252. Admission: £2.50 adults, £1.50 senior citizens, £1 children. Open Mon.-Sat. 9-5.30 Oct.-April; 9-7 May; 9-7.30, June, July, August; 9 6.30 Sept.; 9.30-5.30 Suns.)* was built by Dermot MacCarthy (1411-1494), a chief of the powerful local clan, in about 1446. It is 85 feet tall, and was known as the strongest castle in Munster, an impression which endures today when looking up at its strong keep surmounted by machicolations. Like all castles, it is built on high ground, a limestone bluff (which has caves under it that you can explore), in a strategically important position near a source of fresh water - a river in this case.

A castle of this kind was basically a defensive machine, as can be seen from the removable stone, known as a murder hole, above the narrow entrance lobby, its only entry. The murder hole enabled those holding the castle to pour boiling oil, or in later times, release musket fire, on unwlecome intruders. The staircase is narrow for the same reason; if intruders penetrated they could only climb in single file, and it was easy from above to repel them. The ground floor chamber had a wooden ceiling, and was used as sleeping quarters for the MacCarthy retinue, young men and warriors. Because it is vulnerable at ground level, there is only one slit window. The existence of fireplaces at Blarney reveals that it was a fairly luxurious castle; in others a fire was lit in the middle of the room creating a very smokey atmosphere. Private sleeping quarters were allocated only to the lord and lady of the castle and the young females, and can be seen on the way upstairs. The garderobe, a small chamber protruding on the side facing the main approach, was the overnight toilet. As you ascend the castle's five storeys, the windows become more generous in size, as they were less likely to be attacked. The penultimate storey contained the great hall, which was the main social centre and dining area. The kitchen is on a mezzanine just above it. The top storey was used as a chapel, and from here you emerge on to the parapet, which has excellent views of the Lee Valley, and was therefore used as a look-out post.

You can enjoy the view while you wait your turn to kiss the Blarney Stone. To do this you must first empty your pockets, then lie on your back (while an attendant holds on to you), and put your head backwards and downwards to reach the stone. (Remember you are over 85 feet up here). The stone is scrubbed with disinfectant three times a day to prevent any risk of disease. There is no official charge for kissing the stone, but most people leave a pound coin for the attendant.

Just why the Blarney Stone is supposed to confer the "gift of the gab", nobody really knows. The word "Blarney" has entered the English language to mean a special kind of talk which persuades or even deceives the listener, but without causing offence. The 19th century antiquarian, Crofton Croker, came up with the explanation that is derived from an attempt by Elizabeth 1 to extract firm promises from the then Lord of Blarney, Cormac MacCarthy, to hand his castle over to the (English) Lord President of Munster. He refused to do so, while simultaneously placating the Lord President with elegant excuses, which became known as "Blarney talk". A less likely explanation claims that Elizabeth I finally lost her temper over these protracted negotiations, and exclaimed of MacCarthy's explanations: "This is all Blarney; what he says he never means".

Many visitors enjoy The **Rock Close**, which is included in the admission price to the castle, as much or more than the castle itself. The gardens contain strangely shaped limestone rocks which were landscaped in the 18th century (when the castle first began to attract visitors), and a grove of ancient yew trees said to have Druidic connections.

Next door to the Castle is **Blarney Castle House** (*Admission £2 adults, £1.50 senior citizens, £1 children. Open Mon.-Sat. 12noon-6, June-Sept.*). It is a turreted grey-stone Scottish baronial-style mansion built in 1784 by the Jeffreys family and still lived in by their direct descendants, the Colthursts. The interior is attractively furnished in period, and features a fine stairwell and many family portraits.

Retrace your tracks to the main road on the R579, and turn right, i.e. west, rejoining the N22 Killarney road. It passes through the village of Ballincollig, which has grown in the past 20 years to a prosperous suburb of Cork with a population of around 11,000. The big gates on the right belong to the **Ballincollig Powder Mills**. This large military complex was once a British Army base. Part of it is now occupied by the Irish Army, but the old gunpowder mills on the site are being refurbished, and will be open to the public shortly. (Check with Cork TIO, Tel. 021/273251). Further on, at **Inniscarra Bridge**, clearly signposted to the right, is the **Ballincollig Regional Park** (*Open 9-5 1 Oct.-1 March; 9-8 April and Sept.; 9-9 August; 9-10 June and July*). It consists of land adjoining the River Lee which previously formed part of the military complex. There is an excellent 2-mile WALK along the river's edge within the park, with car park and picnic tables near the bridge.

The road now leaves city and suburbs behind and runs roughly parallel to the River Bride across open country. A one mile detour to the left, about a mile and half beyond the bar, Tatler Jack's, will take you on the Kilcrea-Aherla road to the attractive ruins of **Kilcrea Abbey**, a 15th-century Franciscan friary. It can be seen from the minor road, and is signposted along a footpath about 100 yards off it. It was built in 1465 by the same Cormac MacCarthy who built Blarney Castle, and his tomb can be seen here. The friary survived until 1614 when the friars were expelled following the dissolution of the monasteries. The ruins are exceptionally attractive both in location - an out of the way riverside field - and in the decorative windows of the sacristy and scriptoria. These are to the north of the church which, in contrast, is rather austere. Among those buried here is Art O Laoghaire, who inspired the wonderful Irish poem *"Caoineadh Art O Laoghaire"* - "The Lament for Arthur O'Leary" -which was written by his widow, Eileen, after his tragic death in 1773.

Return to the main road, and about half a mile along on the right is a signpost for **Farran Forest Park**. This park is situated on the lower shores of the reservoir which was created by the Inniscarra Dam (built between 1952 and 1957 as part of the hydro-electric development of the River Lee between Cork and Macroom). It is one of the major forest parks in the county, and has a wildfowl refuge, a small interpretative centre and a herd of deer, as well as good trails for WALKS.

From Farran you can continue to Macroom via Coachford, a very scenic road which runs alongside the River Lee and takes you past **Carrigadrohid Castle**. The castle stands on a rock in the middle of the river beside an ancient bridge, and was once a stronghold of the MacCarthy clan. It is chiefly remembered for an incident in 1650 when the Bishop of Ross, who had been captured by Cromwell's troops was promised his freedom if he could convince the Carrigadrohid garrison to surrender. Instead he shouted to them: "Hold out to the last for religion and country", and was immediately hung from a nearby tree by the reins of his horse, in sight of the whole garrison.

However, if you wish to see the Michael Collins Memorial, you must follow another route to Macroom. Return to the main road and head west. About two miles later, on the approach to the village of Crookstown, is a signpost for **Beal na mBlath**, which is about two and a half miles off the main road. Further signposts will direct you through the village of Crookstown on to the Dunmanway-Drimoleague road (R585). The castle visible on the right as the road climbs out of Crookstown is **Cloghda Castle**, a relatively small castle dating from the 16th century which is on inaccessible private land.

The **Michael Collins Memorial** consists of a large stone Celtic cross on a red brick dias at the side of the road simply inscribed in Irish with Michael Collins' name and the date of his death - 20 August, 1922. Every year on that date a memorial service is held here, and the road was widened at this point to accommodate the crowds. Michael Collins is still held in great respect by the people of Cork, especially the older generation who believe that, had he survived, the course of modern Irish history would have been less troubled. He was, of course, a Corkman, and his birthplace is visited in Chapter Eleven. As leader of Sinn Fein, he was largely responsible for negotiating the 1921 Treaty which left Northern Ireland under British rule. More extreme Republicans saw this as a betrayal of their ideals, and so they ambushed him here and killed him. The same border dispute is behind the violence of today's IRA. The Civil War (1922-23) was fought with particular bitterness in Cork, especially in the west, which is the area we are now entering. The local people engaged in guerilla warfare (1918-21) against the Black and Tans of the British Army (so called because of their parti-coloured uniform which was a result of shortages caused by the 1914-18 war), and against each other. The Treaty question divided families and provoked a bitterness which is only now beginning to die down, 70 years after the event.

There are several other memorials in the area to those who died in the Civil War. If you take a left to the village of **Kilmurry** on your way back to the main road you will find a memorial to Michael Collins and two other men on the wall of the graveyard, and, shortly beyond it, a small **Museum**, which may or may not be open, containing material relating to that period.

On the way to Macroom, the main road crosses a causeway over the Inniscarra-Carrigadrohid dam scheme, and runs along beside a wide stretch of water. When the water level is low you can sometimes see the tops of branches of trees on the flooded land sticking up above water level. The direct road to Inichigeela and Gougane Barra (R584) is signposted to the left at this point, but we continue on to Macroom, and approach Gougane Barra by a back road, returning on the R584.

Macroom is an old-fashioned market town 23 miles west of Cork on the banks of the River Sullane. Park in the main square to have a quick look around. On Tuesdays a **market** is held in the square, which sells mainly vegetables, fish and agricultural clothing. The **Castle Gates** are the main feature of the town centre, and give access to the **Town Park**. The gates are all that remain of the castle, which was burnt in 1922. To the right of the castle gates is a small museum with items of local historical interest, the **Museum Peadar O Laoire**. Macroom has some good shop fronts, some of which have not changed for years. Note the haphazard arrangement of the window displays, for example in A. Golden, to the north of Market Square.

Leave Macroom on the main N22 Killarney road. Shortly out of Macroom the scenery turns suddenly rugged as you enter the mountains of the West Cork *gaeltacht* (Irish speaking area). Houses are few and isolated, and exposed rocks stand out on the hillsides. Three and a half miles outside Macroom on the left of the road is **Carragaphooca Castle**. It can be reached by crossing the bridge on foot. The name means "fairy rock", and refers to the rock on which the castle is built. The rock was said to be haunted by a puca, or malicious spirit. It is a 16th-century tower of four storeys, which was built by a MacCarthy. There is also a small stone circle of five stones two fields to the east of the castle.

The Shrine of Saint Gobnait is signposted to the left in the Irish speaking village of **Ballyvourney**. She lived in the 6th century and founded a convent here. She practised bee-keeping, and was known for her healing powers. She is still an object of devotion and there is a statue of her as a bee-keeper outside the grave-yard made by the Cork sculptor, Seamus Murphy in 1951. The remains of the con-vent, including stones from the circular hut where she lived, her grave and a holy well can be found in and around the village. Pilgrims visit each site in turn, especial-ly on her saint's day, 11 February, and Whit Sunday, saying prayers at each "sta-tion" as they have done for hundreds of years.

The road continues towards Killarney, and we will turn off it and take a back road to Ballingeary to reach Gougane Barra. If you do not fancy a scenic drive of about ten miles along remote, very narrow, twisty roads, drive back to the fork of the road outside Ballymakeera (beside a large bar) where there is a gentler road to Ballingeary and Gougane Barra.

The attractive large building in the middle of Ballyvourney, set back from the road among trees, is a former Irish language college, one of several in this part of west Cork. At the west end of Ballyvourney, almost opposite a large bar called The Mills, is a left-hand turn over a bridge across the river Sullane. The road follows the banks of the river Sullane for about three miles to **Coolea**, or **Cuil Aodha**. Like most vil-lages in the *Gaeltacht*, it is not at all picturesque, but consists of scattered houses, many of them quite modern but of modest proportions, with a small village centre consisting of a church and a small shop. Villages were introduced to Ireland by English settlers, and never really caught on in the same way in those areas that did not adopt the English language.

Coolea was the home of the musician Sean O Riada (1931-1971) who did much to revive Irish musical traditions, later popularised by groups like The Chieftains. His own compositions go further back to the very roots of the Irish musical tradition, often sounding almost eastern. His Mass is sung in churches all over Ireland, but there is something very special about hearing it in the small church at *Cuil Aodha,* where his son, Peadar, also a musician, is choir master and organist. The male voice choir is small, and sometimes depleted by unavoidable absences, but the simplicity of the 10AM Sunday Mass (sung and spoken in Irish) is an experience worth seeking out.

To follow the back road to Ballingeary, drive straight through Coolea and take the left hand turn just before a stone bridge outside the village. Follow the road for about three miles until it comes to a T-junction at which you turn left. Another four miles will bring you to another T-junction, where you turn right on to the relatively main Ballymakeera- Ballingeary road. It is an amazing route, on which you are more likely to meet sheep on the narrow road than other cars. The rocky hillsides patched with coarse grass are only fit for grazing sheep, and there is not even a farmstead until just before the Ballingeary road. The views are modest compared with other mountain passes, but the sheer remoteness of the area is impressive.

A right-hand turn in Ballingeary will lead you to **Gougane Barra**, which is about half a mile off the main road. The name means "Finbar's cleft" in Irish, and it was on the island in this little corrie lake that St. Finbar established his hermitage in the 6th or 7th century. It is a beautiful, astonishingly peaceful spot, in a glacial valley sur-rounded by wooded hills. Nothing remains today of the original hermitage. The ruins on the island - which is reached by a modern causeway - were built in the 18th cen-tury when the place was first discovered by modern travellers. The Romanesque-style chapel is also relatively modern, as are the public toilets, which have been built in a circular shape, and thatched, in an effort to keep in harmony with the surround-ings. On the first Sunday after Saint Finbar's Day (September 25), there is a large Diocesan pilgrimage to the island. Readers of Eric Cross's book, "*The Tailor and Ansty*", will be interested to know that the tailor is buried in the graveyard here under a headstone inscribed: "A star danced and I was born". The earthy language of the tailor caused an uproar when the book was first published in 1942.

The hotel in which the writer and artist Robert Gibbings (1889-1958) stayed on his visits here in the late 1940s, Cronin's, is still here, although it has been much extended since his day. In those times, and in Eric Cross's a few years before, the place was still considered extremely remote, and reading his account of the people and their ways one is mainly impressed by how alarmingly fast the place has changed in the space of 45 years. In Gibbings' day, things went on much as they had in the 19th century; today the people around here live in much the same way as anyone else in modern Ireland.

Do not think that you have "done" Gougane Barra by nipping over to the island and having a quick look at St. Finbarr's chapel. The way to appreciate the very special beauty and peace of the place is to go for a WALK. Forest trails long and short have been marked out in the surrounding hills, and you can take your pick.

If you are heading for the coast, you will have a good reason to turn right when rejoining the main road from Gougane Barra, and drive through the magnificent **Pass of Keimaneigh**, which has tall cliffs of stone on either side of the road. It emerges in Kealkil, which is midway between Glengarriff and Bantry, about 12 miles from each. The main road back to the east of Macroom passes through **Ballingeary** and **Inchigeela** along the shores of **Lough Allua**, a picturesque section of the River Lee. Both villages tend to be over-run with adolescent schoolchildren in the summer months, who are boarded out in the area in order to attend Irish language colleges.

About 8 miles beyond Inchigeela, to the west of the road, is **The Gearagh**, an area of alluvial forest and scrub. Its Irish name means "the wooded river", and it is in fact a 3-mile long maze of tiny wooded islands fringed by reeds. It is interesting both botanically, and for the habitat which it offers to wild life, which is unique in Ireland and Britain.

Sporting Facilities

Golf: *Muskerry Golf Club*, Carrigrohane. Tel. 021/385297. 18-hole. Green fees Mon.-Fri. *Macroom Golf Club*, Lackduv. Tel. 026/41072. 9-hole. *Village Green Golf Centre* (Driving Range), Inniscarra. Tel. 021/873286. **Tennis**: Macroom Town Park. **Horse Riding**: *Blarney Riding Centre*, Killowen, Blarney. Tel. 021/385854. *Hunter's Lodge*, Killens, Blarney. Tel. 021/38075. *O'Regan's Riding Centre*, Minister's Cross, Crookstown. Tel. 021/336387. *Raleigh Riding Centre*, Raleigh House, Macroom. Tel. 026/41018. **Bicycle Hire**: *Tony McGrath Cycles*, Stoneview. Tel. 021/385658. **Fishing**: The Lee Valley is an important coarse and game angling centre. Salmon angling is generally privately owned or leased and day permits must be obtained from the controlling clubs, both of which let day tickets: *Cork Salmon Anglers*, c/o Mr. John Buckley, Raheen House, Carrigrohane, Tel. 021/872137 and *The Lee Salmon Anglers Club*, c/o Percy Cole, Auto Factor, Douglas St. Cork, tel. 021/311082. There are excellent shore angling facilities for trout in Gougane Barra Lake or boats are available from the *Gougane Barra Hotel* (Tel. 026/47069). Trout can also be found in the Sullane River between Macroom and Ballymakeera. Boats are available for pike angling in Lough Allua from *Creedon's Hotel* (Tel. 026/49012) and *Lake House* (Tel. 026/49010).

PUBS, RESTAURANTS, SHOPS AND ACCOMMODATION
(Price Categories are explained in HOW TO USE THIS BOOK)

BALLINCOLLIG

Bar Food
THE DARBY ARMS
Main St. Tel.021/870854. Lunch 12.30-2.30; light snacks till 8:30.

This solid Victorian building on the main Killarney road was known earlier in this century as "the Hotel" and was patronised by workers from the powder mill and the cavalry barracks. It has three entrances: the middle door belongs to the off-licence, the left leads to the public bar and the right-hand one to the lounge. Lunch is served in either bar. The public bar has a Liscannor slate floor, sugan chairs and bar stools and exposed stone walls on which hang an interesting series of photographs of old Ballincollig. The lounge bar has a warren-like interior with dark red upholstery, divided into alcoves by attractive carved mahogany and stained glass partitions.

The menu includes freshly-made sandwiches, a selection of cold plates, a choice of meat or fish main courses and a daily special such as savory chicken pie. Don't miss the beautiful hand-painted sign (by Tomas Tuipear of Clonakilty) outside the door to the lounge bar.

BALLYMAKEERA
Shops and Galleries
THE QUILT SHOP
Tel. 026/45235. Open 9-6, 9-7 in summer. Credit Cards: Visa, Access, Amex, Diners.

This factory outlet can be seen on the left on the main N22 as you enter Ballymakeera. The quilts are made on the premises, and a single patchwork one can cost as little as £80 - and will, presumably, last forever. Most people choose their own fabric from a selection on the premises and have a quilt made to order. They also sell locally knitted Aran sweaters which are a bit out of the ordinary in colour and pattern and very good value, mohair throws, tweed hats, an interesting selection of hand made lace and crochet, and smaller quilted items like pot holders.

MACROOM CARPETS
Udaras Industrial Estate. Tel. 026/41140. Open 9-4.45, Mon.-Fri.

The industrial estate is on the left-hand side as you enter the village from the Macroom direction. This is the factory outlet for these superb hand-made chunky woollen carpets which will be found in many of the better craft shops of Cork. Special sizes or colour combinations can be made to order.

BALLYVOURNEY
Bar Food/Restaurant/B & B
THE MILLS INN
Tel. 026/45237. Bar food to 9PM. Restaurant open from 6PM. Credit Cards: Visa, Amex, Diners. Moderate.

Many of the bars and hotels in the *gaeltacht* look (and, alas, probably are) rather poverty stricken and can be a disappointment if you do not speak Irish. The Mills is an exception, a thriving and stylishly decorated complex ideally situated for a break on the Cork-Killarney journey. In summer it gets its share of tour buses, but the front bar also has a good local trade, and at weekends - or indeed at any time - you are likely to run into a genuine seisun.

The front bar is the place to be, a large cement floored room with an open fire, large stone jars and copper churns dotted around, and paintings by Pauline Bewick blending in surprisingly well with framed collections of advertising ephemera and photographs of the local GAA teams. There is a smaller, plusher back bar for stuck-up people. The all-day bar food menu has the usual staples like lasagne, plaice and chips, smoked salmon platter, and lunchtime specials which include an outstanding Irish stew. The coffee is real. The restaurant serves simple but pricier food: typically, prawn cocktail, steaks and salmon.

The six bedrooms (5 with bath) are pleasantly decorated in keeping with the age of the house (1755), but have all mod. cons. including satellite TV, phone, hair dryer, and tea and coffee making facilities. Free bicycles are available to guests, a nice touch that other "country inns" might copy. There is also a Craft Shop in the Mills courtyard, clearly labelled "Tourist Craft Shop" which specialises in expensive porcelain. There is also a castle and a transport museum on the premises; a small fee for guided tours of these will be introduced in 1992.

BLARNEY
(For pubs near Blarney see also CARRIGROHANE, WATERLOO)

Bar Food/Music/Restaurant/Hotel
THE BLARNEY PARK
Tel. 021/385281. Bar food 12.30-2.30; restaurant 12.30-2.30 and 6.30-9.30. Music nightly from 9.30 May-Sept., Thurs.-Sun. Oct-April. Credit Cards: Visa, Access, Amex, Diners. Moderate.

A 70-bedroom hotel adjacent to Blarney's village green, the Blarney Park is one of the most pleasant and well run modern hotels in the Cork city area, absorbing a heavy tour bus trade while remaining an active part of the surrounding community. You will need to book a room well in advance in the high season, and it is also busy all year at weekends.

There is always a good buzz in the Earl's Bar, a large room with red turkey carpet overlooking the gardens, even in the depths of winter. In summer, bar food is laid out buffet style; off-season it will be fetched from the kitchen as you order. The Clancarty restaurant seats 120 in a wood-panelled room with plate glass windows and discreet framed prints on the walls. The decor is in pale green and pink, and the tables are set with white damask. The menu offers a better-than-average hotel choice, for example, roast half duckling with peach and orange sauce, grilled cod fillet topped with herb breadcrumbs, a vegetarian main course option and a tempting selection of rich puddings.

There is a separate annexe in the grounds, The Cottage, for music and dancing, so the goings-on should not disturb residents. The function room, which is in great demand for weddings, is also entirely self-contained.

The bedrooms are in two-storey blocks, and are small but comfortable with light oak fittings, quilted bedspreads and relaxing pastel colour schemes. They all have fully tiled bathrooms, TV, telephone and writing desk and views over the gardens; there is one room adapted for the disabled. The leisure centre is one of the best around, with a 20 metre pool, a gigantic 40 metre water slide, paddling pool, sauna, steam room, gym and two all-weather tennis courts.

Shops and Galleries
BLARNEY WOOLLEN MILLS
Tel. 021/385280. Open: 7 days a week from 9-6, later from mid-May to mid-Sept. Credit Cards: Visa, Access, Amex, Diners.

The Woollen Mills annual sale is the only time most natives of Cork - especially female ones - will be found visiting Blarney. This vast, family-run craft shop, sited in a converted woollen mill, has been one of the biggest retailing success stories of the past decade, and now has branches in Dublin, Killarney, Windsor and Cambridge. To label it a craft shop, however, is an understatement. It also sells an excellent range of Irish-made high fashion, and classics like camel hair coats and belted raincoats, as stylish as anything you'd find in Grafton Street, and usually more reasonably priced. Then there are acres of shelf-space dedicated to sweaters in all price ranges, all kinds of good quality Irish-made glass and tableware - from Waterford Crystal to Stephen Pearce pottery - rugs and scarves in mohair or tweed, linen shirts, skirt lengths of tweed, mens'clothing, caps, books of Irish interest, blackthorn sticks - the whole spectrum of crafts, right down, alas, to plastic leprechaun key rings. Not all of their goods are Irish-made, so keep an eye on the label if you want to buy Irish. Those with a taste for kitsch will love the special section assembled near the far door for the American tour bus trade - Kerry Green trousers and caps, shamrock-bedecked sweaters and T-shirts and other embarrassing Paddywhackery.

CARRIGROHANE

Bar Food/Restaurant
THE ANGLER'S REST
Tel. 021/871167. Bar food 12-2.30 Mon-Sat. Restaurant Lunch 12-2.30, Dinner 5.30-9.30. Restaurant open daily May-Sept. Dinner Thurs.- Sat. and Sunday lunch only Oct.- April. Credit Cards: Visa, Access. Moderate.

This riverside pub is a very popular summer lunching place with workers in Cork city. It is well under ten minutes' drive from the city centre, if the traffic is on your side. Take the main Killarney road (N22) and turn right at the end of the straight stretch, signposted Blarney. This is also an excellent stopping place on an expedition to Blarney, especially when the village is swarming with tourists.

In summer you can eat or drink outside, overlooking the river. The bar itself is fairly plain but pleasant enough with a quarry-tiled floor, an open fire in the exposed stone wall and Tudor-style stick back chairs. The bar menu has daily hot specials at lunchtime, along with regulars like salmon steak, roast beef, egg mayonnaise, minute steak. The cosy, wood-panelled restaurant is in a small room adjoining the bar; there is additional seating upstairs. The tables are set with dark green place mats and paper napkins. The menu is reliable rather than adventurous featuring steak, chicken, veal and fish. In the long summer evenings there is an added attraction here: boules or petanque, the French bowls game, is played in the car park, and the keen local players would welcome a challenge from other enthusiasts.

COOLEA

TOP OF COOMB
Also known as "the highest pub in Ireland" (although there is another in County Wicklow making the same claim), the Top of Coomb is right out in the middle of nowhere on a mountain peak in the West Cork *gaeltacht* on the Cork-Kerry border. You will find it by driving through Coolea and following the mainest-looking road in the straightest line uphill for about 5 miles. (This is also a very scenic way of getting from Ballyvourney to Kenmare). I was once told that in the gents of this pub you can stand in Cork and piss on Kerry, but that is not the reason for going there. The reason is that it is an informal headquarters for musicians and set dancers from all over Cork and Kerry, and sometimes, I assure you, the crack is mighty. At other times you mightn't meet a soul. Summer Sunday evenings are a good bet, because of musicians returning from gigs further west. It is run by an Irish-speaking family who will remember you for years once they get to know your face.

FARNANES

Bar Food
THE THADY INN
Tel. 021/336379. Bar food available until 10PM, 7 days.

If you are struck by hunger or thirst midway between Cork and Macroom, look out for this pub on the right-hand side just beyond Farnanes. A top-hatted hurler with a pint in his hand swings in an old-fashioned pub sign outside the door. It is a simple country pub with horse brasses hanging behind the bar. All sandwiches are made to order with meat carved from a home-cooked joint. Choices include roast beef, gammon ham, and ox tongue, which are also served as meat platters. Soup, sirloin steak and smoked salmon are also available.

GOUGANE BARRA

Bar/Restaurant/Hotel
GOUGANE BARRA/CRONIN'S

Tel.026/47069. Open mid April-mid Oct. Bar open Suns. only off season. Credit Cards: Visa, Access, Amex, Diners. Moderate.

This is the same establishment that received such high praise in Robert Gibbings' books about Cork. Having seen its location, right beside the lake at Gougane, over-looking Saint Finbarr's hermit's cell, one can understand why Gibbings arrived planning to stay for days, and was still there three months later. It is still run by the same family, but the original Cronin's has been extended by the addition of a modest black and white painted hotel, the Gougane Barra. It attracts people looking for a quiet walking and fishing holiday, but Gougane is no longer the remote and sequestered spot it was in Gibbings' day - the 1940s - so be prepared for a lot of day trippers dropping by if you choose to stay here. There is a limited selection of bar food - cold platters, soup and sandwiches - available all day, and set lunch and dinner menus of unpretentious hotel fare are served in the restaurant. There are 25 rooms all with private bath and telephone, and TV is available on request.

MACROOM

Bar Food/Music
FUREY'S
Castle St. Tel. 026/41603. Bar food from 12.30, 7 days, lunch menu 12.30-2.30.

A small exposed stone facade just below the castle gates leads to a characterful bar with rough hewn tables supported by tree trunks, a flagstone floor, low beams and dim lighting. On sunny days head for the first floor patio which is something of a surprise. Furey's was Pub of the Year in 1988 (under the previous owner) and is still the most popular place in town with the stylish young. The bar food comes in generous portions, and the menu is more imaginative than usual - chicken in a curried mayonnaise sauce, for example, or pork chops baked in apple. Soup, toasted sandwiches and various salads are available on the all day menu. Have a look at the right-hand wall inside the door which is covered with old Guinness ads, framed prints and photos of old Macroom, and other interesting bits and pieces.

Cafe/Deli
CAFE MUESLI
Main Square. No tel. Open 9.30-6, 9.30-10PM May-Sept.

No prizes for guessing that this is a wholefood shop and restaurant, headquarters of Macroom's alternative society. The pleasant, light and airy room is dominated by a large pine refectory table designed to encourage conversation. They had only been open for 4 weeks when I visited, and were serving a limited self-service snack menu - vegetarian toast, garlic bread, home-made soups, sandwiches or (presumably in deference to local taste) sausage, egg and ham. They plan to have a more varied menu of light dishes by Easter 1992. The wholefood, mainly pulses, grains, tea and coffee, is displayed in pine cupboards at the far end of the shop.

B & B
LISSARDAGH HOUSE
Lissarda. Tel. 021/336080. Open all year, but book in advance. Wine Licence - dinner by arrangement (book before 12 noon). No credit cards. Inexpensive.

The gates of Lissardagh House are on the N22 6 miles outside Macroom on the Cork side, opposite the memorial statue to Michael Galvin (shot on that site in 1920 during the War of Independence). He was, incidentally, the uncle of the present owner, Sean O'Mahony. Sean, a retired chemical engineer, describes the 3-storey Victorian house which appears at the top of the hilly, beech-lined avenue, as "a nice medium-sized home", yet it is big enough for he and his wife, Julia, to confine themselves to the basement and give their guests the run of the upper stories. The house is set in 15 acres of gardens which have an abundant growth of mature shrubs. There is a tennis court, and free salmon and trout fishing.

The interior has the atmosphere of a family home by-passed by all recent trends in interior decoration - chintzy armchairs with crocheted anti-macassars, gas fires in the grates, a case of stuffed game birds in the breakfast room, a dinner gong in the hall, a baby grand and a large old radiogram in the sitting room. The 4 bedrooms upstairs have a mixture of wonderful Victorian antiques, picked up for almost nothing 30 years ago when everyone else was throwing them out, and fairly utilitarian post-war stuff. Frankly, new carpets and bedspreads and another bathroom or two (the 4 rooms share one on the landing) would bring the whole place up a bit, but then they would also take away something of the very pleasant, genuinely homely atmosphere that dominates at the moment. This is particularly appreciated by European visitors, who comprise the majority of summer guests.

Guesthouse
COOLCOWER HOUSE
Tel. 026/41695. Fully licensed. Credit Cards: Visa. Inexpensive.
The best thing about this place is its view over the River Lee, which is dammed for hydroelectric power at this height. It is indicated by a nasty red, yellow and white sign a mile outside Macroom on the main N22 from Cork. It is well off the main road, up a long straight track across fields. The front bar, furnished with undistinguished brown modern pieces, has an open fire and leads to a small conservatory overlooking the river view.
There are 10 bedrooms, 4 with bath, whose decor has a 1950s feel to it, with plastic headboards, candlewick bedspreads, an occasional antique piece and a dazzling assortment of patterned carpets. The best ones overlook the view, but if you fail to secure one of these there is a comfortable sitting area for residents with the same view at the top of the stairs. There is bar food available in high season, and the restaurant serves dinner and Sunday lunch all year. There is one tennis court and salmon and trout fishing can be arranged for guests.

B & B
FINDUS HOUSE
Ballyvoige, Kilnamartyra. Tel. 026/40023. Open 1 Apr.-1 Sept. Evening meal by arrangement. Credit Cards: Visa, Access, Amex. Inexpensive.
You will see a signpost for this farm off the N22 about 4 miles west of Macroom. Findus House won the regional "Farmhouse of the Year" title in 1990 for the high standard of its food and accommodation. The six bedrooms (three en suite) are in a modern extension and are simple and uncluttered with matching duvets and curtains and velvet padded headboards. The dining room is in a modern conservatory overlooking the open country, and has separate, modern pine tables. There is a TV lounge for the use of guests. The O'Sullivan family's farm, which is within the *gaeltacht*, is a dairy and chicken enterprise, and also keeps horses and ponies which can be hired out.

Shops and Galleries
MACROOM BOOKSHOP
West Square. Tel. 026/41888. Open Mon.-Sat. 10-15-6, closed Weds. Credit Cards: Visa, Access.
This small, well organised, well-stocked bookshop is something of a surprise in Macroom, and only opened in November 1991. Visitors are welcome to browse while listening to the classical music which owner Joan Lucey plays most of the day. There is a very good selection of children's books, a good choice of books of Irish interest, gardening books and enough fiction to suit most tastes, some of the latter being second-hand.
CUCULAINN CRAFT CO.
New. St. Tel.026/41198. Open 9-6 Mon.-Sat., 2-6 Suns. Credit Cards: Visa, Access.

As you leave the town heading west, you will see the distinctive arched facade of Cuculainn on your right. The shop claims to have the largest selection of handmade pottery in Munster, most of it originating in Ireland, but a small amount of striking imported designs are also stocked for those who want something a little different. There is also a selection of Irish crystal and designer jewellery. Their tea room serves home-baking, including scones, muffins and savories such as prawns in pitta bread, in an unusual loft above the shop.

VANGARD GALLERY
Tel. 026/41700. Open Mon.-Sat 9-6.
As you enter Macroom from the Cork side and the road narrows, this small gallery is on your right-hand side. It sells original works of contemporary Irish art, and has a new, usually mixed, exhibition every month. Prices start from about £50 upwards, with many of the works under £250. As well as promising young local painters like Gerry Ryan, Mairead Dennehy and Elizabeth Comerford they have works by better known artists like Mick Mulcahy, Maud Cotter, John Phillip Murray, Veronica Bolay and Tim Goulding.

OVENS

Bar Food/Restaurant
TATLER JACK
Shreelane. Tel. 021/331659. Food served in bar or restaurant from 12 noon-10PM daily. Booking essential at weekends. Credit cards; Visa, Access, Amex, Diners. Inexpensive - Moderate.
This large roadside pub is six miles from Cork on the main N22, and makes a very convenient stopping place if you get hungry on your way back from the west. The theme of the interior is taken from the mock-Tudor beams of the exterior: open fire, Tudor beams and chintzy drapes in the restaurant, (shame about the mock-veneer table tops), a flagstone floor and Tudor-style stick back chairs in the cosy front bar. This is a busy pub, well-geared to cope with its flourishing passing trade, and yet one which manages to remain friendly. There is a 3-course set menu at lunch, a 4 course one at dinner, or choose from the a la carte which incudes chicken cordon blue, roast duckling, escalope of veal parmigiana and a wide selection of steaks and seafood. Lighter bar snacks include sandwiches and scones.

WATERLOO

Bar
THE WATERLOO INN
Tel. 021/385113.
At the moment this Victorian waterside pub is not very widely known, but it looks as if the new road from Blarney to Mallow is going to bring it to the notice of a lot more people. At the time of writing it is still an ideal place to escape from the crowds in Blarney on a hot summer's day. Drive straight through the village of Blarney, following signposts for Mallow and Waterloo, and its about a mile up the road. A walk along this quiet wooded road would be even more pleasant. The interior is not much to write home about: the point of this place is that you can take your drink into the beer garden and sip it on the leafy banks of the River Martin, a tributary of the Lee.

8 | **CHAPTER EIGHT**

To Bantry Bay via Bandon

This chapter follows the N71 to Bandon, and from there takes the inland route across country to Bantry Bay. At Inishannon the road meets the Bandon river and follows it into the rich farming lands to the west of Bandon. Beyond Dunmanway the landscape becomes more rugged as we approach Bantry Bay. Outside the town is Bantry House with its magnificent tapestries and furnishings, built on an idyllic site overlooking Bantry Bay. We follow the road west along the wooded edge of the Bay, taking a diversion in Ballylickey to explore the pre-historic stone circle near the mountain village, Kealkil. It takes about an hour to drive to Bantry direct on this road (38 miles); how long you take will depend on how many of the detours you decide to follow along the way.

Leave Cork city by following signs for West Cork, which will lead you on to the N71. Just before crossing the Owenabue River is a village called **Halfway**, a name that sometimes puzzles visitors, especially when it appears on signposts. It is, in fact, half way between Cork and Bandon. At the bridge is a signpost for **Crossbarry**, site of a famous ambush during the War of Independence.

Inishannon, the next village, is a pretty place surrounded by woodlands at the head of the navigable tidal section of the River Bandon. The Bandon makes a sharp turn here and runs out to the sea at Kinsale, 7 miles to the south. For a very pretty riverside walk, follow the road on the left as you leave Inishannon, signposted Kinsale, for about 3 miles, stopping at the ruin of **Shippool Castle**. The path beside the castle leads to a small waterfall and the banks of the river, which opens into a wide pool at this point.

Inishannon is an unusual village, a mixture of modest little terraced cottages, (some now unoccupied, but painted cheerfully to keep up appearances) and larger Georgian houses, with two elegantly spired churches. In the 18th century it was a prosperous place with a colony of Huguenot silk weavers, who had been brought in by the landlord, the Earl of Shannon (he is the reason why a village with Shannon in its name is to be found on the Bandon river). Eventually the industry died out, but the houses remain.

• Its most famous resident today is the author **Alice Taylor.** Her best-selling book, "*To School Through the Fields*", describes her childhood near Newmarket in north Cork at the time of the Second World War, but she writes about Inishannon in her verse. At the time of writing, the residents of Inishannon are awaiting her next book, entitled "*The Village*", with curiosity. She lives in the house above the supermarket, which is run by her family.

Just across the bridge at the top of the village is an optional detour, which is also an alternative route from this point to Kinsale. Take the sharp left, which runs along parallel to the bank of the river. The first left, about 3 miles along, brings you down to **Kilmacsimon Quay**, a beautifully quiet spot (see below) on a wide, wooded bend of the Bandon River. Up until the 1950s this was a busy dock to which coal and other bulky goods were brought by barge for distribution to the surrounding area. Nowadays the only people to use the river are the local rowing team, visiting pleasure craft from Kinsale, and users of the boatyard at the far end of the quay, which will soon be moving to a new location. There is one row of houses, among which the recently abandoned Post Office can still be seen. There is good deep-water swimming off the pier beside the bar at high tide, and plenty of bird life on the mud flats at low tide.

Return to Inishannon Bridge, and continue on the main road to Bandon. This is a very pretty stretch with wooded banks where the river flows over shallow rapids. On the opposite bank are the remains of the 15th-century **Dundaniel Castle**, a romantic, ivy-covered ruin. The road runs parallel to the old Cork-Bandon railway, and the tunnel still visible on the left was one of the first to be cut in Ireland. The first section of the line opened in 1849, and it closed in 1961.

Bandon, or Bandon Bridge in a direct translation from the Irish, *Droichead na Bandan,* is an agricultural centre with a large livestock mart which can be seen on the left as you enter. Until the 1960s, cattle fairs were held in the streets of various towns, and marts were established to improve conditions of trading and lessen the inconvenience caused by the Fair Day. The town was founded by Richard Boyle (see Youghal, Chapter Four) in 1608, and "planted" with English Protestants. It was a walled town up until 1688, and one of its gates allegedly carried the inscription "Turk, Jew or Atheist may enter here; But not a Papist". A local wit, Papist, one assumes, added below: "Who wrote it, wrote it well; For the same is written on the Gates of Hell". Such was Bandon's reputation as a Protestant stronghold that up into this century it was referred to as "Bandon, where even the pigs are Protestant".

A sure sign of changing times is the fact that one of Bandon's Protestant churches, **Christchurch**, which dates from 1610, was deconsecrated in 1973, and is now the **Bandon Heritage Centre** *(Tel. 023/44193. Admission £2 adults. Open Mon.-Sat. 10-6; Sun.2-6. July-Sept.).* The exhibitions vary, but usually include an introduction to the pre-historic archaeology of the west Cork area.

The main N71 arrives in Bandon at a T-junction, recently endowed with a set of traffic lights (they are few and far between west of Cork City). Ahead is the town's Methodist church, which dates from 1821, and is a reminder of John Wesley's successful mission in the area. The shopping area of the town is on the left; we turn right, following signs for Bantry. Notice the tall, elegant late Georgian town houses with decorated fanlights over the front doors as you climb the hill out of town; some of them are now being restored after years of neglect. If you would like to see inside one, drop into R & J Forrester's craft shop (see below).

The Bantry road follows the walls of the demesne of Castle Bernard (burnt down in 1921), and across the river, the Bandon Golf course can be seen. At the bottom of one of the hills is a large "creamery", or milk-processing factory. Visitors often ask why such places have road signs warning "Danger - Creamery". It is not that there is anything inherently dangerous about milk; it is the heavy lorries delivering the raw product and removing the processed one that constitute the danger.

The road passes through rolling countryside until it reaches the conjoined villages of **Enniskeane-Ballineen**. A five-mile diversion to the right at the crossroads in Enniskeane leads to **Kinneigh Round Tower**. It is in the grounds of the Parish Church of Kinneigh. It is unusual in that it has a hexagonal base for the first 18 feet. Its conical cap was removed when it was converted into a belfry, and it stands 72 feet tall. It is believed to date from 1014 when a monastery was built on this site.

Return to the main road (if you're feeling adventurous, try one of the smaller roads leading in that direction) and continue for about a mile and a half beyond Ballineen. Here a diversion to the left crosses the Bandon River at Manch bridge and leads, half a mile on, to **Ballinacarriga Castle**. This is a fine, four-storey castle which is believed to be older than the date 1585 given in a window recess on the top floor. It is in such good condition because its top floor was used as a church in Penal times, that is until the beginning of the 19th century, and restoration has been carried out in recent years. The walls are over 6 feet thick for most of its height. There are intact bartizans, or corner turrets, at first floor level on diagonally opposite corners. Its vaulted ceiling supports the top floor which would have been the "best " room in the castle's lifetime, judging by the elaborate carvings and decorations in the windows. One shows a woman with three roses, and is thought to represent Catherine Cullinane, who married Randal Hurley, the builder of the castle. Her initials are inscribed above another window. There are also representations of the Crucifixion and a number of geometric patterns.

Dunmanway, is a market town consisting of two diamond-shaped squares.

There are some well-restored shop fronts here, and until Bandon got in on the act it boasted the only traffic light in west Cork. By turning right off the main road between the two diamonds you will discover an alternative route to Bantry via Kealkil which crosses the Shehy Mountains via Togher Bridge and the Cousane Gap (726 ft.), and is particularly suited to cyclists and walkers.

The main road continues on through a more rugged type of country to **Drimoleague**, celebrated in *The Drimoleague Blues* by the contemporary Cork-born poet Paul Durcan. It is bordered in the south by a particularly spectacular stretch of eclectically-designed modern bungalows, many favouring a kind of Spanish hacienda effect, a feature of rural Ireland which appals city-dwellers, but pleases those who live in them.

The next ten miles across country bring you downhill into **Bantry**. Look out on the right for a signpost near the West Lodge Hotel to **Kilnaruane Pillar Stone**, which is just off the main road. The stone is on the crest of a hill which was the site of an early monastic settlement. Faint outlines of its foundations can be seen. The carved pillar is thought to have formed part of the shaft of a high cross. Despite the weathering, details of the sculptures can still be identified. On the west side, the most weathered, there are delicately carved panels with Celtic interlacing, and a praying figure, with an unusual square-shaped cross. On the other side the carvings show a boat with four oarsmen facing upwards as if sailing to heaven.

The road runs along the foreshore of **Bantry Bay**, and on the right, before the town, is the entrance to **Bantry House** (*Tel. 027/50047. Admission: £2 adults, £1.50 senior citizens, 50p children. Open daily 9-6, till 8 in summer*). The house is on high ground above the road with an unforgettable view of Bantry Bay. "Were such a bay lying upon English shore, it would be the world's wonder", wrote Thackeray on his 1848 visit.

The house is built of stone and brick and consists of a central block and two wings, the wings being almost as big as the centre. It was built in 1771 by Richard White, the First Earl of Bantry, and is still occupied by his descendants. It was the first house in Ireland to be opened to the public. Its porticoed entrance stands on a wide gravel terrace overlooking the sea, and in front of the house is a lawn with a ring of old cannon. Behind it an Italianate garden rises up terraced slopes, its trellises hung with blue wisteria, to reveal another view of the bay from a vantage point above the chimneys of the house. The interior is furnished with an extensive collection of European works of art, brought back from his Grand Tour by the second Earl of Bantry. The mosaics in the entrance hall came from Pompeii; in the sitting room four panels of Royal Aubusson tapestry made for Marie Antoinette hang on the walls, and there is also a Gobelin tapestry. Most of the furniture is also 18th century, some of it oriental. The dining room is perhaps a little too full of furniture, but one of the nice things about Bantry House is that, for all its grandeur, it still manages to feel lived in; the dining room can in fact be hired for private dinner parties. However, as it receives no help from the government, parts of the house must sometimes be closed while repairs to the fabric are undertaken, and visitors occasionally complain that some of the furniture looks a bit shabby. Others find that this only adds to the considerable charm of the place.

In the stable-yard is **The French Armada Museum** dealing with Wolfe Tone, who arrived in Bantry Bay in 1798 with 15,000 French soldiers under the command of General Hoche, who were supposed to lead an uprising against the government. Bad weather prevented them from landing. One of the frigates involved in the attempted invasion has been located by divers on the sea floor, and material from her excavation will be displayed here.

The town of Bantry is fairly dull in comparison to its "Big House", but there is a lively **market** in the main square on Friday mornings. Bantry has never really recovered from the *Betelguese* disaster on January 8, 1979 in which 50 people died when the oil tanker of that name caught fire at the jetty on **Whiddy Island** in Bantry Bay.

Gulf Oil, who had brought a measure of prosperity to the town, pulled out. However, Whiddy Island is again is use as an oil storage depot, and successful efforts are being made to develop mussel cultivation in the bay.

If you go to the Friday market, you may be surprised at the number of "hippies" who have settled in the area. These are mainly young people disillusioned with urban life, and others, not so young, who left England and Wales during the "Thatcher years", seeking a more rural retreat than that island could offer, where they would not, in their own words, be "hassled".

In Main Street and Barrack Street, at the back of the market square there are some good hand-painted shop fronts - MacCarthy's Butchers, Paddy O'Donohue, J. Keohane - some of them adorned with naive animal paintings. The **Bantry Museum** is at the seaward end of the market square, at the place where the old railway line ended. It is run by volunteers, and if it is closed contact Donal Fitzgerald at the Super Valu supermarket in the town.

Leave Bantry on the N71 Glengarriff road, which travels around the edge of the bay. A sign to the right after about two miles indicates **Donemark Falls**, a pretty waterfall on a wooded hillside, and a good place to stop for a WALK.

Ballylickey is not really a village, but a succession of houses situated in wood-land on either side of the road. Leave the N71 where the road bends to the left, and follow the right fork three and a half miles inland to **Kealkil**, a small village at the foot of the **Shehy Mountains**. In Kealkil, turn right at the Catholic church (leave the car here and WALK if you prefer), and take the first left which is signposted "Stone Circle". At the top of the ridge, about half a mile on, are two square gateposts. About 200 yards inside is the **Kealkil Stone Circle**, an alignment of two large standing stones, a circle of five stones, and a stone cairn. From here you will also have a wonderful view of Bantry Bay, and get a better idea of its size.

From Kealkil you can return to Cork through the Pass of Keimaneigh and Gougane Barra (see Chapter Seven) by following signposts to Macroom.

Special Events: Bantry Mussel Fair, early May, contact Failte Bantry c/o Eileen O'Shea, tel. 027/50360.

Sporting Facilities
Golf: *Bandon Golf Club*, Castle Bernard. Tel. 023/41111. 18-holes. Green fees 7 days. *Bantry Golf Club*, Cahir. Tel. 027/50579. **Horse Riding**: *Skevanish Riding Centre*, Inishannon. Tel. 021/775476. *Dunmanway Riding School*, Dunamanway. Tel. 023/45604. *Bantry Horse Riding and Training Centre*, Coomanore South. Tel. 027/51412. *West Cork Horse Trekking Co. Ltd.* Rooska Farm Stables, Bantry. Tel. 027/50221. **Bicycle Hire**: *J. O'Donovan*, South Main St., Bandon. Tel. 023/41227. **Indoor Pool**: *Dunmanway Sports Centre*, Dunmanway. Tel. 023/46347. *West Lodge Hotel,* Bantry. Tel. 027/50360. **Fishing:** There is free fishing on the Bandon river between Inishannon Bridge and Kinsale; above the bridge most fishing is con-trolled. Details available from: *Bandon Salmon and Trout Anglers Association,* c/o Mr. Michael J. O'Regan, Oliver Plunkett St., Bandon, tel. 023/41674. *Ballineen and Enniskeane Anglers Association,*c/o Tom Fehilly, Bridge St. Ballineen (no tel.), *Dunmanway Salmon and Trout Anglers Association,* c/o Patrick MacCarthy, Yew Tree Bar, Main St. Dunmanway. Brown trout and rainbow trout in Driminidy Lake (midway between Dunmanway and Drimoleague); boats available from South Western Regional Fisheries Board, tel. 026/41222. There is free fishing on Ballinacarriga Lough beside the castle (see above) which holds a good stock of brown trout.

PUBS, RESTAURANTS, SHOPS AND ACCOMMODATION
(Price Categories are explained in HOW TO USE THIS BOOK)

BALLINADEE

B & B

GLEBE HOUSE
Tel. 021/778294. Closed 21 Dec.-2 Jan. Credit Cards: Visa, Access. Evening meal by arrangement. Moderate.

This lovely Georgian rectory is in a small riverside village on the Kinsale side of Bandon about 6 miles from both places. The easiest way to find it is to turn sharp left (coming from Cork) off the N71 on the Bandon side of the bridge at Inishannon and follow the signposts for Ballinadee.

The house has a curious asymmetrical facade, and is covered with creepers at the back and surrounded by a well-tended garden. There are 3 rooms, all decorated with highly polished antiques (one has a massive brass bedstead), velvet curtains, plain fitted carpets and duvets. They all have well-equipped en suite bathrooms, tea and coffee making facilities, hair dryer, iron, and shoe-shine kit. The tall gilt mirror and ornate side table in the hall set the tone for the elegantly furnished sitting room, small library and dining room. There is a large mahogany dining table and Georgian sideboard in the latter. Tim and Gill Bracken are especially proud of their breakfast menu which has a choice of no less than 11 main courses including kippers (loud cheers), waffles with maple syrup, and scrambled egg with cheese and rosemary shortbread. There is a four-course dinner menu using seasonal local produce and vegetables and herbs fresh from the garden. There are two apartments for self-catering holidays in the old coach house which are very well-equipped with everything from dishwasher and microwave to electric blankets.

BALLINHASSIG

Restaurant

BAWNLEIGH HOUSE
Ballinhassig. Tel. 021/771333. Open 7.30-9.30,, Tues.-Sat. Closed 2 weeks Oct., 8 days Christmas. Fully licensed. Credit Cards: Visa, Access, Amex. Expensive.

Take the turning signposted Kinsale just beyond Halfway, and continue straight for about four miles. The restaurant is in a large modern house set back from the road behind ranch-style palings. Inside is a large 80-seater room with luxurious cream and eau de nil decor. Although it is deep in the coutnry, it has the ambience of a sophisticated city restaurant, with heavy velvet curtains hiding the view. The tables are a generous size, and well spaced, wtih padded velvet seats. They are formally set up with peach napery and a full complement of wine glasses. The four-course set-menu offers classical French cooking prepared by the owner-chef, Billy Mackesy. Its fancy presentation is influenced by nouvelle cuisine, but the generous size of the portions is not. Sweets are served from an irresistible trolley.

Restaurant/B & B

BLANCHFIELD HOUSE.
Rigsdale. Tel.021-885167. B & B open March-31 Oct.; Restaurant open Tues.-Sat. from 7PM all year. Advance booking advisable, essential, Oct.-March. Wine licence only. Credit Cards: Visa, Access, Amex, Diners. Moderate.

Blanchfield House is clearly signposted on the N71 between Halfway and Inishannon, about 20 minutes from the airport. The undistinguished old house, which has been modernised and extended, stands back from the road beyond an avenue lined with pine trees. The restaurant is in a low-ceilinged room decorated with enormous dressers and a big old sideboard. Rush mats and paper napkins are set on modern pine tables which have chunky tweed-seated chairs. There is a five-course set menu offering a choice of plain, hearty food designed for outdoor appetites.

There are six bedrooms, two with en suite bathrooms and all with peaceful views of the surrounding countryside. They are furnished with old family furniture, some of it antique, and have candlewick bedspreads, patterned carpets and bathrooms with coloured suites. Guests have access to fishing rights for trout or salmon on the nearby Bandon River.

BALLYLICKEY

Guesthouse
BALLYLICKEY MANOR HOUSE
Tel. 027/50071. Fully licensed. Non-residents book in advance for dinner. Closed 3 Nov.-31 March. Credit Cards: Visa, Access. Moderate.

This large country house is situated on a slope beside the main N71 overlooking Bantry Bay. It is one of only 8 hotels in Ireland recommended by the prestigious *Guide Relais et Chateaux*. It is surrounded by beautifully kept mature gardens and has an outdoor heated pool. The main house, parts of which are 300 years old, was recently rebuilt and redecorated after being gutted by fire, but has retained its distinctive line of 3 bay windows. There is something very stylish in a typically French way about the place, which is explained by the fact that the owner, Madame Graves, is French. You can choose between a rustic chalet near the pool, or a room in the main house, both of which are equally attractive in their own way, the chalets offering romantic privacy and the house splendid views and elegant surroundings. All 11 rooms/chalets have en suite bathrooms, direct dial phone and television. French cuisine is served in the candlelit restaurant.

Hotel
SEA VIEW
Tel. 027/50073. Closed 1 Nov-31 March. Non-residents book in advance for dinner. Credit Cards: Visa, Access, Amex, Diners. Expensive.

This large 3-storey, 19th-century house with bay windows overlooking Bantry Bay was a private home until about 12 years ago when the current owners decided to extend it in the same style and turn it into a hotel. It is surrounded by beautifully landscaped gardens. The interior is well cared for, with inlaid antique furniture, highly polished brass and ornate curtains. The front bar has bamboo and cane seating, and there is a large library at the back with television and plump sofas. .

All 17 rooms have en suite bathrooms, TV and direct dial phone, and there is one on the ground floor especially equipped for the disabled. They exhibit varying degrees of luxury, and are furnished with a particularly interesting selection of mainly Victorian antiques, plain carpets and heavy floral drapes. Some of the large bay-windowed ones have their own chaise longue or small sofas from which to contemplate the view. The others have equally nice views of the wooded gardens.

The dining room is an elegant place with crocheted mats and linen napkins on polished tables, its rooms interconnecting through tall arches. The set dinner menu, with the emphasis on fresh country produce, changes daily and light snacks are served in the bar all day. Owner-manager Kathleen O'Sullivan is renowned for her interesting breakfasts and close attention to detail.

Shops and Galleries
MANNING'S EMPORIUM
Tel. 027/50456. Open daily 9-6.

If you know no better it is easy to assume that this roadside shop (on the N71) is just another grocery-cum-newsagent-cum-off-licence, but a closer look at the enticingly displayed range of exotic fruit and veg piled high, continental-style, outside the window will tell you otherwise. Val Manning runs one of the best delicatessens in Cork, and has been a pioneer in promoting local farmhouse cheese, locally smoked salmon and chicken, home-made salamis and pates, and organically grown vegetables. If you're in the area in July then phone to find out when he is holding his two-day Food Fair, at which you can sample all that is best from local producers who display their wares in a marquee on the forecourt. Meanwhile, if you need to find ingredients for an exotic dinner party, or simply to assemble an unusual picnic, this is the place to stop. His selection of wine is small but carefully chosen, and with his range of farmhouse cheeses, charcuterie and organic vegetables - including such hard-to-find items as corn salad, oak-head lettuce, endive and spinach - you will be spoilt for choice. (If you don't believe that it's hard to buy fresh spinach in this part of the world, just try).

BANDON

Hotel
THE MUNSTER ARMS
Oliver Plunkett St. Tel.023/41562. Bar food available to 10PM, lunch specials 12-3. Credit Cards: Visa, Access, Amex, Diners. Moderate.

The Munster Arms claims to be one of Munster's oldest hotels. It was recently totally refurbished in the neo-Victorian style which interior decorators seem to think is *de rigueur* for old coaching inns, and now has a facade in two shades of pink with art nouveau lanterns suspended from wrought iron brackets. The large bar is pleasant enough, with daylight pouring in through the top of the windows, the usual quota of stained glass partitions, mahogany panelling and etched glass mirrors, and a magnificently solid bar of dark wood adorned with barley sugar twist pillars. It really is the best place to eat or drink in a town not over-endowed with good bars and devoid of anything approaching a serious restaurant. Coffee and scones are served in the morning, and there is an all-day menu of hardy perennials like mussels in breadcrumbs, quiche, lasagne and sandwiches. The lunchtime specials always include an old fashioned roast of the day. There are 27 comfortable bedrooms, all recently refurbished, with TV, direct dial phone, tea and coffee making facilities, fitted furniture in dark wood, brass bedside lamps, colour-co-ordinated quilts, curtains and carpets, and fully tiled bathrooms. If you're easily disturbed by traffic noise, ask for an interior room.

B & B
(See also BALLINADEE above).
BALLYMOUNTAIN HOUSE
Inishannon. Tel. 021/775366. Open 1 March- 15 Nov. or by arrangement. Evening meal by arrangement. Credit Cards: Visa, Access. Inexpensive.

Although the postal address here is Inishannon, it is actually only two miles from Bandon on a back road (and about 25 minutes from the airport). The best way to find it is to follow the signposts for Ballymountain House from the bridge at Inishannon on the N71, turning sharp left on the Bandon side of the bridge.

The modest, Georgian-style farmhouse is right in the heart of the country, surrounded by mature trees and a big lawn on which sheep and lambs or mares and foals or cattle will be grazing. This is a 120-acre mixed farm, and there are some excellent walks in the immediate area, including one to a prehistoric grave on the Cummins' land. The front porch-conservatory is filled with thriving geraniums, and the whole house retains that elusive genuine old farmhouse feeling. There is a sitting room with TV and piano, large comfortable armchairs and an impressive display of sporting and stock-breeding trophies. The dining room has a loudly ticking clock and separate tables with solid 1930s upholstered chairs.

The bedrooms have views of the rolling countryside and are gloriously quiet. All six rooms are pleasantly old fashioned and well-maintained, with duvets and floral wallpaper. They share two showers and two toilets on the landing. Sheila Cummins provides a five-course evening meal of plain farmhouse cooking and home baking (bring your own wine) which must be ordered in advance. Dutch visitors are especially fond of this place, but it would suit anyone looking for a simple, inexpensive country retreat.

Shops and Galleries
R & J FORRESTER - THE BANDON POTTERY
82-83 North Main St. Tel. 023/41360. Open 9-6 Mon.- Sat. Credit Cards: Visa, Access, Amex, Diners.

Jane Forrester is one of the best potters - or ceramic artists - working in Cork, producing both sturdy table ware and more delicate decorative pierced bowls. Her studio is behind this tall 18th-century town house (you will find it in the town by following signposts for Bantry) which also contains a craft shop, coffee shop and art gallery. They stock a range of the best of Irish crafts, including Jerpoint glass, jewellery, soft toys, turned wood, candles, Kinsale smocks, knitwear and leather. There is also a good range of Irish books and unusual postcards. The gallery on the top floor has changing exhibitions of carefully selected artists, many of them working in County Cork. The coffee shop concentrates on home baking and home made soups.

ALADDIN'S CAVE
Tel. 023/41974. Open 10.30-5.30, Mon.-Sat., Sun. 3-6, Closed Thurs.

This second-hand furniture warehouse is signposted to the left as the N71 from Cork approaches Bandon. You never know quite what you will find here, but if you're furnishing a house on a budget, or just fond of bric-a-brac, it's worth a look. Some of the stuff might be new - like small pine shelf units - some of it may be near the end of its useful life, but there is so much of it that real flea-market addicts will seldom come away empty-handed.

MARTIN CAREY - MASTER BUTCHER
82 South Main St. Tel. 023/42107. Open 9-6, Mon.-Sat.

Apart from excellent local meat, this butcher's shop is also a delicatessen with a wide selection of Irish farmhouse and continental cheeses, locally made salami, smoked salmon, freshly assembled pizzas, game and venison pies from Rosscarbery Recipes, and oven-ready meals like stuffed mushrooms. They also sell sheepskins, presumably from the same animals whose heads can be found on the butcher's counter on the opposite side of the shop.

BANTRY

Bar
THE ANCHOR BAR
New St. Tel. 027/50012.

If you came into Bantry from Drimoleauge you will have seen this establishment advertised by an enormous anchor set up beside the road. The name "The Anchor" is intended to remind owner Billy O'Donnell of his resolution to stay put, but he still finds sailing an irresistible attraction, and recently completed a circumnavigation of Ireland. I had better come straight out and admit that this is one of my favourite Cork bars, even though I understand that it might not be to everyone's taste. It was built in 1886 just off the main square, and has undoubtedly seen better days - but not, I think, better hosts than Billy and his son. The theme is vaguely nautical with a ship's lantern above the door, but usually the company is so interesting and the light so dim that the decor, or what there is of it, fails to register. There is a special display of hand-made cards with meaningful inscriptions like "When O'Donnell drinks, everybody drinks and when O'Donnell pays everybody pays" (which those who know the owner's unpredictable moods will appreciate) or, more revealing, perhaps: "Anchor Bar: elected official Screwball Headquarters for West Cork". When I asked one rainy December day if they did bar food I was told to go to the cafe down the road and fetch a sandwich, but first to get warm and dry by the fire. You go to this bar to talk to people, and at times the conversation can be great. Love it or hate it, its not a bar that many people easily forget.

Bar/Bar Food/Restaurant
O'CONNOR'S SEAFOOD RESTAURANT

Wolfe Tone Square. Tel. 027/50221. Open 9.30-10.30 Mon.-Sat. Lunch 12.30-2, dinner 6.30-10 plus all day menu. Booking advisable for dinner high season. Fully licensed. Credit Cards; Visa, Access. Inexpensive-Moderate.

The bar is in the back, and the modest little restaurant overlooks the square through a curtain of fishnets and floats. You can eat at one of the booths in the bar, but the front room is more atmospheric, with pine top tables, rush mats, a candle in a brass holder, and an open fire in cold weather. There are about six options featuring Bantry mussels, also "catch of the day" cooked to order, scallops, oysters or an excellent seafood pie. For non-fish eaters there are steaks or shepherd's pie. Live lobsters are available all year round.

Restaurant/B & B
LARCHWOOD HOUSE

Pearson's Bridge. Tel.027/66181. Open from 6.30 Mon.-Sat. Easter-Oct., Thurs.- Sat. otherwise, but phone to confirm. (B & B open all year). Wine licence only. Advance booking advisable. Credit Cards: Visa, Access, Diners. Rooms: Moderate; Restaurant: Expensive.

The restaurant is signposted to the right off the N71 about 2 miles beyond Bantry in the Ballylickey direction and is actually on the back road to Kealkil. It is situated in a room at the back of a modern house overlooking the River Ouvane.

Pre-dinner drinks are taken in a small ante-room with large wood-framed sofas and a brimming china cabinet. The oak-panelled dining room looks out over the prettily landscaped garden to the river. There are bentwood chairs at small tables set with pink and white damask napery. The price of the main course chosen from the extensive four-course set menu determines the price of the meal. Owner-chef Sheila Vaughan practiced her trade in Dromoland Castle before setting up on her own here in 1991, and is fast gaining a reputation locally for imaginative and ambitious food. Among the more unusual main courses you might find are fillet of brill with elderflower sauce, breast of duckling with kumquats and honey or loin of veal with port and cream.

There are four bedrooms with en suite bathrooms, comfortably furnished with modern built-in cupboards and peaceful views of the gardens and the river, which can be heard in the distance.

B & B
BANTRY HOUSE

Tel. 027/50047. Closed 23-26 Dec. Wine licence - dinner for residents available Mon.-Fri. May-Oct., book by 12 noon. Credit Cards: Visa, Access. Expensive.

Bantry House is to the right of the road from Cork as you reach the waters of Bantry Bay just outside the town. The house has been open to the public since 1945, and now the East and West Wings have been converted to provide a unique experience of bed and breakfast. There are six double and twin rooms in the East Wing and a two-room suite and a two-room family apartment sleeping four in the West Wing. There are thriving house plants and red pine floors throughout the public areas, which include a basement dining room, a mezzanine TV landing, a small sitting room with an open fire, and a billiard room.

Old and new are cleverly combined in the bedroom decor to give an impression of uncluttered sunlit space: pale yellow walls with white skirting boards are complemented by pale green carpet. Pine and wicker pieces relieve the effect of heavier antiques, dressing tables are prettily skirted in gingham. Rooms 22 and 25 have sea views, and the others overlook the newly restored Italian garden with its fountains, parterres and the "stairway to the sky". Guests have free access to the house and gardens, and one of the best things about staying here is being able to wander about outside at any hour and savour the truly magnificent view of Bantry Bay.

Bantry House provides the grand surroundings that are expected in an expensive country house hotel, without the pressure to live up to your surroundings which some people find so constraining.

Shops and Galleries

IRISH SCENE SWEATER SHOP

Wolfe Tone Square. Tel. 027/51264. Open 9.30-1 and 2-5.30, Mon.-Sat. Credit Cards: Visa, Access.

This is the factory outlet for attractive locally made sweaters which are predominantly in bright colours with busy striped or patterned designs, although there are also some plainer models.

BANTRY CRAFT SHOP/THE GREEN GALLERY

Glengarriff St. Tel. 027/50003. Open 9.30-6, Mon.- Sat.

These two small shops are at the top end of town on the main N71 to Glengarriff. The craft shop has a selection of modestly priced goods, mostly made locally including enamel and ceramic jewellery, shoes and other leatherware, ceramics, prints and traditionally made baskets. When the Green Gallery is closed you can get the key at the craft shop. The gallery specialises in original work by west Cork artists such as Norah Golden, Pat Connor, Birgitta Saflund, Tim Goulding and Terry Searle.

GILMANI

Glengarriff Rd. Tel. 027/50684. Open 10-6, Mon.-Sat. Credit Cards: Visa, Access.

Anyone with the slightest interest in high fashion will be intrigued by this boutique which sells the work of Fergus Gilman, one of Ireland's brightest young designers, who just happens to be from Bantry. (He has another shop in the Savoy Centre in Cork city). There is lots of exotic evening wear for women and some amazing lines in menswear, such as double-wrap over trousers and skeleton shirts.

DUNMANWAY

Hostel

SHIPLAKE HOSTEL

Tel. 023/45750. Open 15 March-15 Nov. or by arrangement for 4 or more people. Inexpensive.

This place is well off the main road way up in the mountains, but once you have left Dunmanway on the right road it is well signposted. So stop in Dunmanway and ask for the Shiplake Road, which leads off the main diamond in the centre of the town. Accommodation is in a typical stone-built farmhouse, with dormitory beds for 15 people and a gypsy caravan for couples or families. Its remoteness and its friendliness make it a favourite among hostellers. Free bicycles are provided, and there is lake swimming and hill walking. Telephone bookings are accepted, and as it is an independent hostel there is no curfew and no membership requirement.

ENNISKEANE

Shops and Galleries

HOSFORD'S GERANIUMS

Cappa, Enniskeane. Tel. 023/39159. Open 10-6 Mon.-Sat. all year; 2.30-5.30 Suns. March-June and mid-Sept. to Sunday before Christmas. Closed 25, 26 Dec and 1 Jan. Credit Cards: Visa, Access, Amex, Diners.

This garden centre lies midway between two main roads, the N71 and the R586 and is clearly signposted from both of them. The climate of West Cork is particularly suited to geraniums, and the best ones come from Hosfords - both the kind grown for their flowers properly known as pelargoniums, and the delicately scented real geraniums. I mention it here for the benefit of keen gardeners, who might like to visit the county's "geranium headquarters". Hosford's specialise in geraniums and roses; the nursery was set up in 1980 on the family farm by John Hosford who trained with the Royal Horticultural Society at Wisley, and is a source of very sound advice. He also stocks the normal range of bulbs, bedding plants, perennials, shrubs and trees, and has a mail order service for credit card customers.

INISHANNON

Bar/Bar Food
SULLY'S
Tel. 021/775619. Bar food available all day, 7 days a week.
Arriving from the Cork direction, you will see Sully's restrained dark green facade on your right hand side in the middle of the village of Inishannon. Owner Pat O'Sullivan is known as Sully to his friends, hence the name. He and his wife Marie, originally from Dublin, gave the pub a total facelift in 1988 using a Victorian theme with black and white tiles around the bar area and shades of dark green in the upholstery. It functions both as a stopping place for passing travellers and as a popular local, hosting the local GAA teams among others. The bar food is limited to sandwiches and cold platters, which, given that all the meat is cooked at home by Marie and served in generous portions, makes a welcome change from the ubiquitous microwave. Their "beef special" sandwich really is something special, with a lot more than just beef inside, including locally made Round Tower cheese.

Hotel
INISHANNON HOUSE HOTEL
Tel. 021/775121. Lunch 12.30-2.30, dinner 7-9, booking advisable. Credit Cards: Visa, Access, Amex, Diners. Restaurant: Expensive; Rooms: Very Expensive.
Conal O'Sullivan, who bought this hotel in 1989, likes to advertise it as "the most romantic hotel in Ireland", and he has a point. It is a compact white Georgian house dating from 1720 with an unusual circular bow, built in a secluded spot on the banks of the Bandon River and surrounded by colourful gardens. A terrace has been built out over the river which is a heavenly place for coffee after dinner on a summer evening. Inishannon is the nearest town, and the hotel is only 15 minutes' drive from Cork Airport, while Kinsale is ten minutes' drive in the opposite direction. Inishannon House is very well signposted on all approaches.

The hotel itself is small, with only 13 bedrooms, each one decorated in a different version of period country house style - antique furniture, heavy chintzy curtains, original paintings. Not only do all bedrooms have TV and direct dial phone, there is also a phone extension in the bathroom. Guests also have the use of a charming sitting room on the first floor overlooking the river. Residents can fish for trout or salmon from the hotel lawns, and the hotel also has the fishing rights to a stretch of the nearby Brinny River.

The restaurant is in a downstairs room overlooking the rose garden and river and the tables are set with heavy peach-coloured linen. It is adorned, as are all the rooms, by extremely interesting paintings from the owner's private collection which includes works by contemporary Dutch, Irish and Jamaican artists. The a la carte menu has some unusual starters like Witlof salad - a Belgian endive salad with garlic mayonnaise to which hot sauteed prawn tails are added, and a wide selection of main courses including "Catch of the Day", lobster, steaks with a choice of sauces, veal, lamb in season and fresh salmon from the Bandon river. The owner is especially proud of his wine list which has no fewer than 12 house wines among 125 choices.

Shops and Galleries
THE SURPLUS STORE
Main St. Tel. 775037. Open: 9.30-5.30 Mon.-Sat.
Here is another place for people who like finding antiques in unusual locations. The size of the small roadside shop is misleading: behind it is a huge warehouse which sells a mixture of restored antiques, unrestored antiques and good quality

second-hand furniture, including little-used desks, sofas, armchairs and tables. They also usually have a good selection of old whiskey and stout jars, basketware, reproduction brassware, and smaller stuff like canvas shoulder bags, gardening gloves, sweaters and gumboots.

KEALKIL

Bar Food / Music
THE BROWN PUB
Tel. 027/66147. Food served all day from noon, May-Oct. Inexpensive.
This was one of the first pubs to adopt the now commonplace tactic of exposing old stone walls and emphasising rustic features instead of ripping them out. The present owners have extended the pub but maintained its character by using old pine, and have kept the open fire. The most popular items on the bar food menu are seafood sandwiches - smoked salmon, crab or fresh salmon mayonnaise - and there are also home-made pizzas. There are music sessions 3 or 4 times a week in summer and most weekends in winter.

Shops and Galleries
FUTURE FORESTS
027/66176. Open 10-6, Sundays from 2.30.
Take the Macroom road in Kealkil, and after two and a half miles you will see a thatched building on the left-hand side of the road. On the hill behind it is a large tree nursery, laid out in alphabetical order from arbutus through oaks, plum and poplar to rowan, walnut and willow. If you are looking for a particular tree, you'll probably find it here, but it is an education just to wander around. They also stock shrubs, and have a wide range of rare and exotic dwarf conifers. Mike Collard, the master-mind behind this project, originally came to the area to work as a forester, and is fanatic about wood, whether in trees or timber. He has a collection of bog oak and bog fir for sale; he supplies rare hardwoods, and elm, oak, ash and beech for boat-builders. There is also an unusual range of rustic wooden tubs, window boxes, trellises and garden sheds.

KILMACSIMON QUAY

Bar
KILMACSIMON BAR
There are some places that even the most generous travel writer is tempted to keep to herself, and this is one of them. However, assuming that readers of this book are civilised people who will not turn up at this heavenly spot and pollute it by playing the car stereo full blast, nor perplex the kindly owners by ordering Harvey Wallbangers, here it is. Coming from Cork, turn sharp left after the bridge at Inishannon and keep on for about 3 miles. A small road on the left, which may or may not be signposted "Kilmacsimon Boat Yard", but is the first one you come to, will bring you down to the pub. Try to arrive at high tide, when the trees on the opposite bank will be reflected in the calm waters of the wide river-bend outside the pub's strange triangular bay windows. The bar is perched on the water's edge, and consists of two small rooms, with a snooker table in the back one. The best thing to do on a sunny day is to take your drink outside to the high quay at the river's edge and sit on the grass savouring the amazing peace of this idyllic spot.

9 CHAPTER NINE

KINSALE

Kinsale is one of the biggest success stories in the history of Irish tourism. While it may not get as many visitors as Blarney, those that go to Kinsale tend to stay longer, and its attractions and facilities are so good and so numerous that it merits a chapter to itself. It is very much the sort of place where you may well book into a B & B for one night and find yourself still there a week later. It is known for its restaurants, the best of which have formed themselves into the "Good Food Circle", and host an annual gourmet festival in October. It is a popular yachting centre with a marina, and also has excellent facilities for deep sea fishing. The harbour itself is a large one with great natural beauty, and the town, much of which is Georgian, climbs up the slopes of Compass Hill at the top of the harbour on the estuary of the River Bandon. While most Cork towns are "twinned" with modest little places in Brittany, Kinsale has managed to twin itself with Antibes-Juan-les-Pins on the French Riviera, which gives some idea of the town's aspirations. There is a great sense of civic pride in Kinsale, and in the summer its shops and houses are enhanced by window boxes and other floral displays which help it to win prizes regularly in the national "Tidy Towns" competition.

But it was not always so. Thirty years ago Kinsale was a run-down fishing port, its Georgian houses crumbling away, its roads muddy and pot-holed. It has had a bad name historically since the Battle of Kinsale in 1602, generally referred to as "a turning point in Irish history". In October, 1601, a Spanish force arrived in the harbour to support the Irish chieftains in their fight against the forces of Queen Elizabeth of England. The Spanish occupied the walled town, and, while they were waiting for the Irish army, under Hugh O'Neill, the Earl of Tyrone, and Red Hugh O'Donnell, to arrive from Ulster, English forces led by the Lord Deputy, Mountjoy, blockaded the town and harbour. In early December O'Neill and O'Donnell at last arrived in Kinsale, and blockaded the English army which was encamped around the town. Urged on by the Spanish commander, Don Juan de Aguila, O'Neill agreed to a surprise attack at dawn on Christmas Eve. The plan was betrayed - legend has it that a soldier named Mahon sold the information to the English for a bottle of whiskey - and the Irish army was attacked by the English instead. By 2 January, 1602, Kinsale was again in English hands.

But there was more than just a town at stake here; the Battle of Kinsale was the last concerted effort by the native Irish chieftains to challenge English rule. O'Donnell returned to Spain with the Spanish army, but died suddenly before he could organise more aid for the Irish. In 1607 O'Neill, with Rory O'Donnell, the Earl of Tyrconnell and about 100 members of leading Irish families left Ulster for the continent, an emigration known as "the flight of the Earls", which, effectively, left Ireland in English hands. Thus, for nationalists, ever since 1602 the name Kinsale has been synonymous with defeat.

Kinsale was also unlucky for James II, who landed there in 1689 to begin his abortive campaign for the recovery of the throne, which ended at the Battle of the Boyne in 1690. After that, the forces of King William under John Churchill, the Duke of Marlborough, descended on Kinsale, which still held out for King James, and attacked its two forts, both of which quickly surrendered. Kinsale remained an important naval base and ship-building centre throughout the 18th century, but was eclipsed in the 19th century by Cork city. The English army retained a large base in the town until 1918, by which time the main business of the town was the seasonal occupation of herring-fishing. By the 1960s even the herring had gone, and it was not until the 1970s that things started to pick up.

Kinsale is 18 miles from Cork, and 13 from Cork Airport. (There is a regular bus service from Cork with at least 6 buses a day). Leave Cork on the South Ring following airport signs. Traffic is heavy in the town, especially in July and August, and the best place to park while you look around is on the quay immediately to your left (around a hair pin bend) as you arrive. The large metal sculpture which can be seen on the seafront in Kinsale was installed in 1989 much to the horror of the majority of the residents of the town, who refuse to recognise any artistic merit in it, and refer to it as "the monument". Ironically, it was commissioned by the Arts Council and presented to the town by the government to celebrate Kinsale's victory in the "Tidy Towns" competition. It is by the Cork sculptor Eilis O'Connell, and is supposed to represent a sea wave.

Head for the **Tourist Information Office**, (*Tel.021/772234, off season Tel. 021/774026*) a distinctive square building with a steep slated roof surmounted by a weather vane, which opened in 1991. It is on the pier behind Cronin's Commercial Hall. Walk up the narrow street across the road which is signposted "Jim Edwards". This leads to the **Short Quay**; in medieval Kinsale the water came right up to **Market Square**, which is at the far end of the Short Quay. The parallel street, Pearse Street, was also a waterway. The land was reclaimed in the 18th and 19th centuries.

Kinsale Regional Museum (*Tel. 021/772044. Admission 30 p. Open Mon.-Sat 11-5, Sun 3-5, or tel. for key*) is located in the Old Courthouse in Market Square. The museum has a collection of items of local historical interest including some mementos of the wreck of the *Lusitania*, which was sunk 14 miles off the Old Head of Kinsale (See Cobh, Chapter Two). The Courtroom was the scene of the inquest on the victims of the disaster. The Courthouse is an amalgam of two buildings, the Market House, which was built in 1600, and a Dutch-style gabled frontage added in 1706.

Walk up the narrow street on the other side of the museum and turn right into Cork Street to take a look at the newly restored **Desmond Castle**, a 16th-century tower house which was used as the Custom House in medieval times. It is also known as the "French Prison", as it was used to detain prisoners, mainly French, taken during the European wars of the 18th century. Up to 600 at a time were squeezed in here, and when the building was gutted by fire in 1747, fifty four prisoners died.

Return to the bottom of the hill in Cork Street, and across the road is **St. Multose Church**, which incorporates part of a 13th-century church. The town stocks, dating from the 18th century, are in the church porch. There is a pleasant, spacious interior with several interesting memorials. Three of the victims of the *Lusitania* are buried in the churchyard, which has several other interesting headstones. St. Multose was a 6th-century saint, also known as Eltin, and to add to the confusion some claim Multose was female. When he or she was building an earlier church on this site, he or she appealed to the people watching for help in shifting a huge stone. The only one who came forward was a stranger, and St. Multose, in the time honoured tradition of early Irish saints, put a curse on the town, saying that only strangers would ever prosper there.

St. Multose is a good place from which to set off on the **Compass Hill** WALK. This is a most unusual circuit, leaving the town at one end, and walking around the back of the hill on which Kinsale is built to enter it at the other. It takes about half an hour, and offers excellent views of the Bandon River and Kinsale Harbour. Turn left out of the gates of the church and follow the walls through a narrow bit of road, continuing straight up the hill. At the top of the hill a signpost indicating "Compass Hill Walk" will send you out into the country.

You re-enter the town on **The Mall**, which is above the town hall. A footpath leads into the pretty gardens, known as the **Bowling Green**, in front of this striking Victorian Gothic building, which was once an officer's mess for Charles Fort. Charles Fort is visible from here on the left hand side of the harbour.

Charles Fort is well worth a visit, and also offers the chance of two more very good

WALKS. It is a mile and a half down the harbour, along the road that runs beside the Scilly Dam below the entrance of the main road from Cork. If you choose to WALK you should go in one direction along the **Lower Road**, (as it is known locally) which is signposted "Scilly Walk" beyond the Spaniard Bar, and, for the sake of the view, come back on the road above it, the Higher Road. This part of town is known as **Scilly**, and was lived in by fishermen who came here from the Scilly Isles and Cornwall. The Lower Road is a footpath running above the water's edge under a wooded hill. It emerges in **Summer Cove**, a waterside village of tall Victorian houses on two steep hills which was originally built for the families of soldiers serving in the fort.

The fact that **Charles Fort** *(Tel. 021/772263. Admission £1, senior citizens 70p, children and students 40p. Open mid-April-mid-June, 10-5 Tues.-Sat., 2-7 Suns.; mid-June-mid-Sept, 10-6.30 daily; rest of the year Mon.-Fri. 8-4.30 except public holidays. Guide service mid- April to mid-Sept. only)* encloses nine acres of land will give some idea of its scale. It was designed as a star-shaped fort by William Robinson, architect of the Royal Hospital at Kilmainham in Dublin. It was built in 1677 as a coastal defence, so the fact that it was overlooked by high ground on the landward side, making it vulnerable to attack from there, was not considered important. However, when the fort held out for King James II in 1690 (see above) Williamite forces under the command of the Duke of Marlborough took only 13 days to bring it to surrender. Repairs and improvements were made throughout the 18th century, and the fort was garrisoned throughout the 19th century, although it was used mainly as a training centre for new recruits, being something of a white elephant given the diminished importance of Kinsale as a port. It was burnt out by the IRA in 1921, shortly after the British had handed it back to the Irish Government. It stood derelict until 1972 when it was taken into state care as a National Monument, and the restoration work that continues today was started.

If at all possible, join one of the guided tours which take place hourly in the summer. Otherwise, there is a useful exhibition on the fort's history and lay-out in a small house just inside the gate. The fort is mainly impressive for the size of its five hollow bastions, two of which face the sea, but there is also fine stonework on many of the buildings within it, especially the arsenal and the barrack stores.

The little sentry box near the modern light house is the one associated with the ghost known as "the white lady". Like most good stories, there are several variations to it, but the most common version tells that the newly married husband of the governor's daughter sent the sentry on duty in this box into Kinsale on an errand, and took his place while he was gone. The husband fell asleep at his post, and the governor, on a tour of inspection, not recognising his son-in-law, shot him dead, as this was the usual punishment for the offence. When his daughter heard what had happened, she was so distraught that she threw herself over the cliff here and was killed on the rocks beneath.

There is a very enjoyable WALK along the cliff path at the bottom of Charles Fort towards the mouth of the harbour. There are good swimming places in the little coves along here, and the path crosses two stony strands, **Middle Cove**, and **Lower Cove**. Beyond Lower Cove it peters out at the top of the next hill, which will take about 45 minutes to reach from the fort. From Lower Cove there is an alternative route back to the fort which can be reached by going up the tarmacked road and turning left, and left again at the T-junction. There are a couple of steep hills on this route, which can make it seem much longer than two miles back to the fort.

James Fort (freely accessible), on the opposite side of the harbour, can be reached by driving or walking along the pier past Acton's Hotel to the bridge across the Bandon River about half a mile out of town. Turn sharp left off the bridge, and park beside the Dock Bar. There is a small sandy beach signposted here, about 200 yards away, accessible by foot. The fort was named after King James 1 and built between 1601 and 1603 on the site of an earlier fortification. It has a regular pentagonal shape, but is on a much smaller scale than its neighbour, Charles Fort. A covered way leads from the remains of the old castle, which was stormed by the Duke of Marlborough in 1689, to the ruined blockhouse on the water's edge which had a ten- gun battery above it and formed the harbour's main defence before the building of Charles Fort.

From this side of the bridge it is about 7 miles to the **Old Head of Kinsale**, a narrow peninsula that juts out due south into the sea. The ruined castle on the left, just beyond the bridge, was built by John de Courcey, who owned these lands in Norman times. He had another castle at the Old Head, which is just beyond the car park, and is on the site of a much earlier promontory fort. The other ruined "castle" on the high ground behind it is a defensive tower dating from the Napoleonic wars. From here there is a tarmacked footpath to the new lighthouse, a WALK of under a mile during which you will be exposed to stiff sea breezes, even on the calmest of days. It is an excellent spot for bird watching, and there are also good WALKS to be had along the western edge of the Old Head following sheep paths through the springy grass. The ruins half way to the new lighthouse are of a previous lighthouse building. The bay to the left of these ruins is called **Holeopen Bay**, and if you look down at low tide you will see that there is actually a hole, or cave, running right through, just above water level, to the other side of the peninsula. At the time of writing, the Old Head is freely accessible, but regrettably there are plans afoot to build a golf course on its tip.

Returning from the Old Head turn left at The Speckled Door to discover two long sandy beaches. The first is **Garrylucas**, and the second is **Garrettstown**. They are on Courtmacsherry Bay. There is good swimming here, but stay clear of the rocks between the two beaches, and at either end, and look out for the warning flags which are raised at Garrettstown in bad weather.

The road back to Kinsale from Garrettstown runs through the village of Ballinspittle, famous for its "moving statue". The statue of the Virgin Mary is in a grotto about a mile outside the village on the Kinsale road. It is no different from many other statues erected at similar sites throughout Ireland during the Marian year, 1952. However, in the summer of 1985 thousands of people saw the statue "move", and Ballinspittle was visited by pilgrims from all over the country. People still come here to pray, but not in such numbers. A fundamentalist smashed the statue at the end of her summer of fame, and the replacement is, apparently, immobile.

Special Events
Kinsale Regatta - August Bank Holiday weekend. *Kinsale Gourmet Festival* - last weekend in September - Tel. 021/774026 for details of these, and the many other events on Kinsale's packed annual calendar.

Sporting Facilities
Golf: *Kinsale Golf Club*, Ringanane. Tel. 021/772197. 9-hole. Green fees Mon.-Fri. **Tennis:** *Kinsale Rugby and Tennis Club*, Snugmore. (Enquire at TIO). *Oysterhaven Boardsailing Centre*, Tel. 021/770738 (book in advance). **Horse Riding**: *Sunblossom Stables*, Belgooly. Tel. 021/771397. **Bicycle Hire**: *Mylie Murphy*, Pearse St. (No tel.). **Scuba Diving**: *Denis Kieran*, The Folk House, Main St. Tel. 021/772282. **Boat Hire - Sea Angling**: *Kinsale Marine Services*, Lower O'Connell St. Tel. 021/772611. *Trident Angling and Scuba Diving Centre*, Trident Hotel. Tel. 021/774099. **Boardsailing, canoes, dayboats**: *Oysterhaven Boardsailing Centre*, Oysterhaven. Tel. 021/770738. **Yacht Charter**: *International Yacht Charters*, Trident Hotel. Tel. 021/772301:

PUBS, RESTAURANTS, SHOPS AND ACCOMMODATION
(Price Categories are explained in HOW TO USE THIS BOOK)

GARRETTSTOWN
Hotel
COAKLEY'S ATLANTIC HOTEL
Tel. 021/778215. Open all year. Sunday lunch 12.30-2. Credit Cards: Visa, Access, Amex, Diners. Moderate.

If you would like to be lulled to sleep by the sound of surf pounding on the cliffs beside a long sandy beach, then this is the place to go. It is about 7 miles from Kinsale on the shores of Courtmacsherry Bay. The presence of sandy beaches - there is another one five minutes' walk to the left - makes it a very popular base for family holidays, and from July to September it caters admirably for relays of large families. There are 22 bedrooms with bath, most of them in a modern two-storey block with views over the sea. The food is plain and served in generous portions, so try to leave some room for the old-fashioned sweet trolley. It is the sort of grub that makes an excellent Sunday lunch, but be sure to book in advance.

KINSALE
Bars
THE BULMAN BAR
Summer Cove. Tel.021/772131.

About a mile down the harbour in the Charles Fort direction you will find this water-side pub. There is only the one room, with its original Victorian stone tiles on the floor, wooden-clad brown walls, the bar on one side, an open fire on the other, and a darts board in the back. Mid-week it functions as a friendly local; on sunny Sundays it is swamped by noisy youngsters and bikers who spill out on to the quay outside its front door. On a quiet evening, however, there is no better place than that same quay to enjoy the last of the sun, pint in hand, as you plan your next move.

THE DOCK BAR
The Dock. Tel. 021/772522.

This bar is on the water's edge on the peninsula of land opposite the town, from which point it used to be reached by a ferry. Nowadays you must drive or walk to the new bridge and double back to get there. There is a sandy beach behind it, so at the end of a sunny summer day it can be crowded with families trailing tired children. However, most of the time it is quiet and there is plenty of room outside with seats on the front patio. The interior has been tastefully modernized with heavy pine tables, quarry tile floor, open-weave curtains and a handsome cast-iron Godin stove which heats it in the winter. The landlord is an ex-jockey and there are photos of some of his winning rides on the walls.

THE HARBOUR BAR
Scilly. Tel.021/772528.

This waterside cocktail bar is strictly for grown-ups - no pints are served, and the atmosphere is rather hushed - unless it is being ruined by some loud-mouthed bore. There are tables outside, looking over towards the town, but you really ought to have a drink inside the tiny carpeted bar which has sofas and armchairs by the fire among Platt family heirlooms. Tim Platt keeps the menus of most of Kinsale's restaurants on his mantelpiece, and will book you a table when you've made your choice.

Bar/Music
THE SPANIARD
Scilly. Tel. 021/772436.

This converted fisherman's bar was one of the places that helped to put Kinsale on the tourist map in the late '60s, and is now one of the most famous pubs in Ireland. It's on a hairpin bend above the town on the road to Charles Fort. If you want to meet people, the place to be is the original front bar with its sawdust-strewn floor, large log fire and darts board. There is another, usually quieter bar between this and the back room, which is used for live music. There is a regular Wednesday night traditional music session, featuring local talent, which visiting musicians are welcome to join. It starts around 9.30. Big name bands - rock, folk and traditional - play at the weekend, and usually there is no cover charge.

THE SHANAKEE.
Market St. No Tel.

Visitors and regulars contribute to the ballad sessions which take place nightly during the season at this town centre old-world pub, led, usually, by a keyboard player. On Thursday nights the Kinsale set dancers entertain, and will teach a few steps to anyone who would like to join in.

THE TAP TAVERN
Guardwell. Tel. 021/772240.

This is one of the few bars in Kinsale that has not been modernized or "themed" or turned into more of a restaurant than a pub over the last few years. On Saturday and Sunday nights in the high season and occasionally in winter a professional singer leads an informal "come-all-ye" in the bar's one small, brown room which has a friendly atmosphere more like that of an ordinary small town pub than the glossy up-market resort which Kinsale is fast becoming.

THE LORD KINGSALE
Main St. Tel. 021/772371.

The bar has been extensively refurbished over recent years in a luxurious sort of Tudor style - lots of dark wood, low beams, polished brass, and tapestry-type uphol-stery. At the back is a very attractive function room with a high beamed ceiling and a rustic wrought iron chandelier where entertainment is provided every weekend in the summer, and on many Sunday nights off season. It is usually the sort of thing that will appeal to an older, quieter audience: well-trained voices that sing in tune.

Bar Food
1601
Pearse St. Tel. 021/772529. Bar food 12-2.30 and 6.30-9.30 Credit Cards: Visa, Access.

The theme of the front bar is the Battle of Kinsale (1601), and there is an enigmatic mural which is supposed to explain how it was won or lost, which can provoke many a lively argument. The back bar, which is decorated in chrome and black like an up-market cafe, doubles as an art gallery, and has changing selling exhibitions featur-ing the work of local artists. The bar food is well above average, with chicken dish-es, pasta combinations, stir fries, fresh local seafood and a choice of one or two puddings. There is a real espresso machine, and cappuccino is served all day.

Cafe
MOTHER HUBBARD'S
12 Market Place. Tel. 021/772212. Open 9-5.30, closed Weds. off season and when Trev goes fishing.

This friendly little caff run by a family from Yorkshire is something of a Kinsale insti-tution, and is the place to be seen breakfasting, at any hour of day. Their home-made scones are so popular that they also sell a mix so that you can make them at home. They also do salads, real Yorkshire chips, home-made cakes and freshly-made sandwiches. These can be taken away for a quick and easy picnic.

Restaurant
THE SHACK
3 Main St. Tel. 021/774480. Open from 12 noon till late, 7 days. Reservations advisable weekends in high season. Wine licence only. Credit Cards: Visa, Access. Inexpensive.

While Kinsale is best known for its "gourmet" restaurants, there is also a need for a cheap and cheerful eatery like this one, which manages to keep all main courses (except sirloin steak and fillet of cod) under £4. Yes, £4. There is a crazy ranch theme to the oddly shaped room, which is shaded by narrow Venetian blinds and has heavy pine tables and chairs on a flagstone floor and murals on the walls. Home made burgers, lasagne, chicken curry and shepherd's pie are typical menu items.

PIAZZETTA
Milk Market. Tel. 021/774311. Open 12.30-2.30 and 6-9, mid-March-31 Oct. Booking advisable evenings high season. Wine licence only. Credit Cards: Visa, Access. Inexpensive.

There is a continental atmosphere to this stylish little cafe which is not surprising as it is run by a German, Dagmar Rekkers. The reason that the pizzas are so good is that they are cooked to order in a proper pizza oven. There is a selection of non-pizza dishes including gnocchi with parmesan, goulash, Turkish meat rolls, and a whole range of vegetarian choices. Ice cream sundaes are served in tall glasses with paper parasols to keep the children happy.

Bar Food/Restaurant
JIM EDWARDS
Short Quay. Tel. 021/772541. Restaurant open 12.30-2.30 and 6-9.30, closed Tues. dinner mid-Nov.-mid-March; Bar food available to 9.30. Restaurant - booking advisable weekends and high season. Credit Cards: Visa, Access, Amex, Diners. Moderate.

Jim Edwards is renowned for the quality of his steaks and sea food, all of which he personally selects daily, while his wife Paula supervises the front of house. The dark red bar is relatively spacious and comfortable with some interesting pieces of nautical memorabilia around the fireplace. The separate restaurant is unpretentiously decorated with soft lighting, dark red carpets and curtains, and dark green place mats on the wooden tables. It's worth trying a fillet steak here - plain or in pepper sauce or with garlic butter - or a generous portion of seafood such as king prawns in a basil and garlic cream sauce, or medallions of monkfish with fresh herbs.

Bar Food/Restaurant/B & B
THE WHITE HOUSE
Pearse St. Tel. 021/772125. lunch menu 12.30-3, dinner menu 6-10. Restaurant open 12.30-2.30 and 6-10. Booking advisable weekends and high season. Credit Cards: Visa, Access. Moderate.

Behind the small bar of this old town house is an intimate low-ceilinged restaurant with rough-cast white walls which specialises in steaks and simply prepared sea food like black sole on the bone. Upstairs there are five exceptionally pretty bedroom with brass bedsteads, pink and white matching duvets and curtains, and pine bathroom fittings. They are all en suite with TV and direct dial phone.

Restaurant
THE VINTAGE
Main St. Tel. 021/772502. Open from 7pm; closed Sun. in winter, 14 Jan. - 28 Feb. Booking advisable. Full restaurant licence. Credit Cards: Visa, Access, Amex, Diners. Expensive.

This is one of Kinsale's most famous gourmet restaurants. The low-beamed downstairs front room of an old town house has been cleverly converted into a pretty, romantic little restaurant, which is decorated with antiques and rust-coloured swagged curtains. There is a tiny bar for a pre-dinner drink while you consider the menu. Michael Riese, who was formerly the chef at the Four Seasons hotel in his native Hamburg, uses only local produce, and everything is cooked to order. Hot smoked salmon steak is one of his best known dishes, and his version of oysters in a sauce of dry white wine, cream and sorrel is also highly acclaimed. There is a carefully chosen wine list to complement the food. While the Vintage is the perfect place for a special celebration, the atmosphere remains pleasantly informal, and holiday-makers are not expected to dress up, though personally I feel that food as special as this deserves a jacket and tie and its feminine equivalent.

MAX'S WINE BAR

Main St. Tel. 021/772443. Open 1-3 and 7.30-11; closed 1 Nov.- 7 Dec. and 24 Dec.- 28 Feb. Booking advisable weekends and high season. Wine licence only. Credit Cards: Visa, Access. Moderate.

The food and the service in this tiny but elegant place are closely supervised by the owner, Wendy Tisdall. The small tables and the tall bar are always highly polished, and there is a pretty little conservatory in the back. It is a favourite with the Ladies who Lunch, partly because it is one of the few restaurants around to take salads seriously. There is always a choice of three which can, like most of the starters, also be ordered as a main course. Another popular option is the home-made beefburger, although this might give the wrong idea of Wendy's fashionable and adventurous menu. She was, for example, the first to introduce deep-fried cheese to Kinsale, but this year she will no doubt have moved on. The home-made soup and the brown bread are always excellent; so is the seafood, and there is always an appetizing vegetarian choice.

THE BOAT HOUSE

Summer Cove. Tel. 021/774400. Open from 7 nightly, Suns. 12.30-2.30, mid-March-31 Oct. and 15 Dec.-1 Jan. Booking advisable weekends. Wine licence only. Credit Cards: Visa, Access. Moderate.

Being a converted boat house, this place is right on the water's edge. In high season you can be picked up by speedboat at the town pier - ask when you book. The small restaurant is on two narrow floors with much natural wood about, and spills out on to a terrace or the lawn if the weather is kind. It has become a very popular Sunday lunch venue since opening in 1990, but even in the evening there is usually something going on the water outside - yachts, sailing dinghies, windsurfers, waterskiers and trawlers passing. The kitchen will have a new team for the 1992 season, and the menu has not been finalised at the time of writing, but will certainly feature local seafood and steaks.

Bar Food/Restaurant/Hotel

THE BLUE HAVEN

3 Pearse St. Tel. 021/772209. Bar food served to 9.30 all day menu; lunch menu 12.30-3, dinner menu 5.30-9.30. Restaurant open from 7-10.30. Booking advisable weekends and high season. Credit Cards: Visa, Access, Amex, Diners. Expensive.

The seafood at Brian and Ann Cronin's hotel is internationally famous. The three-storey town house has been lovingly converted into characterful place that is everything a small hotel should be. Bar food is served in the lounge bar, the conservatory and the patio, which are all decorated with swagged curtains, hanging plants and nautical brass. The quiet, pastel coloured restaurant overlooks a romantic little garden whose fountain is adorned by cherubs. The seafood is a must here, whether you choose your own lobster and oysters from the tank or try one of the chef's imaginative seafood dishes - for example, poached fillets of Dover sole with oysters and saffron tagliatelle. Non-fish eaters are not neglected, with a choice of steaks, chicken and veal dishes. If you're eating bar food, do try the acclaimed seafood pancake or the seafood canneloni. There are 10 rooms, 7 with bath, and all with direct dial phone and TV. Some are rather small but they are all decorated to a high standard with original paintings by local artists, heavy curtains and well-cared for antique furniture.

Hotel

ACTON'S

Pier Rd. Tel. 021/772135. Credit Cards: Visa, Access, Amex, Diners. Expensive.

This is Kinsale's biggest hotel with 56 bedrooms and a good location on the town pier. Insist on a room with a sea view when you are booking; they all have en suite bathrooms, phone etc., but not all have a sea view. This is the only hotel in town with a leisure centre including an indoor heated pool, sauna and gymnasium. The hotel was once a private house, and the original weather-slated building has been unobtrusively extended. It is owned and managed by Trust House Forte.

THE TRIDENT
Pier Head. Tel. 021/ 021/772301. Credit Cards: Visa, Access, Amex, Diners. Moderate.

This is a modern, purpose-built hotel beside the town's main pier. All the bedrooms are identical with modern furniture, large plate glass windows overlooking the harbour and the hotel's private marina, and all have en suite bathrooms, TV and direct dial phone. It is very popular with groups (usually all male) on deep sea fishing holidays. The Savannah Restaurant, which overlooks the harbour, does a better-than-average carvery Sunday lunch, and there is bar food available until 9PM in the Fisherman's Wharf Bar.

Guest House

THE OLD BANK HOUSE
Pearse St. Tel. 021/774075. Wine licence. Credit Cards: Visa, Access, Amex, Diners. Moderate.

This large Georgian town house at the entrance of the town was once the Munster and Leinster Bank, and opened as a guest house in 1991. It is owned and managed by the people who run the Vintage Restaurant, and shows the same attention to detail and comfort. The nine spacious bedrooms (all with TV, direct dial phone and bathroom) have double-glazing, and are luxuriously appointed with good quality plain fitted carpets, classically draped curtains on the tall Georgian windows matching the pale yellow walls, and nice details like dried flowers and the occasional framed modern print. The large honeymoon suite on the third floor is the most expensive room, but is still cheaper than the town's hotels, and has a magnificent view over the harbour, a large bathroom and a super-king-size bed. An added attraction here is a very good value package which includes a bed for the night and dinner at the Vintage.

B & B

SCILLY HOUSE
Scilly. Tel. 021/772413. Open Easter-mid-Oct. Wine licence. Credit Cards: Visa, Access. Moderate.

The gates of this large, detached Georgian house are just across the road a few yards beyond the Spaniard. It was built in 1740 and has magnificent views over the harbour as well as a beautifully tended garden. Antique pine furnishings, chintzy curtains, traditional American quilts and folk art, and original watercolours by the American co-owner, Karin Young, combine to give the place an unusual atmosphere, part luxury American home, part Irish country house. Breakfast, for example, features croissants, omelettes and fresh fruit as an alternative to the ubiquitous "fry". There is a large sitting room with a Georgian fireplace, as well as a library with a wine bar and a grand piano. The seven bedrooms are clean and fresh with a tasteful pink and white floral motif, country pine furniture and luxurious en suite bathrooms, but all you will really be looking at is the tremendous view of Kinsale Harbour.

SAN ANTONIO
1 Friar St. Tel. 021/772341. Open all year, but phone to confirm Nov.-March. Inexpensive.

This substantial weather-slated Georgian house is beside the parish church, and up until about 50 years ago was the home of the parish priest. It has a wonderfully old fashioned atmosphere, with a large, cluttered sitting room with a TV just inside the door. Jimmy Conron has six rooms on the top two storeys, the four en suite ones being the nicest, with full length curtains at the double glazed Georgian windows, duvets patterned with Chinese-style birds and flowers, and antique pieces that have been in the house forever. The breakfast room has William Morris wallpaper matching the dark turquoise curtains, and separate tables. Jimmy's breakfasts always feature an offer of porridge; he is a master of this little appreciated traditional food.

TIERNEY'S
70 Main St. Tel. 021/772205. Credit Cards: Visa, Access, Amex, Diners. Inexpensive.

There are ten small bedrooms en suite on the two floors above this traditionally painted shop front in the centre of town. All the rooms have TV and direct dial phone, and are furnished in neutral pastel colours with matching floral duvets and curtains.

HARBOUR HILL HOUSE
Tel. 021/772145. Inexpensive.

At the first "Welcome to Kinsale" sign arriving on the Cork road there is a crossroads; turn left here and keep on for about a mile until you come to the gate on the left hand side which is clearly marked "Harbour Hill House". Do not take the gate before it which is marked "Harbour Hill Farm". The double-gabled brown and white two-storey house is at the end of a half-mile drive, high on a bluff of land overlooking Oysterhaven Creek and outer Kinsale harbour, and is sheltered from the prevailing winds by a belt of mature pines. It is a stupendous location, with cliff-side walks in ten acres of land and garden, and foot-access to a nearby rocky cove with good swimming. There are five rooms, two of them en suite, plushly furnished in the modern style. The breakfast room has an old pine dresser and opens through patio doors on to a terrace overlooking the sea. If you are interested in dogs, ask to meet the Irish wolfhounds, who are normally kept well segregated from guests.

Hostel
DEMPSEY'S HOSTEL.
Tel. 021/772124. Inexpensive.

This is a small, independent hostel with 24 beds in dormitory rooms beside a petrol station on the main road into town. The accommodation is very basic, with 4,6 or 8 bunk beds to a room, coin-operated showers and cooking facilities, but hostellers like this place because it is small, central and friendly.

Shops and Galleries
The town centre is so compact that your best bet is to wander around and look at whatever takes your fancy. Craft and gift shops come and go all the time in such a busy town, but the following places are all well-established, and have something special to offer. **Cronin's Commercial Hall**, Pearse Street, is a draper's shop with a good range of crystal, ceramics, gifts, sweaters, sweatshirts and T-shirts with Kinsale logos, caps, mohair, books and small souvenirs. There is also a bureau de change. **Boland's**, Pearse Street, has a bureau de change and a craft shop behind the newsagents, with a particularly good stock of Irish-made and designed clothing and a well-selected collection of other Irish-made goods including Nicholas Mosse pottery, jewellery and books. **The Gourmet Store**, Short Quay, is a cross between a fishmonger and a delicatessen; assemble a picnic here or buy a cooked lobster and its sauce for supper. **Antiques and Bygones**, Short Quay, specialises in Victorian jewellery and silver, old lace and other attractive bits and also sells a carefully selected range of small, mainly Victorian furniture. **Irish Arts and Crafts**, Main Street, stocks as huge selection of modern jewellery by Renee Rich, as well as unusual hand-knits, hand-made leather shoes, kites and a selection of Irish-made and designed clothing. **The Rattle Bag**, Main Street, concentrates on well-designed contemporary crafts which cannot be found everywhere, including wrought iron candleabra, rush baskets, wood turnings, stone carvings, papier mache and ceramics. **Kinsale Silver**, Pearse Street, sells the work of Kinsale sil-

versmith Pat Dolan and his team, which extends from small pieces of jewellery to cutlery, coffee sets and so on made to order. **Keane on Ceramics**, Pier Road is a gallery featuring a good selection of the witty and adventurous decoratvie ceramics currrently being produced in Ireland. **Giles Norman Photography Gallery**, Guardwell, sells strongly composed orginal black and white prints of unusual Irish scenes. **John MacCarthy Photographer**, Market Street, has a special line in local views and maritime photography. His block-mounted colour prints of Kinsale in all seasons are very popular with both locals and visitors. **Jeffer's Art Gallery**, Main Street, holds regular exhibitions of both established and new artists, some mixed, some solo.

OLD HEAD VILLAGE

Bar Food

THE SPECKLED DOOR
Tel. 021/778243. Bar food available all day.

Signposts for the Old head of Kinsale will bring you past this bar, which is actually about a mile away from the promontory itself beside a little harbour. The decor is basic, but this is a friendly, well-run establishment which has been in the Lordan family for over 40 years, and is now run by their son, John. Bar food consists of soup and sandwiches. Even though they have a busy passing trade in the summer, the bar has kept the atmosphere of a small, friendly local, with a pool table and a darts board in the back bar, and tables outside in the summer. The door really is speckled, but according to John the name is all a mistake owing to inaccurate transliteration of the local townland's name, which actually refers to a speckled rock in the nearby harbour.

10 | **CHAPTER TEN**

Courtmacsherry Bay to Clonakilty

In this chapter we head west by travelling around the edge of Courtmacsherry Bay through the picturesque village of Timoleague, with its ruined abbey, to Courtmacsherry, a small village consisting of a line of colourful cottages along the water's edge, backed by lightly wooded hills. From there we head across country, over the beautiful Seven Heads peninsula, to the market town of Clonakilty at the head of Clonakilty Bay. This is the start of the coast of west Cork, an increasingly popular holiday destination offering a combination of sandy beaches, rocky coves, attractive little villages and generally unspoilt countryside, ideal territory for scenic walks and drives. Kinsale to Clonakilty is 18 miles on the main road; this route is a little longer, but can easily be covered in a leisurely half-day.

Leave Kinsale by crossing the bridge over the Bandon River and following signposts for Ballinspittle. (See Chapter Nine). Drive straight through the village towards Garrettstown strand, ignoring the signpost for Clonakilty at the end of the village. Instead, turn right at Garrettstown strand to take the more scenic route on the seaward side of **Garrettstown Woods**. There is a car park with picnic tables on this road if you would like to stop and WALK along the paths in the softwood plantation. A left turn at the first crossroads and a second left about a mile on leads to **Howes Strand**, a sandy beach with good swimming, and a pleasant WALK to the west of it. The large ruin on the east side of the strand is an old coastguard station.

After about 3 miles, the road past Garrettstown Woods joins the Clonakilty road (R600) at a T-junction. Turn left. After another 3 miles the road emerges on the edge of the inner part of **Courtmacsherry Bay**. If you look back after the first causeway, **Coolmaine Castle** can be seen at the water's edge. The castle is privately owned (by Walt Disney's nephew), but there is a good WALK of a about a mile along the water's edge beside it, and also safe swimming. Just before the causeway there is a signpost for **Kilbrittain** (3 miles), which leads to a small village built around a restored de Courcey castle (privately owned). On the way to the village is a very pretty forest park, Kilbrittain Woods, with good WALKS.

As the road climbs towards **Harbour View** the village of Courtmacsherry can be seen across the water. At low tide there is very good bird life along the silted-up creek on the left of the road. The ruined silhouette of **Timoleague Abbey** at the water's edge forms a striking approach to the town. Park beside it, and walk around the back to find the gate. It was built in the mid-14th century, and is one of the best preserved early Franciscan friaries in the country. The friary was sacked by the English in 1642, but up until that time, the friars were famous for importing Spanish wine, as the creek had not yet silted up, and was still navigable. Until the middle of this century it was used as a graveyard, but, if you ignore the relatively modern headstones, the ground plan of the old abbey can still be traced - chapel, refectory, cloisters and wine cellar. Photographers will enjoy the sea views framed by its arched windows.

From here, follow the signposts for Timoleague Castle Gardens which lead to the other side of town. The large Hiberno-Romanesque Catholic church on the hill-side has a triple stained glass window by Harry Clarke (1889-1931). The smaller Church of Ireland church beside the castle gates is worth visiting as its interior is entirely covered in mosaic and gold leaf - a gift from HRH the Maharajah of Gwalior. The tiny squares of ceramic, some adorned with gold leaf, were laid out on trays on the lawn in front of the castle before being stuck on to the church walls. On the back wall, above the entrance, is a mosaic mural of Christ and the Apostles, and the whole is a good example of the highly decorative style favoured at that time by the Oxford Movement. It is well worth seeing. The church is usually open, but to get the full effect the lights should be turned on, and the name and address of the person who

Nik liked Timoleague — didn't have time to explore gds

can do that is stuck on the inside of the church door.

The gates of **Timoleague Castle Gardens** *(Tel. 023/46116. Admission £1.20 adults, 60p children. Open Easter weekend and mid-May- mid-Sept. , daily noon-6)* are just beside the church. The castle has been replaced by a grey stone house, built in 1923, but the original gardens, part of them beside the Argideen River, have survived. All that remains of the 16th- century tower house are two ivy-covered storeys. There is a mature shrubbery, a riverside walk, and two large walled gardens, one for flowers and one for fruit and vegetables.

From Timoleague follow signs across the bridge to **Courtmacsherry**. The road runs along the water's edge, and the mud flats here are usually teeming with bird life. Courtmacsherry is a good base for deep sea fishing, and there are also plenty of sandy beaches in the area to keep the children happy. It is extremely proud of its life-boat, the nearest to the east being in Ballycotton, east of Cork Harbour, and to the west in Baltimore. It can usually be seen moored off the pier. Courtmacsherry has long been a popular weekend and holiday resort. From 1886 to 1961 it was connected to Cork by a branch railway line, and went into a decline after its closure, from which it has now recovered. About 40 self-catering cottages have been completed in the last few years, about two thirds of them in existing houses, which has put new life into the place without entirely swamping it, and allowed its 3 pubs to stay in business.

The building that is now the Courtmacsherry Hotel was the home of the 2nd Earl of Shannon. He was a keen horticulturalist and planted many exotic shrubs and trees in the demesne, which now forms part of the village. He also laid out the woods which form such an attractive background to the village. To appreciate the landscaping take a WALK from the pier to **Woodpoint Wood**. There are several paths through the wood leading to little coves and the point itself, (2 1/2 miles) which is opposite Coolmaine Castle at the mouth of the open sea.

Another good WALK (about 3 miles), known as the "Fuchsia Walk" can be found by turning right at the Church of Ireland and taking the first left up Ramsey Hill. Take the first left after a group of houses and past the next house turn right at the signpost for "Fuchsia Walk", which runs along a raised ditch.

From Courtmacsherry there are two choices: the inland road to Clonakilty passing Lisnagun Ring Fort, or the coastal road through Butlerstown, exploring the cliff walks and sandy coves and beaches around Seven Heads. If you opt for the latter, leave Courtmacsherry by turning right at the Church of Ireland and following Butlerstown signposts. Beyond Butlerstown there are no more villages, only a network of small roads. Four or five of them lead to the coast at Seven Heads; another good bet is Dunworley Bay, (follow signposts for Dunworley Cottage Restaurant), which has a beautiful sandy beach under a steep cliff, and good WALKS. Clonakilty is signposted to the west at the more important cross roads; to find your way around here, even if you have a map, it is best to use the old method, and "follow your nose". If you want to visit Lisnagun Ring Fort on your way to Clonakilty, turn right in the village of Ring.

The direct route to Lisnagun involves back-tracking to Timoleague and turning left on to the R600. The second turning on the left, which should be signposted by summer of 1992, leads after about 4 miles to **Lisnagun Ring Fort** *(Open 10-6, 1 May-30 Sept. Nominal admission charge to be confirmed)*. This is the site of an early Christian farmstead, which was excavated in 1987. It is now being reconstructed, using information gained from the excavation, by a team of local volunteers. Ringforts, with a palisade built on earth ditches enclosing living quarters - usually thatched huts - were typical dwelling places of nobles and "strong farmers" from around 500 B.C. to 1000 A.D. Cattle raising was the main activity, and wealth and status were measured by the number of cattle owned. To prevent cattle raids, the beasts were kept in the enclosure at night. It is the first *rath* (as they are called in Irish) to be reconstructed *in situ*. There are many hundreds around the country, but usually they are only visible as a circle of raised earth, now grassed over.

Turn left on the R600 and continue into Clonakilty on the main N71. If you are travelling direct to Clonakilty from Cork or Bandon on the N71 you will pass through the
village of **Ballinascarthy**, the ancestral home of Henry Ford, the motor car maker.
In fact his grandparents came from Ballinascarthy; he was not born there himself.
But when he heard that the ancestral home - a modest cottage - was up for sale he
decided to buy it and have it shipped out to America. Then he discovered how
much this would cost, and abandoned the plan.   *lovely market time v· colourful*

It is well worth stopping in **Clonakilty**, so avoid the by-pass and head for the
town centre. Clonakilty was founded in 1614 by Richard Boyle and became a centre
of linen manufacturing and flour milling. In the famine which devastated the surrounding countryside in the 1840s, people crowded into Clonakilty in the hope of
seeking refuge at the workhouse. The workhouse, alas, was impossibly over-crowd-
ed and inadequately prepared for the scale of the disaster, and Clonakilty became
synonymous for miles around with death, so that whenever people said "Clonakilty"
they added "God help us". "Clonakilty, God help us" was still heard among the older
folk when I was growing up in the 1960s.

Nowadays Clonakilty has become something of a show piece due to a local planning policy encouraging hand-painted wooden shop signs with an emphasis on the
Irish language. One of the best places in Cork to hear traditional music in pubs, it is
also a popular centre for people visiting the many sandy beaches nearby.

Turn left off the main street just before the large Catholic church and park in
Emmet Square. Well-proportioned Georgian houses are built around this central
green away from the busy through-traffic. On the road linking the square to the main
street is a small Presbyterian church which is now used as a post office. Behind the
church is a complex of fine 19th century mill buildings which have been cleverly renovated and contain the town's library and council offices.

Back on the main road, almost opposite the Catholic church is the **West Cork
Museum** *(Open 10.30-5.30, Mon.-Sat. in summer)* which has a collection of items
of local historical interest, including mementos of Michael Collins who was born
nearby. (See below - Woodfield).

A mile and a half north of the museum (take the second right -R599- as you drive
through Clonakilty) is **Templebryan Stone Circle**, near the village of
Shannonvale. The circle is near a road junction south east of the village, and
about half the original stones remain: five large standing ones, and a white central
stone. They are much bigger than any of the other stones in the area, and it must
once have been an important site. (See Drombeg, Chapter Eleven). Nearby, on the
hill above, is an 11-foot tall ogham stone with badly weathered carvings on one side
and a cross on the other. This is near the site of Templebryan church, which was an
ancient centre of worship built within the enclosure of a ring fort.

Clonakilty's beach, **Inchydoney**, is a mile and a half south of the town and can
be reached by returning to the roundabout where the Cork road arrives, and following signs off the by-pass. Inchydoney was previously an island, but is now connected to the mainland by a causeway. There is excellent swimming here, and shifting
sand dunes which provide good shelter for picnics. If you are prepared to walk
about half a mile you can escape the crowds who tend to congregate near the hotel
and car park.

From Inchydoney the coast road to **Galley Head** gives access to several other
beaches - **Dunmore, Dunnen, Donnycove**, and **Red Strand** (also known as
Dirke Bay) beside **Galley Head Light House**. There are good cliff WALKS all
around the area, one of the best being the road from Red Strand out to Galley Head
light house (about 2 miles round trip). You can see the scant remains of an ancient
promontory fort **Dunoure Castle**, on the western side of Galley Head. It is almost
on an island, connected to the mainland only by a narrow isthmus which was an
important feature of its defences. Another interesting WALK can be taken along the

eastern headland of Red Strand, which is known as **Dunowen**. The pathway passes **Our Lady's Well**, an ancient place of pilgrimage which is still visited today (about a mile round trip).

This peninsula is a little more heavily colonised with small holiday homes than the Seven Heads in the east, but, until the hotel at Owenahincha in the west, is still a remarkably quiet and unfrequented area by most standards. The coast road continues west passing **Castlefreke**, an extraordinary ruined house which was built in Tudor-Gothic style with turrets and large chimneys, which can be explored by the curious. The basements are still intact, and it is possible to guess at the lay-out of the house. There is a car park near it which also gives access to woodland WALKS. South of the wood is the church of **Rathbarry**, which was built in 1832 and abandoned a century later. Beside it stand the ruins of the 16th century **Rathbarry Castle**. Both can be seen from the house.

In the 18th and 19th century this remote area was populated by a sizeable colony of English settlers, chief among them the Earls of Carbery, whose family name was Freke, hence Castlefreke. It was built in the mid-19th century, and burnt down in accidental fire in 1910. It was then rebuilt with insurance money, but in the 1930s Lord Carbery, a keen aviator, uneasy with the changes that had taken place in Ireland since independence, decided to renounce his title and leave his mansion to make a life for himself in Africa, where he found congenial company in the "Happy Valley" set. He is said to be the person who invented the "sport" of dropping live chickens from aeroplanes. The army took the castle over for a time, and then it was used sporadically for local social events. In the 1950s its roof was removed, and it has been declining ever since, although there is now talk of restoring part of it as an "amenity centre". Beyond Castlefreke is **Owenahincha**, a long, sandy beach, marred by some of the ugliest coastal development in the county, dating from the unenlightened 1960s.

The coast road rejoins the main N71 just east of Roscarbery. Turn left to reach it; if you want to visit the birthplace of Michael Collins at **Woodfield**, turn right on to the N71 and backtrack for about four miles. It is clearly signposted off this road to the north. There is a memorial to Michael Collins (See Chapter Seven - Beal na mBlath) at **Sam's Cross**, which was unveiled by General Tom Barry, himself a prominent figure in the Republican movement. The little homestead at **Woodfield** is about a mile further north. It was opened in 1990, the centenary of Collins' birth, by President Hillery. The homestead was burnt out in 1921 by the Black and Tans, and the remains were restored by Collins' nephew, a solicitor from Clonakilty, with the help of the local historical society. The intention was to create a simple memorial to the man, without the political overtones of Beal na mBlath, and this has been touchingly achieved. The original house, a small two-roomed cottage at the back of the site, has been re-roofed, and temporary exhibitons are mounted here. The cottage is interesting in itself for giving an idea of the mean proportions of the average 19th century family home. The larger house in front, of which only the foundations remain, was built in 1900, and Collins lived here with his family until 1906, when he left for London at 15 years old, like so many other young men from the district. The modest grounds are appropriately landscaped, and there is a bronze head of the famous man on a plinth.

Special Events
Courtmacsherry Regatta - first week in August. *Courtmacsherry Shrimp Festival* - mid-September. Tel: 023/46493. *Clonakilty Busking Festival* - late August - Tel. 023/33220.

Sporting Facilities
Golf: *Dunmore House Golf Club*, Dunmore, Clonakilty. Tel. 023/33352. 9-hole.

Clubs available. **Tennis**: Community Centre, Clonakilty; Courtmacsherry village. **Horse Riding**: *Courtmacsherry Hotel*, Tel. 023/46198 (1 April-30 Sept.). *Ardnavaha House Hotel*, Tel. 023/39135. **Bicycle Hire**: *Jim Healy*, Rossa St. Clonakilty. No tel. **Boat Hire - Deep Sea Angling**: *Courtmacsherry Hotel*, Tel. 023/46198 or enquire at Courtmacsherry Pier. **Trout and salmon angling:** for visitors' tickets on the Argideen river contact *Argideen Anglers' Association,* c/o Peter Wolstenholme, Courtmacsherry Ceramics, Courtmacsherry, tel. 023/46239.

PUBS, RESTAURANTS, SHOPS AND ACCOMMODATION
(Price Categories are explained in HOW TO USE THIS BOOK)

BALLINASCARTHY

Hotel

ARDNAVAHA HOUSE
Near Clonakilty. Tel. 023/39135. Credit Cards: Visa, Access, Amex, Diners. Expensive.

Ardnavaha is way out in the country in the middle of a triangle with Bandon, Clonakilty and Timoleague at the apexes. The best way to find it, coming from Cork or Bandon, is to follow the signpost for the hotel to the left in the village of Ballinascarthy, which is on the N71 about 7 miles west of Bandon.

The house, which has two storeys over a basement and a large fanlight over the front door, was built in the Georgian style in 1812 on the site of an earlier MacCarthy castle. The 40 bedrooms are in a modern block which is well concealed by the facade of the house. It is set in 40 acres of park, meadow and woodland, and has an equestrian centre in the grounds, an outdoor heated pool, sauna, mountain bikes for hire, and facilities for croquet, tennis and volley ball.

The interior is disappointing after such an attractive facade, with an intrusive reception desk built in the finely proportioned hall. Bedrooms in the modern 3-storey extension block all have bathrooms en suite and direct dial telephones. The decor schemes feature veneered built-in furniture, with hessian covered walls, floral duvets with matching curtains, and variously patterned carpets. There are good views from all rooms over the rolling countryside. Above the entrance hall of the old house is a spacious chintzy sitting room for residents, and next to it a separate TV and video room.

The Stable Bar overlooks the courtyard and its swimming pool. It has a high pitched roof, a large open fire and exposed stone walls on which old harnesses and saddles hang. In summer bar food is served, which can be eaten at outdoor tables. The dining room is in the main house, in two interconnecting rooms. The linen-draped tables have white leatherette low modern chairs which contrast oddly with the formally elegant dark red curtains. At dinner there is a five-course French-influenced set menu.

BUTLERSTOWN

B & B

SEA COURT
Tel. 023/40151. Open 8 June-20 Aug. Moderate.

Butlerstown is a tiny village in the middle of the Seven Heads peninsula, and is best approached initially by following signposts from Timoleague for 4 miles. Sea Court is a Georgian mansion built in 1760 with a fan-lighted doorway beneath a pillared porch. It is set in ten acres of wooded gardens, and has a view of the sea across its terraced lawn. The interior has been simply and tastefully restored by an American architect. Rooms are uncluttered with pale pastel walls and carpets and some very attractive pieces of antique furniture. There are 4 rooms, each with private bathroom and all have peaceful views. Outside the B & B season the entire house can be rented by the week or the month.

Restaurant
DUNWORLEY COTTAGE

Tel. 023/40314. Open 6.30-9.30 Weds.-Sun.; Sunday lunch from 12.30, but check by phone for extended hours in high season. Advance booking advisable. Full restaurant licence. Credit Cards: Visa, Access. Moderate.

This is one place that I am not going to attempt to give precise directions to, because I usually get lost myself on the way there. From Timoleague, Courtmacsherry or Clonakilty follow the signposts for Butlerstown or Barryroe where you should pick up the restaurant's own signposting system. The cottage is right on top of a cliff, so if you're heading for the sea you should be going in the right direction.

It is a very beautiful part of the coast, which is one good reason for going there. The other is the highly unusual food served by the owner, Katherine Noren. From her predecessor, Otto Kunze, she inherited a restaurant committed to fresh, high quality organic produce with each dish freshly prepared as it is ordered (so be prepared for a longer than average wait). The menu indicates vegetarian, vegan, gluten-free, and low cholesterol options, something which the purely sybaritic may find rather tedious. Nettle soup and mussel broth were among the favourite starters in Otto's day, and to these Katherine, who is Swedish, has added her authentic gravadlax with mustard and dill sauce, and marinated herring. It is the sort of menu that tempts you to make a meal out of three or four starters. On a budget the best bet is to stick to the set menu of the day. There is a full selection of organically-raised meat for carnivores; fish and shellfish are excellent, and include brill, salmon, and a very special crab gratin. The bread, which is all, of course, made on the premises, is especially tasty. Fresh herbs are grown in the cottage garden and all other vegetables come from local organic suppliers. I did not ask whether they also eat the geese which roam freely outside the windows of the conservatory section of the dining room. If you book far enough in advance you can specify a table here (preferable on warm summer evenings) or in the small inside dining room (warmer in the winter) which has an open fire. Tables and chairs are of all different sorts, with cheery gingham cloths in the conservatory and white napery with mats inside. The walls are plastered with framed testimonials from an international selection of food writers, many of whom are as stunned by the beauty of the location as they are by the discovery that rural Ireland can boast a restaurant of such gastronomic sophistication as this. Vaut le detour (which is considerable).

COURTMACSHERRY

Bar
PIER HOUSE

Tel. 023/46180.

John Young recently inherited this bar from his aunt, whose cheerful if mildly eccentric hospitality will be remembered by past visitors to Courtmac. John has refurbished the interior of this simple little pub (which overlooks the Pier) replacing the familiar old brass-railed bar with a new pine-clad one, and installing glass chandeliers and red velvet bar stools. You may or may not approve of his renovations, but he has nevertheless established himself as one of the most helpful hosts a visitor could hope to find, and the bar is effectively an informal tourist information bureau. He also serves a very good pint.

Restaurant/B & B
TRAVARA LODGE

Tel. 023/46493. Open 15 March-1 Nov. Dinner from 7.30-9. Wine licence only. Credit Cards: Visa, Access. Inexpensive.

This is a small Georgian house at the far end of the village just across the road from the sea. The restaurant is in a front downstairs room, and has original paintings by local artists on the wall, and solid 1920s wooden chairs at tables covered in a pink cloths. The a la carte menu concentrates on local seafood which is prepared by a cordon bleu cook. There are four bedrooms with shared bathrooms.

Hotel
COURTMACSHERRY HOTEL
Tel. 023/46198. Open 1 April-30 Sept. Credit Cards: Visa, Access. Moderate.

The hotel is at the far end of the village behind a low ivy-covered crenellated wall, and looks out over the harbour. This is one of the better family-run seaside hotels in Cork, aimed firmly at the solvent but not exactly rich holiday-maker. The house was originally built in the Georgian style as the family home of the Earls of Shannon, but nowadays it's not at all grand, just comfortable in a homely sort of way. There are 15 bedrooms, 10 en suite and all with TV and direct dial phone. There is a riding school in the grounds, (run by Carole Adams, one of the owners) tennis court, and boats for deep sea fishing can be arranged. The dining room appears to be just another better-than-average plain hotel food place until you get a look at the wine list which is both extensive and fascinating. Wines are personally chosen by the owner's father, an enthusiastic connoisseur, and prices are extremely reasonable. The hotel also manages a new self-catering complex next door: details from Terry Adams on the above number.

Shops and Galleries
COURTMACSHERRY CERAMICS
Tel. 023/46198. Open 10-6, Mon.-Sat. mid-March 1 Nov.

Peter Wolstenholme, originally from Yorkshire, has made Courtmacsherry his home for over 20 years now. He is highly regarded as a ceramic artist, and has exhibited widely in Ireland and the UK. His work is strongly influenced by his interest in birds and fish, although his best known work is probably the small ceramic animals which are on sale in nearly every craft shop in Cork. You'll find them here too, but this is the only place where you will also see his tableware, oven-to-table dishes and large ornamental pieces. You can buy a hand-made ashtray for as little as £1.50, or just contemplate the amazingly delicate blue and white bowls with a myriad of birds and fishes under the glaze which represent the finer side of Wolstenholme's work. He also has self-catering accommodation; anglers are especially welcome.

THE GOLDEN PHEASANT CRAFTS,
Tel. 023/46182. Open: April-June and Sept.-Dec. daily 10-6; closed Tues.; July and Aug. daily 10-7. Credit Cards: Visa, Access, Diners.

The craft shop is in a building in the middle of a small but richly planted garden, with an aviary of exotic birds beside it. There is a particularly good display of unusual, old-fashioned fuchsias, which thrive in this climate. The shop specialises in "original and traditional Irish crafts", which covers tweed, ceramics, basket-ware, sweaters, woodwork, candles and much else. There are usually also a few unusual potted plants for sale, if you can convince them that you are capable of taking good care of them.

CLONAKILTY

Bar/Music
DE BARRA
Tel. 023/33381.

This bar, in the middle of Clonakilty's main street, is a Mecca for traditional musicians from the nearby *gaeltacht* and beyond. It was one of the first places to revive the traditional hand-painted bar sign and to see the decorative value of old whiskey jars and enamel cigarette ads. Continental visitors are generally thrilled with the place, as indeed are most visitors, as Clonakilty has only recently put itself on the map for traditional music. Friday to Sunday are the best nights for music, though in the high season there will probably be something going on every night. This is also the headquarters of Clonakilty's Folk Club. For rainy days, it is worth remembering that they have a snooker table in the back room.

Bar Food/Restaurant

AN SUGAN

Wolfe Tone St. Tel. 023/33498. Bar food 11-10.30; restaurant 12.30-2.30 and 6-10 daily. Booking advisable high season. Credit Cards: Visa, Access. Inexpensive-Moderate.

If you follow the signs for the town centre coming in from the Cork direction this is about the first commercial premises on the road. The large corner house is adorned with Celtic-style hand-painted signs. Downstairs is an-L-shaped bar with natural daylight pouring in the windows, decorated in the modish rustic style with a large collection of old stone jars and the daily menu chalked up on a blackboard. An Sugan specialises in fresh fish including lobsters and oysters from their own tank. Owner Kevin O'Crowley takes the food side of his business seriously, and is usually on hand to ensure everything goes smoothly at meal times. Bar food includes home made pie of the day, and an imaginative selection of lighter dishes like stir fry chicken oriental. The upstairs restaurant is in a corner room with rustic beams and Tudor stick-back chairs. There is a four-course set menu, or you can eat a la carte. Starters often include the famous Clonakilty black pudding or dishes like seafood mousse or garlic mussels and there is a wide choice of imaginative seafood main courses, with rack of lamb or steak for meat eaters. Vegetarian and gluten-free dishes are also served.

THE SANDLIGHTER

Strand Rd. Tel. 023/33247. Bar food 12-9.30; 7 days; restaurant open from 6pm Mon.-Sat, Sunday lunch only. Booking advisable high season. Credit cards: Visa, Access. Inexpensive-Moderate.

Even though the street addresses differ, the Sandlighter is just across the road from An Sugan. The bar is nicely decorated with pine partitions framing modern stained glass, an open fire and a quarry tiled floor around the U-shaped central bar. The bar food menu has choices like seafood chowder, home made chicken and ham bouchees and roast leg of lamb with mint sauce. Upstairs there is a choice of 3 menus - a la carte, gourmet or set dinner, the gourmet being a more elaborate and expensive set menu. The restaurant has a black, red and grey colour scheme, with modern chairs at black tables set with red paper napery. Fresh fish is served according to availability: John Dory, salmon, trout, and the main alternative is steak - sirloin, T-bone or fillet. Vegetarians are also catered for.

Restaurant

DOLOREE HOUSE

Lisavaird. Tel. 023/34123. Open from 6PM Tues.-Sun. and 12.30-2.45 Sun. Booking advisable high season and Sunday lunch. Credit Cards: Visa, Access, Diners. Moderate.

This restaurant is on the N71 four miles west of Clonakilty. A modern extension and conservatory have been built onto a pink-painted traditional farmhouse by the owner-chef Joe Dolan and his wife Paula. The room is divided by banks of real house plants, and has pale pink walls and modern tweed-seated chairs at properly laid tables. The menu - choose from set or a la carte - is based on seasonal produce and is interesting without being wildly adventurous - for example, supreme of salmon poached in white wine and vermouth, or (in winter) medallions of venison in a mushroom and cranberry sauce. There is a decent wine list which features Chilean, Australian and American choices as well as French and German, with nearly all bottles under £14.

Shops and Galleries
WEST CORK CRAFT AND DESIGN CENTRE/GRAINSTORE GALLERY
Emmet Square. Tel. 023/34125. Open 10-1 and 2-6 daily. Credit Cards: Visa, Access.

This place has the best selection around of locally made crafts, displayed in a spacious old grain store in the nicest part of Clonakilty - a Georgian square hidden away behind the Catholic Church. Their stock is an impressive testimonial to the high standards of craftsmanship and the variety of products that are now being made in the area. Look out for traditionally made sally-rod baskets from Ballingeary, beeswax candles from Kealkil, cottage tweed sweaters from the Sherkin Island Co-op, pottery from Cape Clear and Bandon, kites from Ballydehob, compressed peat sculptures from Kinsale, quilts from Ballymakeera, Irish music cassettes from the Sulan Studio in Ballyvourney - and much else. Upstairs is a spacious gallery which exhibits watercolours and oils by local artists of varying degrees of accomplishment, most of which are priced at under £100.

CLONAKILTY BLACK PUDDING CO./TWOMEY'S BUTCHERS
16 Pearse St. Tel. 023/33365. Open Mon.-Sat. 9.30-6.

Confusingly, the authentic Clonakilty black pudding advertised as "made to the original Harrington's recipe", is actually produced nowadays by a butcher called Edward Twomey. You will find it on sale in his shop, and at other outlets around the county. If you really like the stuff you can also buy a "Clonakilty Black Pudding" T-shirt here. Seriously, Mr. Twomey is to be congratulated for rescuing a traditional food which was in danger of being replaced by a mass-produced, plastic-wrapped tube of bland slime. Black pudding sold here is everything it should be: a robustly seasoned concoction of pigs' blood and barley encased in pigs' intestines. Up-market Irish chefs have gone mad about it, and serve it with oysters, in mustard sauce and, no doubt someone somewhere has served it on a fruit coulis. Personally, I like it the way my grandmother served it: as one element in a mighty fried breakfast with bacon, egg, tomato and its less celebrated relative, white pudding, which is a far more subtle and unusual product altogether. Try them both and see.

HARBOUR VIEW

Bar Food/Restaurant
THE PINK ELEPHANT
Harbour View, Kilbrittain. Tel.023/49608. Restaurant open 5-6.30 for high tea and 7-9.30 for dinner, daily, and Sunday 12.30-2, April-Sept.; closed Mon. & Tues. Oct.-March. Bar food available all day. Credit Cards: Visa, Access. Inexpensive-Moderate.

The Pink Elephant's head and paws peeping over the hedge are a much-loved landmark on the Kinsale-Timoleague coast road (R600). The bar and restaurant are above him, above a sloping lawn on a height overlooking Courtmacsherry Bay. The view is absolutely spectacular, and it is worth stopping just to sit for half an hour watching the distant boats across a wide expanse of sea going in and out of Courtmacsherry harbour. The bar is in the left hand-side of the modern pink house and has an unusual bar counter modelled on an old clinker-built rowing boat. In summer there are tables outside. There is always a home-made soup of the day, served with excellent, nutty-tasting home-made brown bread. Open sandwiches are served on the same bread, or you can have a closed white one. There are also mussel dishes, smoked salmon and pates.

The dining room is pleasantly lit with pink linen cloths on tables that can be pulled together to accommodate the large parties that frequently gather here to celebrate some family occasion. The high tea menu features mixed grills, steaks and chicken dishes. At dinner there is a choice of set or a la carte menu with more sophisticated offerings like roast duckling and orange, chicken cordon bleu, or scallops mornay.

TIMOLEAGUE

Bar Food
DILLONS
Tel. 023/46390. Bar food available from 12 noon to 9.30PM June-Sept; closed 2-6 off season.

This small bar in the centre of the village serves unusually good food because it is supplied by Dunworley Cottage Restaurant (see BUTLERSTOWN above), and includes the famous mussel broth and nettle soup plus main courses like salami pizza, beef casserole and chicken in white wine sauce and apple strudel for pudding. The Victorian bar has a heavy lace curtain in the window and bistro-style tables on one side of the room.

Restaurant/Hostel
LETTERCOLLUM HOUSE
Tel. 023/46251. Restaurant open daily from 7PM and Suns. 12.30-2.30; advance booking advisable; Thurs.-Sun. only Oct.-Dec. and phone in advance to confirm. Wine licence only. Hostel and restaurant closed Jan.-Feb. Restaurant: Moderate; rooms: Inexpensive.

This place is signposted just outside Timoleague off the main Clonakilty road (the R600, not the scenic route). In its previous incarnation the large Victorian Gothic house was a convent; before that it was a private home. It was bought five years ago by a group of young people disillusioned with Dublin, who have been restoring and renovating the house, its gardens, farm and outbuildings ever since. Two of them, Con McLoughlin and Seamus O'Connell, built up an enthusiastic following while they were cooking at the 1601 in Kinsale, and their admirers have been increasing steadily since they opened the restaurant here, while strangers are dumbfounded to find such professional cooking in such strange surroundings.

The dining room is in the front room of the house, which was a chapel in the nuns' time, and still has a devotional stained glass window at one end. Nowadays it is a cheerful place hung with large contemporary paintings above a stripped pine floor, with assorted tables set with white napery. The food is freshly prepared from local produce and the produce of their own garden and farm. It is the judicious saucing of these high quality ingredients that gives the cooking such distinction- lamb with a yoghurt-based tarragon sauce, for example, or salmon with sorrel sauce. There is always a vegetarian choice on the menu prepared with just as much thought and care as the meat and fish; puff pastry filled with spinach and cream cheese or Indonesian style vegetable curry with tofu are typical, and will probably be the work of a third member of the team of chefs, Karen Austin.

Upstairs there are 6 private rooms, 3 doubles, 3 family rooms (all at £7.50 per person, £4 per child) and 2 dormitories of 8 and 10 beds at £4.50 per night. The rooms are large and very plainly furnished with sanded floors and rugs and all have big windows overlooking Timoleague estuary and the open country. You can eat breakfast in the restaurant (home-made croissants are baked daily) or make your own using the self-catering kitchen. There is a large, comfortable sitting room for residents opposite the dining room. Guests are free to wander around the 12 acres of grounds where there is a walled organic herb and vegetable garden in the early stages of restoration, and free-ranging poultry, pigs and goats. Children absolutely love it, and so do their parents, as they can feed them in the self-catering kitchen and leave them safely asleep upstairs while they eat a more indulgent meal in the restaurant below. Not surprisingly, it is advisable to book non-dormitory accommodation well in advance, especially in summer. In the autumn residential workshop weekends are held with courses in cooking and drawing; write or phone for details.

11 **CHAPTER ELEVEN**

INTO WEST CORK

There are endless arguments about where west Cork actually begins - some say Kinsale, others Clonakilty. For many it is that moment when the main road from Clonakilty to Skibbereen climbs through a cutting faced with bare rock on either side and emerges at the brow of a hill, with Rosscarbery's wide estuary spread out below. This chapter covers the most popular places on the coast of west Cork - Rosscarbery, Glandore, Castletownshend, Baltimore and Schull - its inland centres, Skibbereen and Ballydehob, and the islands of Roaring Water Bay. The distances are not great - the drive from Rosscarbery to Schull on the main road takes about an hour - but there are numerous side attractions, such as a visit to Cape Clear island, or an exploration of Lough Hyne, which would make a good day's outing in themselves.

Rosscarbery is a little cathedral town, part of the diocese of Cork, Cloyne and Ross since 1617. It is situated at the head of a shallow, landlocked inlet of Rosscarbery Bay, across which a causeway runs. The lagoon, on the inland side of the estuary, is home to a large number of swans, who enhance the already picturesque little town which is built on a bluff above its cathedral.

To visit the Rosscarbery you must detour off the main road to the right for about 500 yards. It has become a popular holiday centre, partly because of the nearby sandy beaches and now has about 70 holiday cottages, most of them new, but sympathetically designed. This has given the rather run-down village a great economic boost in recent years. It has a pleasantly old-fashioned central square which was once its market place. From here it is a short walk downhill to **St. Fachtna's Cathedral**, a small church, incorporating parts of a pre-Reformation cathedral. St. Fachtna was a 6th or 7th century bishop who founded a monastery and school here, of which only fragments remain.

There are several good beaches and cliff WALKS beyond Rosscarbery Quay. To reach the quay, turn left off the N71 at the end of the causeway. This also makes a pleasant WALK of about a mile, with much bird life on the shallow estuary beside the road - herons, curlew, plover, swans and cygnets in season. Steps lead up from the pier to the cliff top which gives a wonderful panorama of Rosscarbery Bay. Cross the stile at the top of the steps and head up the fields. Following this path will lead you back to the village (about 3 miles round trip) past the ruins of Downeen Castle, with spectacular views of the coast and the village along the way. Beware, however, of the cliff edge; there is much erosion in the area, and it is a dangerous stretch of coast for walkers. You may hear the sea rushing into the many "blow holes" around here, but be very careful if you decide to investigate more closely.

Downeen Castle is below the path on a rock which was once joined to the mainland. When this was eroded by the sea, it took half the castle with it, and what stands today is virtually a cross-section of the original building. Not much is known about the origins of the castle, which dates from at least the 15th century. In pre-historic times forts were often built on such promontories, as the narrow causeway was easily defended, so it is very likely that there was a much earlier castle here. The watchtower on the hill behind the castle dates only from the early 20th century. The path leads to a road after about a mile; turn right here for the village.

From Rosscarbery the main road to Skibbereen and Roaring Water Bay runs inland to **Leap**, a village that straggles along the main road for about a mile. Pronounced "Lep", it is named after a ravine which has now been bridged. Until the bridge across the ravine near **Myross Woods** was built in the early 19th century, people fleeing from the law could escape by urging their horses to take the "leap", thus shaking off their pursuers, as only horses familiar with the locality could manage the jump. There were no regular law-enforcers or garrisons beyond this point at that time, and so the expression "Beyond the Leap, beyond the law" came into being.

ↄ   An alternative and more scenic route to Skibbereen through Glandore, Union Hall and Castletownshend can be taken by turning left at the signpost for Glandore just beyond the causeway at Rosscarbery. This route is especially spectacular in high summer when the fuchsia is at its best. Although this plant, originally imported to England from Chile by a sailor in the 1780s, grows wild all over the coastal areas of the county, it is especially profuse in this area. Many of the tall roadside hedges are fuchsia, and it is so invasive that many people refuse to have it in their garden.

A well-signposted detour of about 3 miles off the Glandore road leads to the
Worth a visit **Drombeg Stone Circle**. Even if you are not especially interested in antiquities, this is a sight worth seeing, a remarkably intact circle, beautifully situated in a sunny open space between the surrounding hills. It is not actually visible from the car park; walk about 300 yards up the little lane. As this circle is intact, it is easy to spot the correct entrance: between the two tall uprights opposite the flat altar. An old super-stition says that to enter a stone circle any other way will lead to bad luck. Whatever about that, if you do go into this circle the right way, you will get a good understand-ing of its orientation, and its ritual design. This circle is placed so that the rays of the setting sun fall on to the flat "altar" stone at the winter solstice. The first time that I visited Drombeg it happened, accidentally, to be near the winter solstice, and the sight of weak winter sunlight penetrating through scudding clouds and coming to rest just above the flat stone was unforgettable.

These circles were used for an unknown, presumably ritual purpose about 2000 years ago. A small stream runs through the site at Drombeg, and leads to the *fulacht fiadh* - "deer roast" in literal translation, a cooking place used initially, perhaps, as part of the ritual. This works by filling one pit with water, and heating stones in fire in the other. The meat is wrapped in straw, and when the stones are hot they are put into the water to make it boil, and the meat is added.

There are records of this method of cooking large quantities of meat being used up to the 17th century, and the pit at Drombeg was recently in use for a TV docu-mentary. By all reports, the meat cooked in that way was delicious.

Return to the main road and head on for Glandore. The large ruin with tall chim-neys in a valley beside the road is **Coppinger's Court**, a fortified house built around 1630 by William Coppinger, a Cork merchant. He hoped to establish a town here, but the wars of 1641 put an end to his plans, and it has stood in ruins ever since. Mullioned windows can still be seen, with especially good ones on the fourth floor, and there are some well-preserved turrets and chimney stacks. It is rather eerie to find such a large ruin in the middle of nowhere.

 small but pretty view **Glandore** is a delightful little fishing village built on a steep hill which runs down to the edge of the water at the head of **Glandore Harbour**, a land-locked haven about one mile across and three miles long. The islands in the harbour are little more than rocks, but have been given names. The large one at the harbour mouth is Adam, and the small one further in is Eve. In the old days sailors used the expres-sion "avoid Adam and hug Eve" to remember how to get into Glandore; the modern sailing directions say the same thing in a less sexist way.

Glandore is a very popular holiday base, mainly with fairly affluent visitors, as there is no cheap rented accommodation here. Most of the holiday-makers own their own houses, or arrive by boat, with the result that the place is almost deserted in winter. It is a heavenly spot at any time of year, sheltered from the worst gales, and something of a sun trap in summer, with lovely views across the harbour to the heav-ily wooded headland opposite.

The village was improved in the mid-19th century by a progressive landlord, James Redmond Barry. Together with his neighbour, the political economist, William Thompson,(1785-1833) he made great efforts to establish a model community at

Glandore with co-operatives for fishing and industry, and a good education for girls as well as boys (in spite of Adam and Eve!). Thompson's writings were greatly admired by Marx, and there are several statues of him in Eastern Europe, but he is strangely neglected in Ireland, and you need not look for a statue of him in Glandore.

To follow the scenic route, cross the narrow bridge upstream from Glandore which leads to Union Hall, another little fishing village, very pretty in its way at high tide, but rather eclipsed by its neighbour. The name leads most people to expect a big house either in the village or nearby. In fact it was named for the 1801 Act of Union, a generally unpopular piece of legislation which deprived Dublin of its parliament. It was near here that Jonathan Swift stayed during his visit to the area in 1723. It is said he wrote his poem *"Carberiae Rupes"* while sheltering from the rain in nearby Castletownshend.

Follow the main road through Union Hall by turning left at the entrance and right at the T-junction. Follow the right bend past the church for Castletownshend. This is a particularly lovely stretch of road, passing **Rineen Woods**, where there are picnic tables and a choice of forest and seashore WALKS.

Signposted just off this road is **Ceim Hill Museum** (*Tel. 028/36280. Admission £2 adults, £1 children. Open 10-7 daily, 2-7 Sundays, but phone in advance to confirm off season*). This is a most unusual folk museum, a one-woman show, created by a herbalist, Teresa O'Mahony, in the farmhouse which has belonged to her family for generations. Her collection ranges from Iron Age farm tools to west Cork cloaks and the post-1921 Civil War.

Castletownshend, with its main street descending steeply to the sea, lined by large, stone-built, 18th- century houses is quite unlike anywhere else in Cork, or in Ireland, come to that. It grew up in the 17th and 18th centuries when a number of soldiers who had enriched themselves in the Cromwellian wars settled in the area, brought their families over from England, and set themselves up as merchants. One of the old warehouses on the quay has recently been converted into apartments. In summer the village's population of 104 is swelled to 3 or 4 times that number, but all accommodation is in existing houses, so its considerable charm remains undiminished.

The large "flower pot" in the middle of the road containing two young sycamores, is one of its many unique features. A short WALK along The Mall, which runs off at right angles here, will give you a feeling of the village. The large gates on the right-hand side of the mall belong to a house known as Glen Barrahane, which has now gone, although the gardens are still tended. It is one of several places in the village associated with Edith Somerville (1858-1949) and her family. Her own home was Drishane House, which is still in the Somerville family, whose gates can be seen at the top of the village. Edith Somerville, together with her cousin, Violet (Martin) Ross, wrote the humorous Irish R M stories, and the more serious novel, *"The Real Charlotte"*, among other books. A recent pictorial biography of the two by Gifford Lewis gives a vivid picture of the lively social life here around the turn of the century.

Somerville and Ross are buried in **St. Barrahane's Church**, which can be reached by turning left at the bottom of the village and climbing 52 steps. The graves are behind the altar end of the church, Edith's being a specially selected slab of rough granite. The view of **Castlehaven**, as the village's sheltered harbour is called, the village itself, and the off-shore islands, is well worth the climb. Have a look inside the church at the stained glass window behind the altar. It is by Harry Clarke, and was commissioned by Edith. It incorporates a black and white cow: Edith and her sister, Hidegarde were among the first to import Friesian cows into Ireland. Hildegarde also had a violet farm, which is pictured in the window too. In the church porch is an oar from one of the *Lusitania's* lifeboats, a rather poignant memento. Bodies and debris from the wreck (See Chapter Two) were washed up around this coast for months after the event. If you are interested in history you will want to take half an hour to read the inscribed plaque in the church which gives the history of the leading families of the parish, who apparently considered changing sides when it became obvious that they were on the losing one, as a matter of pride. The castle that gives the village its name is on the waterfront below the church. It is still in the Townshend family, but is private property now run as a guest-house (see below).

There are several choices when leaving Castletownshend: a sandy beach at **Tragumna**, fine for the kids, but its car park and concrete breakwaters are not to all tastes. Less frequented small coves can be found by driving around **Toe Head** (where the remains of a promontory fort can be seen). If you are keen on pre-historic remains, you will want to visit **Knockdrum Ring Fort** which is signposted on the approach road to Castletownshend. This is an early iron-age fort, with a stone wall enclosing an area 95 feet across. It was restored by Thomas Somerville in the mid-19th century, when the thick stone walls were rebuilt. This fort has a souterrain - an underground passage - originally used for storage and as an emergency escape route. It contains three chambers, and is cut from solid rock and roofed with large slabs of stone. Some of the free-standing stones have interesting markings. If you cross the fields in the opposite direction from the signpost for Knockdrum you will come to the **Garranes "Finger Stones" Alignment**, four fingers of stone set in the brow of a hill, three of them tall and thin, and one squat, which presumably once had some ritual purpose. Edith Somerville described the tall uprights as "looking like three stern priests of a forgotten religion". Originally there were five stones here, but in the last century the wife of the Somerville who restored Knockdrum had one of them removed for her rockery, where it still stands. Gardeners will understand the temptation.

Whichever option you choose here, **Skibbereen** is well-signposted from all directions. This is a busy market town (pop. 2000), the main shopping centre for the surrounding area. Irish-American visitors are often disappointed to find that Skibbereen is nothing great, as it is celebrated in one of their most popular songs, which lists "the reasons why I left auld Skibbereen". The reasons were mainly to do with failing farms and lack of other employment; between 1911 and 1961 almost half the population of the Skibbereen district emigrated. It is also widely known for its weekly paper, *The Southern Star and Skibbereen Eagle,* which shot to fame earlier this century when it warned Bismark that the *Skibbereen Eagle*, as it was then, was keeping an eye on the Czar of Russia. It is still a very effective local paper, and visitors from more metropolitan areas will find most intriguing matters of local interest, especially court cases, reported in its pages.

From here we head for Baltimore via Lough Hyne, both of which are well signposted at the east end of town. **Lough Hyne** - or Lough Ine, as it is sometimes spelt - is a marine nature reserve, a land-locked saline lake with many unusual species of marine life, and is not to be missed if you enjoy good scenery and quiet out-of-the-way places. Its wooded hillsides and sheltered location give it a very special atmosphere, something which the ancients noticed too, as there is a holy well at the top of the lake which has been a place of pilgrimage since pre-Christian times. There are also ancient remains on the island. There is excellent swimming and scuba diving here, but swimmers are warned to wear foot protection, or better still, swim in the deep water off the pier without touching the lake's bottom, as some of the sea urchins have poisonous spines. The marine life is explained in displays near the picnic tables. Water ski-ing and high-powered boats are not allowed on the lake.

There are excellent WALKS all around Lough Hyne. Follow the path up the west side to see the place where the tide surges in up a narrow gulley. If you climb the wooded hill to the south of it for about a mile, following the road past the old schoolhouse, you will get a wonderful view of Roaring Water Bay.

On the way from Lough Hyne to Baltimore you will pass the entrance to **Creagh Gardens** *(Tel. 028/21267. Admission £1.50. Open 10-6, 1 April- 30 Sept.),* an informal garden of light woodland which features many of the frost-tender plants that flourish in the west Cork climate. Parts of it are right beside the sea. There are some unusual fuchsia cultivars, good rhododendrons, camellias and magnolias, and a water garden inspired by the jungle paintings of Rousseau.

Baltimore is 8 miles from Skibbereen, and about 6 miles beyond the Lough Hyne road. **Ringarogy island**, signposted on the right just before the village, is now connected to the mainland by a causeway, but is still a good place to explore, and well off the beaten track, especially if you leave the car once you are on the island, and WALK. — break !

Baltimore is the end of the road for motorists, but worth the round trip if you plan to visit Sherkin or Cape Clear Islands. The ruined castle in the middle of the village is an O'Driscoll castle, one of several in the area built by its dominant clan. In the early 17th century Baltimore was an English settlement. In 1631 Algerian pirates raided the harbour and carried off some 200 inhabitants. Not surprisingly, the few English left in the area decided to move inland, and founded the town that is now Skibbereen. Baltimore subsequently became an important boat-building centre with a large fishing fleet. Today its economy is chiefly reliant on the holiday trade, and the numbers of newly-built self-catering units for seasonal visitors exceeds those houses occupied by permanent residents, who numbered 158 in the 1986 census. It is a lively place in summer, and at weekends throughout the year.

There is a good WALK up the hill behind the village, which takes about 20 minutes, and gives an excellent view of the islands -"Carbery's Hundred Islands" - as they are known, and the whitewashed Baltimore Beacon, often called "Lot's Wife".

Baltimore is the main departure point for the islands. Both ferries take only foot passengers and bicycles, and one of the attraction of the islands is the relative lack of traffic. (Boats also leave from Schull during July and August). **Sherkin Island** is a 5 minute trip across the sound. *(Tel. 028/20187 for details: half-hourly service in summer, about 7 ferries a day rest of the year.).* There are several small sandy beaches on the island, and abundant wild life. The picturesque ruins which can be seen as you walk up from the pier are of a 15th- century Franciscan abbey. Sherkin's marine life can be studied in detail at **Sherkin Island Marine Station**. which has an excellent **Natural History Museum** *(Tel. 028/20187. Admission £1.25, children 50p. Open daily May-Oct.)*

A visit to **Cape Clear Island** is a more serious excursion, a boat trip of about an hour through the rocky islands of **Roaring Water Bay**. *(Tel. 028/39119 for sailing times. There is usually a boat out at 2.30, returning at 5.30. Cost is about £7 return).* It is an exciting ride, most of it spent wondering how the skipper manages to avoid holing the boat on the sharp black rocks which stick up on either side of the channel. There is a Youth Hostel and a few B & Bs on the island, and it is also a popular destination for campers and yachts. It is a great place for walking, with good swimming in the south harbour, and is small enough to explore in an afternoon. It is the most southerly point of Ireland, about three miles long by one mile across, an Irish-speaking area with a population of about 170, which has remained steady for the last 20 years. The landing pier is in the north harbour, not far from the remains of **St. Kieran's Church**, a 12th- century church built on the site of the early Christian saint's original foundation. Some claim that Christianity was strong in the area before the arrival of Saint Patrick. There is also a well near the harbour - **Tobar Ciaran** which is still visited on his saint's day, 5th March.

Fifteen years ago there was only one simple pub in the North Harbour; now there is a Heritage Centre, pottery shop, craft shop and restaurant. Leave it all behind by walking up the only road. Keep straight on downhill for the South Harbour, or turn right uphill to visit **Lough Errol** and the O'Driscoll castle. The lake was once believed to have magical cleansing properties; in fact it contains rare micro-organisms which will eat away the dirt of anything soaked in it - a handy thing to know if you're camping here for a few days. On the rugged western coast of the island is

Ballyieragh, a 14th century O'Driscoll castle, built on a rock jutting out into the Atlantic. Like Downeen, (see Rosscarbery) the rock was once connected to the mainland by a causeway, and is the site of an earlier, pre-historic fort. Bird lovers will want to seek out the **Cape Clear Observatory** which keeps records of rare migrants and the sea birds which abound along this stretch of coast. Others may be interested in the windmill, which is part of an experimental electricity generating project.

From Baltimore return to Skibbereen, and drive through it heading west. The main N71 runs alongside the **River Ilen** beyond Skibbereen before turning inland and running through low hills to **Ballydehob**, 11 miles on. From the approach road, the brightly painted cottages of Ballydehob seem set among mountains; in fact they are at the head of an inlet of Roaring Water Bay which is crossed by a tall 12-arched viaduct (a relic of the West Cork Railway). It is a lively little place with something of a name as a retreat for writers, crafts-people and good-lifers. Like most of the west Cork coast, it is certainly a cosmopolitan place, with numbers of English, German, Dutch and American settlers in the area. Until the 1930s it was the chosen marketing centre for the islanders of Roaring Water Bay, and as the islands lost their population, it diminished in importance, being revived only by the arrival of tourism and foreign settlers.

There are some good WALKS hereabout. An unusual short one takes you out of town on the road beside Levis's Bar, down to the quay, and across the viaduct - a 20-minute circuit. A longer one carrying on straight in the same direction will bring you, after about 3 miles, to Rossbrin, an isolated headland with a few cottages and a ruined castle overlooking Roaring Water Bay.

From Ballydehob the road runs straight across open bogland, parallel to the line of the old West Carbery Tramway and Light Railway, a short-lived venture which opened in 1886 and closed due to shortage of fuel during World War II. It is about 6 miles to **Schull**, a fishing village on its own little land-locked harbour beneath Mount Gabriel. The two white domes on the top of the mountain are radar tracking stations; most transatlantic flights heading for Heathrow use it, including Concorde. Echoes of the "boom" as Concorde goes supersonic way out over the Atlantic can sometimes be heard in the area.

Schull gets its strange name from the Irish *Scoil Mhuire*, St. Mary's School, which was said to be an early Christian foundation linked to that of Rosscarbery. Nowadays the little village positively buzzes, and even suffers from traffic jams and parking restrictions in July and August. Several clusters of holiday homes have helped to increase the village's prosperity. There are numerous good beaches in the area, most of them small rocky coves; it is an ideal base for water sports. If you get a rainy day you might like to visit **The Planetarium**, the only one in Ireland, which is on the Colla road. *(Tel. 028/28552. Star show times subject to seasonal demand, as advertised locally, or by appointment for groups).*

There are plenty of good WALKS in the area. One of the best is to the west of the town; follow the signs for **Colla Pier**. The road runs along the west side of the harbour, and continues parallel to **Long Island**, one of the bay's inhabited islands. By taking a right turn shortly beyond the Colla Hotel you can return to Schull across country through Gubbeen - a circuit of about 3 miles with wonderful sea views. At the other end of Schull, near the point where the road from Ballydehob arrives, follow the signs for the golf course, but keep on past it and take the first right. The road passes a fully restored mill-wheel, and leads to **White Castle**, a most picturesque ruin overlooking the other side of Roaring Water Bay, and there is a little strand with good swimming just beyond. It's about 3 miles from the town centre. If you want to climb Mount Gabriel (1339 ft.), leave the town to the north, past the convent, and go up Gap Road. The return journey can be made down the other side of the mountain through Rathcool and Glaun - a fairly strenuous ten mile circuit. Walkers on Mount Gabriel are warned to look out for disused mine shafts.

From high ground around Schull the **Fastnet Light House** can be seen, standing on a large rock ten miles out to sea. A writer who visited the area in 1896 reported that "the coast peasantry have a superstition that the rock sails a mile to the westward at daybreak on the 1st of May every year". The first light house built there was finished in 1854, but was swept away by gales in 1865. It was replaced by a building of granite blocks, imported from Cornwall, which was completed in 1906. A helipad can be seen beside it. It is the furthest point reached by the Fastnet race out of Cowes. It is also used as a mark in local races during Schull's regatta, which, in recognition of the town's size relative to Cowes, and the fact that there are islands of that name in the bay, is known as "Calves Week".

Special Events
The whole area is alive with regattas and festivals from mid-July to mid-August, with Schull, Baltimore, Castletownshend and Cape Clear having regattas, a rowing regatta on Lough Hyne, and festivals in Rosscarbery, Skibbereen, Ballydehob and Schull. Entertainment can range from piggy-back races to open air concerts, and is generally free. Check local advertisements for dates and events.

Sporting Facilities
Golf: *Skibbereen and West Carbery Golf Club*, Skibbereen. Tel. 028/21227. 9-hole. *Schull Golf Club*, Cusheen. No Tel. 9-hole. **Tennis**: Public courts at Castletownshend and Schull. **Bicycle Hire**: *N.W. Roycroft & Son.*, Ilen St. Skibbereen. Tel. 028/21235. *Andy's Restaurant*, Cotter's Yard, Schull. Tel. 028/28165. **Boat Hire** (Deep sea fishing, diving or pleasure cruises): *George Salter-Townshend*, Castletownshend. Tel. 028/36268. *Sea Angling Centre*, Baltimore. Tel. 028/20319. *Schull Watersport Centre*, Pier Road. Tel. 028/28554. **Fishing**: There are salmon, brown trout and sea trout on the River Ilen; contact Skibbereen TIO for permit details, tel. 028/21766. In Schull fishing permits for Schull Reservoir (wild brown trout, rainbow trout and rudd) are available from *Newman's Bar and Shop*, at the top of the road between the town and the pier, tel. 028/28223.

PUBS, RESTAURANTS, SHOPS AND ACCOMMODATION
(Price Categories are explained in HOW TO USE THIS BOOK)
BALLYDEHOB
Bar
LEVIS
Main St. Tel. 028/37118.
The name is pronounced "Leev-iss" in these parts, and belongs to two sisters, Julia and Nell, who run this little grocery store-cum-bar. Its just across the road from Annie's Restaurant (see below), and Annie encourages her clients to read the menu over a drink in here before taking their table in the restaurant across the road. The facade is unpromising, but inside you will find one of the most friendly and unspoilt bars in the area, (some would call it quaint), which explains why many people prefer this place to more flashy establishments up the road.

Restaurant
ANNIE'S
Main St. Tel. 028/37292. Open 12.30-2.30 Tues.-Fri., 7-9 Tues.-Sat. Booking essential for dinner. Wine licence only. Credit Cards: Visa, Access. Moderate.
Young Annie Barry has been running this archetypal "front parlour" restaurant for 8 years now, and her enthusiasm and warm welcome show no signs of diminishing. The restaurant is in a small front room with a shop window on to the street, and still has the low cottagey ceiling, and walls clad in white painted wood. There are small

tables with red cloths and ladderback sugan chairs on the glazed stone floor, and charming naive watercolours of farm animals by Keggie Carew on the walls. There is a light lunch menu with fresh crab, seafood or smoked salmon open sandwiches, and dishes like home made steak burger or vegetable and cheese quiche. The four course dinner is a more substantial affair, with main courses like scallops mornay, medallions of beef with green pepper sauce, pork and chicken kebabs, and some irresistible puddings: hot chocolate fudge cake, Bailey's Cream ice cream. If you are not up to all four courses you can pick and choose and pay pro rata - an excellent idea. The menu changes monthly, and is varied by different daily specials. Be warned: this restaurant is so popular that in the high season you should book days, not hours, ahead.

Shops and Galleries
MINIATURE GALLERY
The Bridge. Tel. 028/37430. Open Mon.-Fri. and Sun. 2-6; Sat. 10-6. Credit Cards; Visa, Access.
As you will gather from the name, they specialise in original miniature paintings.

BALTIMORE
Bar
BUSHE'S BAR
Tel. 028/20125
This is a lovely old bar overlooking the harbour. Nautical folk will enjoy the amazing collection of marine artifacts in the narrow left-hand bar, which includes framed Admiralty charts and tide tables, ships' clocks and compasses, propellers, lanterns, rowlocks, pennants and much more. A limited range of bar food - open or closed sandwiches, soup of the day and salads - is available in the summer.

Bar Food/Restaurant/Music
MACARTHY'S BAR
The Square. Tel. 028/20263. Bar food available till 9PM; restaurant open high season only. Moderate.
Macarthy's is the place to go if you are looking for a music session. Musicians who would like to find others to play with are especially welcome. It is a relatively large bar overlooking the harbour. Bar food - curries, lasagne, local seafood - is served all year round, and in the summer the first floor restaurant, *The Pride of Baltimore*, serves a more formal menu featuring steaks and seafood.

Restaurant
CHEZ YOUEN
Tel. 028/20136. Open daily Easter-Sept. lunch and dinner, otherwise dinner and Sunday lunch only. Closed Nov.1-Dec.15. Credit Cards: Visa, Access, Amex, Diners. Set lunch Moderate, otherwise Expensive.
Youen Jacob, a large, energetic Breton, is the mastermind behind this superb seafood restaurant which overlooks Baltimore harbour. The room itself is simple and rustic, with a beamed ceiling, a cluttered pine dresser and copper pans hanging on the walls, but the napery, glasses and comfortable chairs are quietly elegant. Youen's seafood is the very freshest, and lobster is available year round. Fish and shellfish are served in ways that accentuate their freshness and quality - ray in black butter, for example, wild salmon or monk fish grilled and served with fennel sauce, poached lobster with lemon and butter, or a magnificent seafood platter of assorted delicacies.

Bar Food/B & B
THE ALGIERS INN
Tel. 028/20145. Bar food high season only, 4PM -10PM. Inexpensive.

The name of this establishment commemorates the sacking of Baltimore in 1631 when 119 residents of Baltimore were kidnapped into slavery by Algerian pirates, and has always struck me as a prime example of west Cork's bizarre sense of humour. The bar has been pleasantly restored and has one exposed stone wall, and a beamed ceiling that is apparently held up by cast iron pillars. There is a quieter back area with an old kitchen range still in situ. The food is all home-made, and all main courses are under £7, excellent value for dishes such as chicken Kiev, steak, and a choice of 3 or 4 fish dishes. There are ten rooms in an adjoining building which has its own separate entrance and large sitting room, all with private bathrooms, TV and direct dial phone. All rooms have a view of the sea, if not from the room itself then from the shower! They are furnished with old, not quite antique furniture, velvet curtains, patterned duvets and plain walls and carpets, and were entirely revamped by the Algiers' new owner for the 1992 season. There are also 5 cheaper rooms above the bar itself with shared bathrooms.

B & B
RATHMORE HOUSE
Tel. 028/20362. Evening meal by arrangement. Wine licence. Credit Cards: Visa, Access, Amex, Diners. Inexpensive.

You will see Rathmore House on your left about a mile outside Baltimore. It stands on high ground overlooking the harbour and the islands. It is a large detached house which at first glance appears to be Georgian, but was in fact only built in 1987 by Marguerite O'Driscoll's husband, a builder. The inside is as authentic as the outside, with moulded plaster cornices on the ceilings. There is a sitting room with TV and piano for the use of guests. All six bedrooms have a private shower and toilet, and are plainly decorated with duvets, floral cotton curtains and nice traditional furniture. The front ones enjoy a magnificent view of the harbour and islands, and there is one ground floor bedroom. Mrs. O'Driscoll is a very friendly hostess, and her home has an exceptionally pleasant atmosphere.

Shops and Galleries
BEACON DESIGNS
Tel. 028/20148. Open Mon.-Sat. 10-6.

A small craft shop near Bushe's Bar, Beacon Designs stock mainly Cork-made crafts - Jane Forrester's pottery, Bebhinn Marten knitwear, silver jewellery and smaller items like pot pourri and natural cosmetics.

CASTLETOWNSHEND
Bar Food/Restaurant/Music
MARY ANN'S
Tel. 028/36146. Bar food 12.30 3 and 0-7.30 Mon.-Sat.; restaurant from 6.30 Mon.-Sat., advance booking essential Nov.-Mar.; advisable high season. Credit cards: Visa, Access. Moderate.

This is one of west Cork's most famous olde worlde pubs, but even a constant stream of tourists has not spoilt its charm. Try to go there in the depths of winter when the owners Fergus and Patricia O'Mahony will have time to talk. Nobody quite knows how old Mary Ann's is, but its location 3 minutes' walk from the harbour suggests that it has long been a haunt of seafaring visitors. The front room has low beams and small round tables and leads into an oddly shaped back room where there is an open fire, a darts board and TV, and a door out to the patio and garden. The food served here is mainly determined by the availability of local seafood. In the bar they serve mussels, seafood crepes, steaks, fish of the day, lasagne, chicken Kiev, soups and pates, while the restaurant has a four course set menu using the best available seafood - scallops, prawns, crab, lobster - with steak, pork or lamb as alternatives. In the summer you can eat in the garden; there is also a kind of loft above the back bar, and an open fronted summerhouse out in the garden, all of which make a memorable setting for a meal. There is music every Sunday from 5 to 7, sometimes played very loudly in the garden which totally wrecks the *olde worlde* charm bit - especially if, as so often, it is played by an over-amplified rock band.

Guesthouse

THE CASTLE

Tel. 028/36100. Lunch and dinner by arrangement. Moderate.

The family seat of the Townshend family is a double-fronted stone-built mansion with mock castellations in its own extensive grounds right on the water's edge. Part of the house dates from about 1700, but most of it was built in Victorian times following a fire. It is one of Cork's most atmospheric guest houses, absolutely crammed with family heirlooms in various states of repair. There is a wonderful library of readable books (i.e. not just for show) behind the entrance hall. The latter, on my last visit, had a disused billiard table as a centrepiece, and probably still does. Tidiness and modern notions of interior decoration are not the great strengths of this establishment. Nevertheless, people find its informality so beguiling that, if you want the best room in the house, The Studio, you will have to book at least a year in advance for the most popular dates. This is a large, nay, vasty, room above the front door with two beds and a day bed and a couple of armchairs in the window overlooking the harbour. It is decorated, as are all five rooms, (no en suite bathrooms, God forbid!) with well-worn Indian carpets, chintz curtains and an amazing assortment of antiques. The next best is Army, or the one which has access to a positively Victorian bathroom, the likes of which you will not see again. Meals, including breakfast, are taken at the family dining table, usually with the family, next to a sideboard laden with family silver. Your hostess, Mrs. Rosemary Salter-Townshend, is a mine of information on the history and antiquities of the area. She is also the person to talk to if you are looking for self-catering accommodation in the area. This is available in the two wings of the Castle and in several other properties in the village which she manages.

B & B

BOW HALL

Tel. 028/36114. Evening meal by arrangement. Moderate.

This 17th-century house is in a courtyard just before the village's famous trees in the middle of the road. Like many houses in the village, it has a terraced garden behind it and overlooks the sea. It is run by an amiable American couple, who have been here for nearly 20 years now, dispensing American-style hospitality which includes a choice of pancakes and hot muffins at breakfast as an alternative to the usual "fry". Home-made bread is baked daily. The house is beautifully decorated with the Vickery's own antique furniture which they imported from America. There are three bright, cheerful bedrooms en suite with views of the garden and the sea. Dinner is freshly prepared by Barbara Vickery using herbs and vegetables from the garden and the best local fish and meat.

GLANDORE

Bar

P. CASEY

This bar is at the top of the hill in Glandore, and only those who know about it resist the allure of the trendier establishments further down. It is, for some reason, one of those bars where extraordinary things always seem to happen - one time it was a Danish folk singer with a guitar giving a most professional performance of her own compositions, another time it was sea shanties from a group of English yachtsmen, and best of all, an elderly local man one autumn night who gave us umpteen verses of a ballad of his own composition about local events of which I cannot remember a single word. These sort of goings-on cannot, of course, be guaranteed, but if they are going to happen, they seem to happen here more frequently than anywhere else.

Bar Food/Hotel
THE MARINE HOTEL
Tel. 028/33366. Bar Food:12.30-2.30 and 6-9. Open Easter-30 Sept. Moderate.
The Marine is in a prime location right beside the quay at the bottom of Glandore's hill, just across the road from the sea. Bar food is served in a large room on the raised ground floor, the front part of which faces the sea. The emphasis here is on seafood, with an excellent crab salad, fresh salmon mayonnaise, seafood chowder and mussels in garlic breadcrumbs. The bar has decent sized tables with comfortable stick-back chairs. There are 16 recently modernized rooms, all with TV and bathroom en suite.

B & B
KILFINNAN HOUSE
Kilfinnan. Tel. 028/33233. Evening meal by arrangement. Inexpensive.
This farmhouse is signposted at the top of the hill on the Rosscarbery side of the village and is about a mile down this beautiful cliff top road. It is a small dairy farm on 45 acres with hens and turkeys pecking around the yard. They also raise their own pigs and beef cattle for the table, and vegetables are organically grown in their own garden, as they have been for generations. The old but modernised farmhouse has four bedrooms, one with ensuite bathroom, simply decorated with candlewick bedspreads. Most rooms overlook the farmyard or the garden, as although the sea is very close, the house was built in the old style in the shelter of a hill. There are very good walks in the area, and several small rocky coves and beaches for swimming can be found within a mile's radius. Guests have the use of a comfortable sitting room which has a piano but no television: Margaret Mehigan says she wouldn't have any time to watch it, which is understandable as she bakes soda bread and scones every day for breakfast, the eggs are from her own hens, and she also makes the jams and looks after the garden.

HARE ISLAND
ISLAND COTTAGE
Tel. 028/38102. Open mid-May to mid-Sept., dinner only. Booking essential. Wine licence only.
Hare Island is one of the inhabited islands of Roaring Water Bay, with a population of about 15, plus a few holiday homes. It has no pub and no guest house, but it does have a restaurant. The place has been a great talking point since it opened in 1990, its location giving its patrons a mild sense of adventure. The restaurant seats 20 people in parties of three, and once 8 people have booked, smaller groups will be taken. The nearest boat is from Cunnamore, off the main road between Ballydehob and Skibbereen, a five minute ride. From Baltimore it takes about 25 minutes. The boat is negotiable, but the shortest crossing costs about £3 return per person. The chef, John Desmond, is no amateur, but has had along career in the catering business, and taught at the famous La Varenne cookery school in Paris. His wife, Ellmary is an experienced restaurant manager. Wisely they stick to a four-course set menu, followed by coffee, and cheese if you want, and featuring only freshly prepared local produce. In 1992 the price is a very reasonable £14. Such is the charm of the location, a whitewashed cottage with goats tethered outside, reached by walking up a fuschia-lined boreen after your boat ride, almost anything would taste good, but in fact their fresh and imaginative food compares very favourably with any meal you could find on the nearby mainland.

RINEEN

Restaurant

THE MILL HOUSE

Tel. 028/36299. Open from 7.30 Tues.-Sat. and Bank Holiday Mons. Easter-31 Oct. Booking advisable. Wine licence only. Credit Cards: Visa, Access, Amex, Diners. Moderate.

From Union Hall follow the signposts for Castletownshend and you will find this restaurant right out in the country on a very scenic back road. The house is beside a picturesque old mill, and the restaurant is in the old part of the house which dates from the early 18th century. The low-ceilinged room has high windows and candle-lit tables with wicker chairs. A typical meal might consist of seafood provencale in choux pastry, a bowl of spinach soup, steak au poivre, or scallops in a brandy and cream sauce followed by Bailey's Irish Cream and burnt almond ice cream. All ingredients are locally grown or reared.

ROSSCARBERY

Bar Food

CALNAN'S THE COURTHOUSE

Tel. 023/48117. Bar food available all day from mid-May-mid-Sept.

This bar is on the right hand side just after crossing the causeway. The traditional exterior gives no hint that inside it has been unusually refurbished with specially commissioned wood carvings forming partitions, enhanced by original stained glass inlays. The bar food consists of soup, sandwiches and scones. In summer there are tables outside, or you can take a drink over to the little park opposite. Owner Bob Kelly is a great source of information on the locality, and spends so much time in the summer months giving people directions that in 1992 he hopes to have a proper tourist information point installed in the old fashioned wooden barn-top caravan that stands outside the pub.

SCHULL

Bar

T. J. NEWMAN'S

Main St. Tel. 028/28223.

This tiny bar on the corner of the main street and the road down to the quay is a favourite with visiting yachties (being the first bar they come to after disembarking) and with people who like old-fashioned bars with genuine character. I don't think the interior, with its tall bar clad in turquoise plywood, has changed since I first drank here in 1968 or thereabouts.

Bar Food/Restaurant/Deli

THE COURTYARD

Main St. Tel. 028/28209. Restaurant open Weds.-Sat. from 7.30, possibly more days in summer; bar food served all day. Deli open 9.30-6 Mon.-Sat. Moderate.

The bar and restaurant are reached by walking up an alley into the courtyard. They are currently under separate management. The restaurant is in a dark, low-ceilinged room with different shaped tables, including a lovely big round one in the window, and has a good off-beat country restaurant atmosphere. There is plenty to choose from on the menu with dishes such as scallops in garlic butter, roast duck with prunes, and ray with black butter being typical. The bar is to the left, and has a large open fire in almost all weather. There are tall stools at the wooden bar and an odd assortment of low chairs and tables. On the walls are some very interesting old photos and lithographs of Roaring Water Bay and the Fastnet Lighthouse. The bar food comes from the Deli on the street side of the bar (see below) and is way above average with open sandwiches of crab or other available seafood on brown bread, Irish-made salami, ploughman's platter with farmhouse cheeses, all kinds of home baking and a freshly made soup of the day. The same food is served at four quiet tables at the back of the deli which interconnects with the bar. They also have a brilliant stock of local farmhouse cheeses, traditionally-made sausages and salamis, organic vegetables, hand-made bread, olive oils, chutneys, coffees, mustards, herbs, spices and all kinds of wholefood, as well as a good range of wines.

Bar Food
THE BUNRATTY INN
Upper Main St. Tel. 028/28341. Bar food: 12-4 and 6.30-9.30 Mon.-Sat. Credit Cards: Visa, Access. Lunch: Inexpensive; dinner: Moderate.

Here is another example of the weird sense of humour that is found in west Cork: under a previous owner this bar had such a flea-blown and deserted aspect that not even the most desperate drinker would approach it, and if he or she did, it would most likely be closed. Bunratty Castle being one of the most luxurious and presumably exotic places in Ireland at that time, Bunratty become the nickname for the biggest dump in town. I suppose the new owners found the name hard to better, and here it still is, but transformed into a very chic pub indeed which serves excellent food. The front bar has highly polished tables and red Turkey carpet with an interesting collection of advertising ephemera and old prints on the walls. In the back there is a small conservatory, a patio and a room with an open fire in the exposed stone chimney breast where tables are set with cheerful gingham cloths for the evening eaters. The award-winning bar menu offers dishes like seafood chowder (almost a meal in itself), devilled crab, roast beef salad, toasted Gubbeen cheese sandwiches and a substantial daily special such as baked gammon with three veg. The evening menu features various steaks, roast half duckling, and a good choice of seafood including scallops and salmon.

Restaurant
ANDY'S
Main St. Tel. 028/28579. Open 10-10 daily Easter-1 Oct. Inexpensive.

This is a cheap and cheerful joint where you can take the whole family for burgers and chips, fish and chips, shepherd's pie, pizza or lasagne without having to part with an arm and a leg when the bill arrives.

Guesthouse
CORTHNA LODGE COUNTRY HOUSE
Tel. 028/28517. Inexpensive.

This place is a real find, a 6-room guesthouse in the newly-built wing of an old farmhouse about a mile outside town. To reach it, follow the main street up to the signpost for Goleen and take the left hand fork (not the Goleen road) and the first right about a quarter of a mile on. The house is set in four acres of land, on which a tennis court and croquet lawn are planned for 1993. The spotlessly clean heavy lace curtain hanging at the window beside the front door of the B & B wing gives an indication of the high standards of housekeeping that you can expect from the owner, Loretta Strickner, an energetic young woman, who will give you a nice warm welcome. All six rooms have lovely new bathrooms and well-co-ordinated colour schemes with the skirts of the kidney-shaped dressing table matching the floral curtains, and plain duvets. They look out on to unspoilt countryside and are miles away from any traffic. One of the rooms is suitable for a guest in a wheelchair. The dining room has small pine tables, a glazed slate floor and warm pink walls. There is a quiet sitting room in the guest wing overlooking the lawn, with a suede-covered three-piece suite and a TV. It is all very pleasing to the eye, clean and comfortable without being overly fussy.

B & B
WHITE CASTLE COTTAGE
Ardintenant. Tel. 028/28528. Inexpensive.

This place is two miles outside Schull, and is signposted to the left just as you reach the sea arriving from Ballydehob. Keep to the road you are on, and do not go to the golf club, and shortly after that bend you will see the second signpost. By the time you reach the cottage you are nearly back at the sea again: it overlooks the romantic ruin of the White Castle, and beyond that the islands of Roaring Water Bay. There is a short walk to the beach at the bottom of the road, just beyond the castle. There are three small double rooms, two of them under the eaves of the cottage and one on the ground floor, and they share two bathrooms. They are simply done up, with duvets and a washbasin in each. Breakfast is taken at one large table in the cottage's main room. The Holts also have a caravan in the back garden which can be rented by the week.

Shops and Galleries
BEBHINN CRAFTS
Cotter's Yard, Main St. Tel. 028/28165. Open 10-6 daily, 10-2 Mon.-Sat. off season; closed 1 Jan.-1 April. Credit cards: Visa, Access.

Brigida Marten's shop looks more like a high fashion boutique than a craft shop, especially if you have an eye for well-designed hand-spun hand-knits in unusual wools like alpaca. On my last visit they were all in shades of black, white and grey and every bit as expensive as I had suspected. Brigida asked me not to mention prices, so I will not, but I will say that whatever they cost, these beauties are pure classics, and not the sort of impulse buy that you'd regret... She also has a selection of sophisticated and very different leather work, baskets, specially made candles and beautifully chosen bits of ceramic and decorative woodwork.

BUSY LIZZIE ANTIQUES
Main St. Tel. 028/37138. Open 11-6 Mon.-Sat.; Mon., Fri. and Sat. only off-season.

You will find a modest, and maybe affordable selection of antiques and bric-a-brac here - stripped country pine, old washing jug and bowl sets, Victorian glass bottles and old enamel advertising signs among much else.

MIZEN BOOKS
Main St. Tel. 028/28414. Open 10-6 Mon.-Sat. Credit Cards: Visa, Access.

Probably the most southerly bookshop in Ireland, Mizen Books have a great selection of all kinds of books with a big emphasis on books of Irish interest and children's books. There is a very good second-hand section in the back which should interest serious bibliophiles.

FUCHSIA BOOKS
Main St. Tel. 028/28118. Open 10-6 daily summer, a few hours daily off season - confirm by phone.

Mary Mackey has a very good collection of second hand books here, everything from thrillers for holiday reading to coveted first editions of Irish authors. She also buys books, from a whole library to a handful of paperbacks. There is a small gallery upstairs with hand-painted T-shirts for sale and some rather nice, inexpensive hand-painted prints of Roaring Water Bay.

GUBBEEN HOUSE
Tel. 028/28231. Open 10-5.

Visitors are welcome at the farm that makes the award-winning Gubbeen cheese between the above hours, where whole cheeses can be purchased. Ask for directions in the town.

WEST CORK NATURAL CHEESES
Dreenatra. Tel. 028/28593.

Bill Hogan and Sean Ferry make Gabriel, Desmond and Raclette cheese and old fashioned butter at their farmhouse plant near Dreenatra pier about 2 miles outside

Schull. Here they sell extra-mature whole cheeses that you cannot buy elsewhere. Phone before going out, to ask for directions and to check that there is somebody there to show you around.

Skibbereen

Bar/Hotel/Restaurant

THE WEST CORK HOTEL

Tel. 028/21277. Restaurant open 12.30-2.30 and 6-9 daily. Credit Cards: Visa, Access, Amex, Diners. Moderate.

Follow the signposts for Ballydehob as the hotel is on that side of town, beside the River Ilen. It used to be the Railway Hotel, and if the railway was still there it would run right through the middle of its new extension - the old viaduct is still standing. This is a famous west Cork institution, best known for its dining room where the food is still served in portions large enough to satisfy the most hungry farmer: try the mixed grill at dinner if you do not believe me. At lunch there is a choice of roast meats and a plain fish dish like grilled salmon or trout. At the a la carte dinner the steaks and lamb cutlets come from locally raised meat, and are accompanied by relays of vegetables and potatoes served from hotel-plate by attentive waitresses. There are 42 comfortable, modern rooms all with bathroom en suite, TV and direct dial phone.

Shops and Galleries

JUG AND REELS

North St. No Tel. Open 10-6 Mon.-Sat.

If you are interested in Irish music you will enjoy their selection of sheet music, cassettes and CDs. The crafts include local ceramics, jewellery and sweaters. The same owners have another shop 8 miles out of town on the Ballydehob road which sells old country pine furniture.

NILO'S ART SUPPLIES

Townshend St. Tel. 028/22488.

This is the only specialist supplier of artists' materials west of Cork City.

WEST CORK ARTS CENTRE

North St. Tel. 028/22090. Open 12.30-5 Mon.-Sat.

West Cork's thriving arts centre holds regular selling exhibitions of work by artists from west Cork and beyond. It is well worth a visit, as prices are generally fairly accessible, with some items in the crafts exhibitions selling at under £5, and most of the paintings in the £50-£500 price bracket.

12 CHAPTER TWELVE

THE FAR WEST

This chapter heads out to the western extremities of County Cork - the Mizen Head, Sheep's Head and the Beara peninsula. The Mizen Head forms the southern shore of Roaring Water Bay, and the head itself is the most southerly point of the Irish mainland. Sheep's Head is the smallest of the two, a finger of land divided from the Mizen Head by Dunmanus Bay, forming part of the southern shore of Bantry Bay. We then cut across the top of Bantry Bay, through the sub-tropical woods and gardens of Glengarriff, to travel down the largest of the three peninsulas, the Beara. The Beara peninsula forms the northern shore of Bantry Bay and overlooks the estuary of the Kenmare river and the Iveragh peninsula (the Ring of Kerry).

The area offers spectacular scenery, from the sub-tropical lushness of Glengarriff to the uncanny glacial rock formations of the Beara. The Mizen Head is the liveliest of the three, the sandy beach at Barleycove attracting large numbers of day trippers and self-catering holiday-makers in July and August. Accommodation on the Sheep's Head is mainly in farmhouse B & B's, and there is not really much to see except the scenery. Glengarriff has been on the tourist trail since the late 18th century, when its attractions were considered on a par with Killarney, and it is the only place in the area visited by large numbers of tour buses. The Beara is popular with people seeking an inexpensive outdoor holiday. It is great country for walking, birdwatching, sketching, picnicking, and swimming in rocky coves. Its main town, Castletownbere, is still a busy fishing port, but also gives a warm welcome to visitors. All three headlands have a very short high season - June, July and August - and outside these months, while you will not have the widest choice of places to stay or eat, you will be able to enjoy the feeling that you have the place very nearly to yourself.

All three peninsulas are dotted with megalithic remains dating from over 2000 B.C. Although some of them are impressive, mainly for their age and their siting, they are all badly weathered, which is understandable, given their age. In the more rocky areas they are hard to distinguish from natural rock formations. I will only point out the main ones which can be easily found from the road.

Mizen head deserves a whole day's exploration; the Sheep's head drive is a short one to two hour interlude. Glengarriff makes a day trip only if you take a boat trip to Garnish island and explore the nearby forest parks. The Beara makes an excellent one day drive, but to get its full flavour you should really spend a night there, especially if you are based east of Bandon.

Leave Schull on the Goleen road (R591) which is at the western end of town, beyond Bunratty's Bar. At **Toormore**, the first little village, in a field beside a restaurant called The Altar, is a megalithic tomb, a dolmen, known as Altar. It dates from over 2000 B.C., and only the large capstone remains. It is similar in style to the dolmens found in the Burren in county Clare.

Soon after Toormore the road skirts the sea in unusual rock formations. The village of **Goleen** is actually on the sea, but you would never guess if you do not stop and take a WALK down to the little harbour (signposted Heron's Cove), which dries out at low tide, and has some interesting bird life.

Follow the signpost for **Crookhaven** in Goleen. The village, which used to be known as "the last town in Ireland" is on a "crook" of land which forms an exceptionally sheltered harbour, and the line of multi-coloured cottages can be seen across an inlet of water as you drive towards it. The remains of a stone quarry are on the road along this north bank; it employed over 100 men up to the 1930s.

Crookhaven was an important place in the 18th and 19th centuries. It had a large fishing fleet and was also a "haven" for shipping, including the West Indian and the

Jamaican fleets, seeking refuge from contrary winds, or putting in for provisions. Earlier this century the Manx fishing fleet would base itself here for months on end. The little Church of Ireland on the outskirts of the village was built specifically for sailors. Its importance increased with transatlantic shipping, which called in here after the crossing for "orders", that is, to report their safe arrival and to be told which port to proceed to. Its most famous resident was Marconi, who came here in 1902 to set up the first transatlantic telegraph service. He set up a station on Brow Head behind the village, which was moved to a better location at Valentia in Kerry in 1906.

The decline of fishing, the disappearance of sea traffic, and the closure of the quarry decimated Crookhaven's population, which is still down to double figures in the winter months. But the development of tourism has saved it from total ruin. Its pretty terraced houses have been renovated and are used as holiday homes, and it is a popular yachting anchorage. In July and August it is one of the liveliest places in Ireland - too busy at weekends for some tastes.

You can WALK up to Brow Head by following the only road out of the middle of the village, beside the "Welcome Back" sign, for a distance of about a mile. From the summit there is a good view of the automatic lighthouse across the water at the entrance to the harbour. You will also find a fairly intact 19th-century signal tower, and the ruins of the old telegraph station.

If you have a taste for narrow twisting roads and coastal scenery, when you rejoin the mainland from Crookhaven, turn left instead of right, climbing for two miles up a tremendous road which skirts the edge of **Barleycove**, crossing its head over a causeway. (Alternately, return to Toormore and turn left for Durrus). Turn left at the T-junction, and you have a choice, each about a mile and a half on, between the light-house at **Mizen Head**, or a WALK to **Three Castle Head**, both of which are on the tip of the peninsula. I would advise investigating both of them. The WALK at Mizen Head is shorter, just a few hundred yards. But the lighthouse (now automatic, like all along this coast) is most unusual, set on a promontory separated from the mainland by a deep rocky chasm which is bridged by a red cast-iron structure. A more extended and adventurous WALK can be taken up the slopes of the hill to the east of the light house, **Corran** or **Cairn Hill**. At 765 feet it is a modest summit, but when you get to the top you will discover that the peak is in fact made of a cairn of stones and boulders. The date is uncertain, but it is possibly related in orientation to some of the other megalithic structures in the area, and if so, it has been there for over 4000 years.

Return towards Barleycove Hotel and follow signs for **Dunlough**. These will bring you to the end of the road at a rather alarming open quay. The car must be left here, and there is a spectacular WALK on a grassy path for about a mile to Three Castle Head. Part of the ruins are on the very edge of a precipice above the sea, and on the inland edge the walls descend into a lake that was probably man-made as part of the castle defences. The earliest of the three towers was built on the site of an earlier promontory fort by the O'Mahony clan in 1207, some 50 years after the Norman invasion. Presumably they retired to this remote spot to avoid Norman sub-jugation.

Return to the Barleycove Hotel, and take a left fork beyond it at Kilmoe church. This leads on to a dramatic road around the north side of the Mizen peninsula. As it falls gradually to sea level, you will see the square shell of **Dunmanus Castle**, a 3-storey structure on a rocky outcrop in Dunmanus Bay. It was built by the O'Mahony clan in the mid-15th century.

The road into **Durrus** along the sheltered inner shore of Dunmanus Bay passes through more familiar, fertile farming land, a pleasant change from dramatic rocky shores. The village itself, at the sheltered head of Dunmanus Bay, is a centre for the surrounding farming communities, and is about 6 miles from Bantry, which is the place to head for if you are not driving around the headland - a circuit of about 40 miles.

To make the circuit of the Sheep's Head, follow the signpost for **Ahakista**. Up to this point the road runs right beside the edge of the bay. In Ahakista there is a memorial to the 329 people who died when an Air India flight exploded off the coast on 23 June, 1985. It is by the Cork sculptor, Ken Thompson, and is in the shape of a large sundial. Beyond the next village, **Kilcrohane**, the road gets more rugged, until it finally ends about five miles further on. There is a good view of Bere Island, the mouth of Bantry Bay, and Three Castle Head from this point, which is also known as **Muntevary Head**. WALK towards the cliff edge for even more dramatic views.

Returning towards Kilcrohane there is a different view of the Sheep's Head with its white farmhouses dotted about the landscape. In Kilcrohane, follow the signpost for the **Goat's Pass**. The road slopes up gently across the middle of the peninsula, arriving at a sudden vista of Bantry Bay and the Caha Mountains on the Beara, then runs steeply down the other side. Shortly after, you join the N71 taking the Bantry direction. (See Chapter Eight for Bantry).

From Bantry the N71 follows the edge of Bantry Bay, climbing steeply into rougher country beyond **Snave Bridge**, and crossing an exposed headland before sloping down into the shelter of **Glengarriff**. In the summer months you will be hailed by men who wait at the roadside offering to ferry visitors across to **Garnish Island**, also known as **Ilnacullin**. *(Ten minute boat trip negotiable - expect to pay about £4 return. Gardens: Tel. 027/63040. Admission £1.50 adults, 50p. children and senior citizens. Open July-Aug. Mon.-Sat. 9.30-6.30, Sun 11-6; Apr.-June and Sept. Mon.-Sat. 10-6.30, Sun. 1-6; March and Oct. Mon.-Sat. 10-4.30, Sun. 1-5. Last landings one hour before closing).*

These beautiful gardens were laid out in 1910 by Harold Peto. At their centre is a formal Italian garden with colonnades, terraces and pools, surrounded by a more natural garden, leading to a long glade called the Happy Valley, which is a riot of colour in late spring when the rhododendrons and azaleas are in bloom. Elsewhere on the tiny island is a clock tower and a Martello tower. There is also a fine double herbaceous border which is at its best in high summer, although the island is best known for its frost tender shrubs and unusual trees, including New Zealand fern trees. But finally, it is the location which makes the garden so unusual - in the midst of all these carefully cultivated plants and architectural embellishments, you will suddenly catch a glimpse of a barren mountain peak or an expanse of open sea.

The village of **Glengarriff** is very much back on the beaten track, with tour buses, craft shops and tea rooms, which may or may not please you. It is a good base for WALKS, as the Glengarriff valley consists of a combination of ancient woodlands, once the property of Lord Bantry, and new plantations. These now form **Glengarriff State Forest** which has two entrances for motorists, one a mile north of the village on the road to Kenmare, and one half a mile west on the road to Castletownbere. Stop at either entrance, both of which have picnic tables and a car park, to explore the paths, which lead variously to a lake, and several streams and waterfalls.

From Glengarriff we head west again along the only road down this side of the Beara peninsula, signposted Castletownbere. The **Beara** has only very recently put itself on the touring map. Previously it was overshadowed by its flashier neighbour, the Ring of Kerry. The Ring has a better selection of up-market hotels and restaurants than the Beara, but I would rather have the quiet, uncrowded charms of the Beara than the over-commercialism of the Ring any day. The Beara gets visitors who have heard about its isolated charms by word-of-mouth, often back-packers and hostellers, bird watchers, hill walkers and other outdoor enthusiasts. Some people find it so empty and quiet as to be positively eerie; others become addicted to its other-worldliness, and find its scenery, its history, and its simple ways an endless source of enjoyment.

Beyond Glengarriff the road opens up to give wonderful views across Bantry Bay to the hills of the two peninsulas that we have left behind. It is one of those humpy, twisting roads that doesn't quite seem to know where it is going. You will meet plenty more like it further down the peninsula. It skirts the lower slopes of the **Sugarloaf Mountain** which rises to 1887 feet in an almost perfect cone shape. In the village of **Adrigole** is the turning for the **Healy Pass**, which leads to Kerry. I prefer to drive it in the opposite direction (see below), as the views are even better coming north to south.

Beyond Adrigole is **Hungry Hill**, which has one of the highest waterfalls in Ireland on its northwest slope. A finger post beside the road points to one of several ways to climb it (2521 feet). Take local advice before setting out, as some of the descents can be treacherous if the weather turns nasty. The name of the mountain was used by Daphne du Maurier, as the title of a novel based on the story of a local family feud. Beyond Adrigole there are good views of Berehaven (also spelt Bearhaven), which is the natural harbour formed between Bere Island and the mainland. Like Queenstown in Cork harbour, this was one of the naval ports which the British held on to after the Treaty until 1938, when Churchill, to his great fury, had to hand them back to the Free State. Berehaven was large enough to shelter the whole British navy, and would have been of great strategic value in the 1939-45 war. Nowadays it is often used by large fleets of factory ships from the Eastern Bloc ("They get angry if we call them Russians now", I was told recently in Castletownbere), who buy fish, (mainly white fish), from the local trawler fleet.

The island has a regular car ferry service which leaves from a pontoon signposted off this road on the outskirts of the town. *(Tel. 027/75009 for ferry times. 5 crossings daily in peak season, July and Aug., 2-3 cars per ferry)*. Bere Island has two pubs and two churches. Remains of the extensive British fortifications, including two intact guns, are scattered throughout the island. There are also several small sandy beaches and sheltered coves.

Castletownbere, or more correctly, Castletown Berehaven, is not really much of a town, but it has a certain appeal if you like a working port with unrenovated Victorian shops and houses. Park in the main square, and take a WALK around its busy quays to get a flavour of the place. As you leave the town heading west there is a signpost to the **Stone Circle**, quite a good example of its kind. (see Drombeg, Chapter Eleven for a discussion of stone circles).

About two miles out of town on the road to Allihies is **Dunboy Castle** and **Forest Park**. Leave your car in the car park, and, for the moment, ignore the large ruined house, and WALK to the end of the little peninsula. Here you can see the badly ruined but clearly excavated remains of the original **Dunboy Castle**. It is within a star shaped fort, and was the headquarters of Donal Cam O'Sullivan Bere (1560-1618), chief of the O'Sullivan sept, and one of the leaders of the rebellion against English rule which was defeated at the Battle of Kinsale in 1601. (See Chapter Nine).

After that defeat, part of the Irish and Spanish forces retreated to Dunboy, where they were besieged by the English forces in 1602. The attacking army forced its way into the cellar of the castle just as the mortally wounded commandant, Richard mac Geoghegan, was about to blow it up, which explains why it is in such a state today. Meanwhile, Donal Cam, who had been hiding out in the Glengarriff area waiting for Spanish reinforcements, realised that they would not arrive, and decided to seek refuge in Ulster. He set out from Glengarriff on 31 December 1602 with 400 fighting men, and 600 women, children and servants to march north. Only 35 of the party survived the journey, including Donal Cam, who sailed shortly after for Spain, where he was created Earl of Berehaven.

The larger ruin is known locally as "the Puxley mansion", and belonged to an unpopular local family who extracted vast amounts of copper from the hills in Allihies. (The same family featured in Daphne du Maurier's *"Hungry Hill"*). The grandiose house, which displays a mixture of styles from Scottish baronial to Italian villa, incorporates part of an earlier mid-18th-century house. Although parts of it were lived in, it was not fully completed when it was burnt out in 1921. For much of the year, cattle are allowed to graze in its ruined halls.

Beyond Dunboy the scenery on the road to Allihies starts to get really spectacular. After about five miles you are faced with a choice of a direct or a "scenic route" to Allihies. The latter gives you a chance to visit Dursey Island, which, because it is the end of the road, involves a detour of an extra 8 miles off the scenic route. The short route is just as good as the "scenic" one, and at 4 miles, about half the distance.

Dursey Island, which is still inhabited, is a humped rock about two miles by half a mile separated from the mainland by the deep and narrow **Dursey Sound**. It is connected to the mainland by a cable car which swings across from one cliff to another on a couple of wires stretched out about 60 feet above the water. It is licensed to carry three passengers or one cow. *(The cable car makes return trips at 9, 11, 2.30, 5, 7, and 8, with extra trips at 4 and 5, on Sundays in June, July and August only. Check these times by phone 027-73016 - if you're keen to get across, as they vary subject to demand - or more usually, lack of demand).*

There are eleven families living on the island, which has no pub. The bird watching is excellent, and there are also good walks, one of which leads to the remains of an O'Sullivan castle which was destroyed at the same time as the one at Dunboy (see above). The three rocks which can be seen from Dursey island are named the Bull, the Cow, and the Calf, according to size.

Whichever direction you approach **Allihies** from, you will not fail to be struck by the strange beauty of its glacially-scraped mountains. You will also notice a strand of shining white sand, **Ballydonegan**, which is in fact not a natural strand at all, but consists of sand used in the process of extracting copper from the mountains. The old engine room belonging to the mine works can still be seen on the hill behind the town. Copper has been mined here since prehistoric times, and was rediscovered in 1810. The mines were opened by the Puxley family shortly after. By the mid 19th-century over 1300 people were employed in the mines, with the skilled workers at first being imported from Cornwall. The ore was taken by horse and cart to Castletownbere and shipped to Swansea. By the end of the 19th century the mines were in decline, and conditions, which had never been good for the workers involved, became intolerable with deeper shaft workings. The miners found that their expertise was in demand in America, and many of them emigrated to Butte, Montana. The mines closed in the 1930s, although they were re-opened a couple of times since, and speculators still turn up looking for other minerals in these hills.

The Allihies Folklore Centre, a restored stone-built cottage right on the beach at Ballydonegan, is a local initiative that produces exhibitions and publications about the antiquities and folk ways of the area, and is well worth a visit *(Open 7 days, June, July and August, or tel. 027/73148).*

If you have the energy for a bit of a climb, there is a truly remarkable walk along the ridge of the hill behind the village above the mine's engine room. Drive or walk through Allihies, and take the right fork at the top of it. There is a car park of sorts under the engine room, and a clear path to follow up the hill. Be very careful of open mine shafts in the area. Some, but not all have been fenced off. At the top of the hill, a green road runs along the spine of the mountains; how far you follow it is up to you, but I would advise you to stick to the path and come back the same way. The views are great, but it is the silence up here that is equally remarkable.

It is not so much the village itself that makes Allihies especially attractive, as the whole district around it, with its combination of strangely coloured and shaped hills and rocky little coves. It is easy to understand why some of Ireland's finest artists choose to have their studios in this part of the world. I suggest WALKING out towards Cod's Head for about a mile, rather than driving straight on to Eyeries.

Leave on the road signposted Allihies, but take time to explore the coves and footpaths on the left, seaward, side of the road. Whether you walk or drive, this is a great piece of road, which crosses the end of the peninsula and emerges on the shores of Coulagh Bay at the outer end of the Kenmare river's estuary. On a fine day you will be able to see the Skellig Rocks, distinctive cone shapes, on the horizon, and the tip of the Iveragh peninsula. Down at the water's edge on the left of the road there are several small rocky coves which make good picnic spots. A **Mass Rock** is signposted on the right. It is a large slab of stone which was used as an altar during penal times in the early 18th century, when Catholics were not allowed to have churches.

Eyeries is a pretty village a little inland from the coast but still in sight of the sea, with an L-shaped line of multi-coloured cottages which are adorned by floral window boxes in the summer. Leaving the village on the road signposted Ardgroom, in a district known as **Ballycrovane**, you will see the tallest Ogham stone in Ireland standing up against the skyline. It is 17 and a half feet tall, and its inscription, in the ancient alphabet comprised of vertical dashes, reads "Of the son of Deich descendant of Torainn". Access is difficult, and it is on private land.

Just near the standing stone is a signpost on the left for a fairly terrifying "scenic route" which is actually a detour of over ten miles to Ardgroom (3 miles direct), along tiny steep roads with precipitous drops on the bends, which are really more suited to walkers than motorists. It does, however, offer great views of the Iveragh peninsula across the water, and there is pedestrian access to several rocky coves.

At **Ardgroom**, the last village before Kerry, there is a pleasant detour of under a mile to **Glenbeg Lough**, a peaceful, narrow mountain lake just over a mile long. The road ends at the top of the lake in a farmyard, but there are good walks on either side. Just beyond Ardgroom, on the right, is a relatively intact **Stone Circle**. The road crosses the border into Kerry and carries on to Lauragh, from where I suggest you return to Cork via the amazing **Healy Pass**, which comes down the Cork side of the mountain in a series of apparently interminable zig-zags and is yet another unforgettable drive.

Sporting Facilities

Golf: *Barleycove Beach Hotel*. Tel. 028/35234. 9-hole. Green fees welcome. *Glengarriff Golf Course*. Tel. 027/63116. 9-hole. Green fees welcome. *Berehaven Golf Club,* Castletownbere. Tel. 027/70299. 9-hole. Green fees welcome. **Tennis**: there are public courts at *Crookhaven* and *Allihies* and the *Barleycove Beach Hotel.* **Horse Riding**: *Allihies Riding Centre*. Tel. 027/70340. **Fishing**: *Deep Sea Angling*: contact Bear Havinga, Crookhaven. Tel. 028/35240. *Shore angling* is freely available all around the area. Ask in the nearest bar for tips. *Salmon and sea trout*: Glengarriff river: for permission contact *Glengarriff Anglers Association*, c/o Mr. Bernard Harrington, The Maple leaf, Glengarriff, tel. 027/63021. There are 10 loughs in the Adrigole-Glengarriff area where permission is considered free. Ask Glengarriff Anglers how to find them. The Adrigole river (Beara): for permission contact *Kenmare Anglers Association*, c/o John O'Hare, Fishing Tackle Shop, Main St., Kenmare, Co. Kerry. Tel. 064/41499.

PUBS, RESTAURANTS, SHOPS AND ACCOMMODATION

(Price Categories are explained in HOW TO USE THIS BOOK)

AHAKISTA (Sheep's Head)

Bar

AHAKISTA BAR

This tiny corrugated-iron shack is opposite the entrance to the Japanese Dinner House (see below) and should not be missed by those with a taste for totally unrenovated bars and meeting the locals - who are frankly puzzled as to why anyone should wish to join them in here.

Restaurant
SHIRO JAPANESE DINNER HOUSE
Tel. 027/67030. Open from 7PM. Reservations Essential. Wine Licence only. Credit Cards: Visa, Access, Amex, Diners. Very Expensive.
   When it opened everyone said it would never catch on; here it still is, and if you want one of their two tables you will have to book days or even weeks in advance in the high season. The large Edwardian house was once a Bishop's summer retreat; now it is home to Tokyo-born Kei Pilz and her German husband, Werner. The rooms are decorated with Kei's own watercolours, and she uses her artistic gifts on the food as well, which looks so beautiful on the plate that it is a pity to spoil the picture by eating it. There is a fixed price four-course menu which makes good use of the fresh local seafood and free range chicken. Only Japanese food is served: there are no "European" options, but vegetarians can be catered for. Sashimi (raw fish) will probably be one of the starters on offer, with other authentic Japanese dishes such as tempura (deep fried squid, prawns, fish and vegetables) yakitori (spit-roasted chicken with a sweet sauce), as main course options. The food is delicious,as well as being beautifully presented, and the whole strange experience is something that you will remember for years.

B & B

HILLCREST HOUSE
Tel. 027/67045. Open 1 April-30 Oct. Inexpensive.
   This farmhouse B & B won two awards in 1991, and it is easy to see why. It is the sort of place people dream of finding - a nicely restored old farmhouse on the top of a pine-covered hill with fantastic views of the sea, secluded but not too remote. (Durrus is about 7 miles, Bantry about 12). It is surrounded by a 40-acre dairy farm. Downstairs there is one en suite family room with a separate entrance. The other three rooms (two of them en suite and the other with its own bathroom just across the corridor) are upstairs in the old farmhouse and have hipped ceilings clad in tongue and groove woodwork, and are fitted out with modern country pine furniture and duvets. The stone-floored dining room is in the old farmhouse kitchen and has exposed stone walls and an open fire. An added bonus here is the "playroom" which has been installed in a nicely restored cow byre with a high-pitched beamed roof. There is an old settee, table tennis and a darts board. There are good walks on the farm's land up the hill-side behind the house, and coastal walks along the road below it.

ALLIHIES (Beara)

Bar
JOHN TERRY'S
Tel. 027/73008.
   This is the only bar in Allihies which opens all day at all times of the year. It's a red building at the top of the village, and was fitted out with pine settles and low-beamed ceilings in a successful face-lift a few years ago. One of the rooms has a stone fireplace, and there is a snooker table in another. Coffee, tea and sandwiches are served officially from May to September but Mrs. Terry can usually produce a sandwich on request outside these months.

Restaurant/B & B
GLUIN
Tel. 027/73097. Open all day till late, June- mid-Sept. No licence: Bring Your Own Bottle. Inexpensive.
   This place is known locally as "the blue house", and is an old farmhouse up above the village beside the disused copper mines. Its a short walk from the top pub in the village. The American owner Larry Messick has a day time menu with light meals

featuring fresh local produce, and is best known for his home-made pizzas. Dinner is served in a new extension to the farmhouse, a large room with mix and match tables and chairs and a view of the mining tower. The menu is limited to fresh local produce, usually salmon or Beara mountain lamb and a vegetarian dish, and the food is simply prepared in one of two new kitchens. There are two large bedrooms above the restaurant for guests who do not mind late night noise: there is a busy trade done here in after-pub pizzas. Early sleepers should ask for one of the other two rooms which are further away from the restaurant. Either way, you'll wake in an exceptionally beautiful mountainside location.

Hostel

GARRANES HOSTEL
Garranes. Tel. 027/73032. Inexpensive.
The hostel is in the grounds of the Dzogchen Buddhist Holiday and Retreat Centre off the main Castletownbere-Allihies road, about six miles from the village itself. Even if you are not interested in hostelling or alternative religion, it is worth visiting this place to see the amazing meditation room and that has been built on the very edge of a cliff overlooking the distant Mizen Head. It is entered through an indoor Japanese garden. The Buddhists, and people attending their courses, stay in neat little white cottages on the cliff. The hostel is an old farmhouse with dormer windows, and sleeps only 12. It is run as a normal Independent Hostel with no curfews or membership requirements. Vegetarian meals are available, and there is a small wholefood shop. It is an excellent base for cliff and hill walking, with access to a secluded beach in the grounds, and there are bicycles for hire.

Shops and Galleries

CORMAC BOYDELL, CERAMIC ARTIST
Coomeen. Tel. 027/73085. Open 12-6, Mon.-Fri. July and August only.
Cormac Boydell is one of Ireland's leading ceramic artists, and his studio can be found outside the village on the Eyeries road.

ALLIHIES GLOBE ARTICHOKE CO-OPERATIVE
Reentrisk. Tel. 027/73025.
Ireland's only pick-your-own artichoke farm is signposted off the scenic road between Allihies and Eyeries. Bring a sharp knife to do the "picking". Tony Lowes also sells artichoke crowns by post: they have attractive grey foliage, and thrive in this climate. The season extends from May to September, and peaks in June and July.

GREAT BARRINGTON POTTERY
Tel. 027/73125. Open June-Sept.
The showroom is just outside the village on the Eyeries road, and sells American-designed tableware.

ARDGROOM (Beara)

Bar Food/Music

THE HOLLY BAR
Tel. 027/74082
Although this bar has been extended recently, it still has an enormous holly tree growing in the front bar, which is a sight to see. The bar food consists of soup and sandwiches, and there is music most nights in the summer and most weekends off-season.

BARLEY COVE (Mizen Head)

BARLEYCOVE BEACH HOTEL
Tel. 028/35234. Open 1 Jan.-20 Dec. Credit Cards: Visa, Access, Amex, Diners. Moderate (Expensive July & Aug.).

The kids will be delighted if you decide to stay here. It is a robustly built modern hotel overlooking a curved beach of golden sand which has a 9-hole par 3 course on its dunes. There is an indoor heated pool, tennis court and games room. All 11 rooms have TV and direct dial phone and en suite bathroom. The hotel also manages 24 self-catering chalets in the grounds which can be rented by the week.

CASTLETOWNBERE (Beara)

Bar

MACCARTHY'S
Town Square. Tel. 027/70014.
This is a good first port of call to find out which fleets are in the harbour and what the trawlers have been catching. This is because the front part of the bar is a grocery store which provisions most of the boats. Opposite the shop counter you will notice one of the last remaining matchmaking booths. It used to form a private room for the matchmaker and the bride and groom's parents to discuss marriage terms, a practice which only died out in the last generation or two around here. Later in the evening you will find that the back bar is a lively place which has a fiercely competitive darts team.

M. O'SHEA
Town Square.
This is the nearest bar to the quays, and if you look up you will see a painting of a bearded sailor and a plaque giving its other name: "El Bar del Marinero". It is the main drinking place of the Spanish and French trawlermen, and when its polyglot clientele is in town it has a certain je ne sais quoi.

JACKIE LYNCH
Main St.
Jackie Lynch used to run a great bar in Eyeries, and moved into town a few years ago and renovated his current premises. He has got it just right, smartening it up just enough, with heavy pine furniture, to create the sort of bar where an urban sophisticate would feel quite at ease, without losing the atmosphere of a small-town local.

Restaurant

OLD COTTAGE RESTAURANT
Derrymihan West. Tel. 027/70430. Open 12.30-2 and 6-9 in summer, off season dinner only and tel. to confirm. Booking advisable. Wine licence only. Credit Cards: Visa, Access. Moderate.
The little cottage is clearly signposted on the top of a hill beside the main road as you enter Castletownbere from Glengarriff. Inside are three pretty inter-connecting rooms with views over the bay. The tables are set with linen cloths, bowls of fresh flowers and delicate white crockery. The Dutch chef, Vincent van Nulck, has been here four years, and is about to install an open oak fire over which to cook steaks and lamb. Main courses come with two kinds of potato and three vegetables, all most beautifully prepared. His other speciality is, of course, seafood. Mariage du mer is a shellfish plate for two with lobster, mussels, crab toes, scallops and caviar served with two sauces, or try darnes de saumon grille, - grilled salmon with garlic butter, anchovies and olives. There is a wine list with 21 choices including champagne. This is the only serious continental-style restaurant for miles around, but even though there is no competition it maintains very high standards.

Restaurant/B & B

JOHN MURPHY
East End House. Tel. 027/70244. Restaurant open 9-9 Mon.-Sat. summer and 9-7.30 off season. No wine licence: bring your own bottle. B & B open year round, but tel. to confirm off season. Inexpensive.

This is the sort of family-run restaurant where tea cups and bread and butter appear on the formica-topped table as soon as you sit down, that used to be the norm around the county, and are now fast-disappearing. When they are good, as this one is, they are very good indeed. At the top end of the menu you can choose from T-bone steak with onions and chips, mixed grill, poached or grilled salmon or seafood salad. Other choices are plaice and chips, sausages and chips and the like, and breakfast is also served. There is a children's menu and I reckon that a family of four could eat here for the price of one starter and a main course at a fancier place. The owner's son John and his young wife, Joan, now run the restaurant which is on the ground floor of a 3-storey Victorian town house, and they also have 5 charmingly old-fashioned bedrooms, with shared bathrooms, some of which look out onto the harbour.

Hotel
THE BEREHAVEN INN
Tel. 027/70357. Credit Cards: Visa, Access. Moderate.
This is not the smartest hotel in town, but it has the advantage of being compact and friendly and right in the middle of the action. From its back windows, it overlooks the harbour and the quays. At the moment there are 18 rooms, 9 en suite, but it is just about to change hands, and the new owners will no doubt undertake some renovations before the 1992 season. I like it for its Jekyll and Hyde character; from the front it could be any old hotel in any small country town, yet from the back it is right on the sea in the midst of a busy working port. There is a door on the staircase opening directly on to the quay which reminds you of its unusual location as you come down to breakfast in the morning, and this is the one thing that I hope the new owners don't change. The rest of it, frankly, could do with a bit of smartening up.

B & B
RODEEN
Rodeen Cross. Tel. 027/70158. Open all year. Evening meal by arrangement. Inexpensive.
Rodeen Garden Centre should be signposted as you arrive in town from Glengarriff; it is on a road running parallel to the main road about a mile outside the town, and has a superb view of the shipping at anchor in Berehaven. As you would expect from a woman who also runs a garden centre, the modern house is surrounded by well-tended shrubs and flowers. There are five en suite bedrooms, four of them overlooking the bay. Breakfast is eaten in the conservatory, and there is a barbecue in the garden. Ellen Gowan has won several cookery competitions, and is happy to cater for vegetarians. She can also run you up an unusual breakfast, if the normal "fry" does not appeal.

Shops and Galleries
THE SHELL
Main St. Tel. 027/70152. Open 10-6 Mon.-Sat.; 10-4.30 off season.
The nicest thing here is the selection of locally-made knitwear; they also have ceramics, candles, books, stationery and cards.

CROOKHAVEN (Mizen Head)
Bar
O'SULLIVAN'S
028/35200
Billy O'Sullivan runs one of the best bars in the county, with a wonderful waterfront location. Unlike the other bars in Crook, he is open all year round. Local lobster fishermen congregate in the front right-hand corner, and the walls are covered in photographs of local characters, past and present. There is an unusual glazed stone floor, and a wooden ceiling. Sandwiches, toasted or plain, and tea and coffee are

available on request. There is a snooker table, and in summer there is music nightly. Visit Crookhaven in the daytime off season, and this is your only option. From June to September there are five small restaurants, and two other bars.

DURRUS (Sheep's Head)

Bar
CASEY'S THE PUB
Beyond the wonderfully strange horse's head lampshade in the window you will find a typical "brown pub" - brown wooden walls, brown ceiling, brown bar, brown chairs and benches - which has a lively cross-section of local residents of many nationalities as its regular clientele.

Bar Food/Restaurant
CRONIN'S
Tel. 027/61144. Bar food: 12.30-8; Restaurant open from 7PM daily mid-May-Sept., otherwise tel. to confirm. Credit cards: Visa, Access, Amex. Moderate.
Cronin's is a friendly village pub with photographs of old Durrus on the walls. The bar menu is better than average, with home-made soup, pates, local seafood served on open sandwiches, and home-made beefburger among the choices. The restaurant is in a small room separate from the bar which has a Tudor-cottage atmosphere with wood-panelled walls, brown and cream chintz curtains, ladder-back chairs and white napery. The wine list has 9 choices, mostly under £10, and the food is fresh and simply prepared: crab cocktail, stuffed mussels, local salmon and scallops, T-bone or fillet steak. Should you find it convenient to stay the night, they have 7 guest bedrooms.

Restaurant
BLAIR'S COVE HOUSE
Blair's Cove. Tel. 027/61127. Open: dinner only Tues.-Sat.; Sun. lunch only. closed Sun. PM and Mon. and Nov.-mid-Dec. and Jan.1-mid March. Reservations advised. weekends. Wine licence only. Credit Cards: Visa, Access, Amex, Diners. Expensive.
This is a most unusual restaurant in the converted stables of a Georgian house overlooking Dunmanus Bay. The stout wooden beams and rough stone walls contrast strangely with the candle-lit formality of the pink napery, and gleaming silverware. Most nights a pianist plays soft background music. In summer you can dine on the terrace overlooking the rose garden and courtyard. The owners are French, which gives a French accent to the cooking, and the emphasis is on fresh local produce. Starters are arranged buffet-style, and the range of smoked or locally cured fish is always interesting. Meat-eaters will be tempted to try steak or lamb from the open oak-wood grill; the other speciality is seafood which can also be grilled if you wish, but is usually offered in a rich and tempting sauce.

Dairy
DURRUS FARMHOUSE CHEESE
Coomkeen. Tel. 027/61100. Open 10-3, Mon.-Sat.
This is a farmhouse dairy where you can purchase mature whole hand-made Durrus cheeses. To find it, drive down the Ahakista road as far as the Protestant church, and drive up the road behind the church for about three miles. Even better, walk there!

EYERIES (Beara)

Bar/Music
CAUSKEY'S BAR
Tel. 027/74161.
The bar is at the top of the village opposite the Catholic church. From the outside

it doesn't look very promising, but the front bar leads to a back room which has a totally unexpected picture window looking out onto an amazing panoramic view of Coulagh Bay. There is music here every Sunday night - "mainly traditional but a bit of everything really" says Mrs. Causkey.

Cafe/Craft Shop
AN CLOCHAN
Eyeries Cross, Inches. Tel. 027/74147. Open Easter-end of season 10.30-9. Inexpensive.

If you're struck by a craving for herbal tea in Eyeries never fear: you'll find one in this interestingly converted old garage on the Castletownbere side of the village. The light, airy room has hand-made tables and chairs on a pale green carpet; besides herbal tea they also serve real coffee, sandwiches, omelettes and home-baked cakes and pastries. The crafts are all Irish, and some of them are made locally. They have dried flowers, stoneware pottery, jewellery, stained glass sun-catchers and a small selection of books of Irish interest.

B & B
THE SHAMROCK
Strand Rd. 027/74058. Inexpensive.

Strand Road in Eyeries is not a street, but a boreen leading to the strand, and is on the left-hand side as you approach the village from Castletownbere. There are four rooms (shared bathrooms) in this cottage which are reached by a steep, narrow staircase. They are small and cosy with stunning views of the sea which is about a hundred yards away. There is one long table and a heavily laden dresser in the farmhouse-style dining room, and an evening meal can be provided by arrangement.

Dairy
MILLEENS CHEESE
Tel. 027/74079.

Veronica Steele was a pioneer in the revival of farmhouse cheese making, and her Milleens is one of the most celebrated. You can buy a mature Milleens from the farm (left at the graveyard outside Eyeries and second right), but telephone first to make sure you call at a convenient time.

GLENGARRIFF

Bar Food/Hotel
THE ECCLES
The Harbour. Tel. 027/63003. Bar food available 10-9, daily. Restaurant open from 6.30 daily and Sunday lunch. Credit Cards: Visa, Access, Amex, Diners. Moderate.

For a tourist honey-pot, Glengarriff is not well endowed with interesting places to stay or to eat, but maybe, like Blarney, they just don't try very hard as there are always people about. Whatever the reason, the only place that I find at all special is the good old Eccles, which has been there for over 250 years. If it is a while since you visited Glengarriff you'll be surprised to find that the Eccles has apparently moved inland: in fact, it is the main road that has moved, on to reclaimed land in front of the hotel, and the Eccles is now about 100 yards from the sea.

The grand beige and white facade with its intricate wrought iron balconies remains unchanged, as do the Grecian pillars in the lobby which has otherwise been smartened up with wing chairs and sofas and a big satellite TV. There are 49 rooms here, all en suite with TV and direct dial phone, overlooking either the bay or the gardens. They have light oak fitted furniture and candlewick bedspreads. The wide corridors creak atmospherically under their acanthus-patterned carpet. Some interesting mementoes of the hotel's long history are displayed in framed collages at the bottom of the staircase.

Although the hotel is very big, its most recent extension, the dining room wing, was built in 1860. It is a vast, high-ceilinged room seating 300, which can be partitioned on quiet days, and has tall windows overlooking the bay. Bar food can be eaten in the Victorian style front bar or at seats on the terrace outside, and it has an extensive menu running from open or closed sandwiches and salads right up to mixed grill or fried cod and chips.

GOLEEN (Mizen Head)

Bar
S. MACCARTHY
Tel. 028/35119.
There is an unusual combination here - bar, off licence and drapery. Sean MacCarthy sells a good selection of caps and heavy weather gear, and many of his bar customers find themselves ordering a hat with their second pint.

Restaurant/B & B/Antique Shop
HERON'S COVE
Goleen Harbour. Tel. 028/35255. Restaurant open from 12 noon, 7 days, June-Sept. Lunch 12-2.30, tea 3-5, dinner from 6PM. B & B Easter-Oct., but phone in advance to confirm. Wine Licence only. Credit Cards: Amex, Diners, Visa, Access. Lunch: Inexpensive; Dinner: Moderate; B & B: Inexpensive.
Sue Hill turns two rooms on the ground floor of her house into a restaurant in the summer. It overlooks a pretty little cove, which is indeed populated by herons. The pine tables are set with mats in the daytime, and there is a children's menu available, and a 3-course tourist menu for £12. At dinner there is white napery, and a full a la carte menu. Mrs. Hill's son Ronan is the chef, and specialises in local seafood including turbot, langoustines, scallops and lobster from the tank. Wine is "off the wall" - you choose a bottle from the wall of wine racks, and it is opened at your table. The selection includes a special collection of Irish Bordeaux. The tiny antique shop is off one of the dining rooms.
Upstairs there are four bedrooms, two with private bathrooms and a little terrace overlooking the cove. They are simply but comfortably furnished in the modern style, with tea and coffee making facilities and large TVs with satellite.

TOORMORE (Mizen Head)

Restaurant/B & B
THE ALTAR
Tel. 028/35254. Open 10.30-3.30 and from 7PM; 1 Oct- mid-May Tel. to confirm. Advance booking for dinner advisable. Wine licence only. Credit Cards: Visa, Access. Moderate.
You will not easily miss this place on the road between Schull and Goleen as it has a colourful mural on the gable end and a London taxi sitting outside. The wine bar and two dining rooms are interconnecting and have stone walls with antiques and bric-a-brac scattered around, and red and white table cloths. There are also some tables outside. It is a cheerful, extrovert sort of place, and on Wednesday nights they do a special £14 Irish menu followed by live music and a sing-song. The name, The Altar, incidentally, is that of the townland, and comes from a 5000 year old megalithic tomb on their land which you can have a look at if you ask. The menu is heavy on seafood - sea trout stuffed with crab meat or prawn tails in garlic butter, and there are also steaks, beef stroganoff and vegetarian specials. There are three rooms en suite (Inexpensive) if it suits you to stay the night.